RECLAIMING ADELAIDE

AN AGE GAP/HACKER ROMANCE

ANN-MARIE DAVIS

Contents

Moreno Mafia Series

Charity's Torment

Protecting Charity

Charity's Vengeance

Charity's Redemption

Blackstone Tech Series

His Obsession, Book 1

Corrupting Ivy, Book 2

Decoding Adelaide, Book 3

Reclaiming Adelaide, Book 4

Do you want to read them in Chronological order?
*His Obsession (**Blackstone Tech**)*
*Charity's Torment (**Moreno Mafia**)*
*Protecting Charity (**Moreno Mafia**)*
*Charity's Vengeance (**Moreno Mafia**)*
*Corrupting Ivy (**Blackstone Tech**)*
*Charity's Redemption (**Moreno Mafia**)*
*Decoding Adelaide (**Blackstone Tech**)*
*Reclaiming Adelaide (**Blackstone Tech**)*

Standalones

The Harbinger

To those who stuck with me for the two years it took to finish this series. You are my reason.

"Betrayal doesn't only break your heart but also darkens your soul. You'll never forget the pain like a fog that forever lingers in the depths of your mind."—*Rahul Jangid*

1

That's not fucking possible. But it was there... my username on her phone.

Blood rushed from my face as I clenched my fist around her phone, resisting the temptation to shatter the offending evidence of her betrayal against the wall into tiny fragmented pieces.

I should wake her.

No.

How could I trust myself to keep control of the rage bubbling beneath the surface?

Catatonia hung like a heavy drape over me until my thumb twitched along the screen, opening the conversation box, showing me all the corruption she'd taken part in—two private chats, a public one, and an invitation-only, with a green man as the icon.

Her sleeping frame raised with steady breaths then lowered on exhale, an invariable pace in contrast to the wild beat that was my heart.

How could she sleep so soundly, knowing she'd betrayed me like this?

My thumb jerked again as I squeezed her phone, clicking on the green man icon.

Scores of conversations between her and five other hackers.

I ground my teeth to powder as I read their congratulatory celebrations and files—files that had my business name on them.

A heavy thrum in my ears quickened as I read more with a deeper understanding of how far this betrayal went. She'd sent me her code on this chat just to use it against me, gain access to my computer systems, and steal from me.

What were they after, though? And for how long?

I clicked out of her chat after going back a month with the mention of something or someone called *Sev Shen*—a name that sparked recognition in me. I searched the rest of her phone, forgoing her privacy.

Her stable breathing filled the room as I looked at her in my periphery, my spine vibrating. How had this evening turned from a successful night of pulling her back toward me to searching through her phone like a jealous lover and wanting to do terrible things to her?

Fuck.

I could wake her up and force her to answer my questions—demand she tell me everything. I wanted to know their agenda and anything else they had planned. But how could I believe a word she said now? I couldn't trust her, not anymore.

Turning back to her phone, I flipped through her ridiculous selfies with her Betta fish and Monica. She'd snapped a picture of my freshly tattooed hand wrapped around my gear shifter...

She'd taken this tonight.

Dammit.

Didn't they say tattoos cursed a relationship? Well, that didn't take long—less than twelve fucking hours.

My knee bobbed, and my jaw ached from the constant pressure against my teeth. I flipped through them until I paused on a photo with two individuals I'd recognize anywhere.

Son of a bitch.

My vision tunneled, the edges pitch black like ink as I swiped up, getting the metadata on the phone. She took it weeks ago, before the incident at the awards ceremony.

I pinched the screen, zooming in on the couple sitting at the same ice cream parlor I'd met her at before dragging her into the park behind it and fucking her.

So that meant... she not only hacked my company and infiltrated my life but also stalked my best friend.

How could I have not known? She'd played me so hard.

I should've known.

What a fucking fool.

Adelaide's breaths shuddered as she stirred, stretching her arms above her head. She squinted in the bright light.

My heart stopped.

This was it. The moment it all came crashing down. The girl I'd fallen for was a snake in disguise. She'd sunk her fangs deep into my skin and poisoned me with her lies.

I sat back against the couch and watched her, not trusting myself to touch her, not when the urge to slip my hands around her slender neck and squeeze the life from her perfect body plagued me.

"Why are you up? Come lay back down with me."

Her drowsy voice pulled me in like a nighttime melody. Instead of laying beside her and burying my face between her breasts, I stood and put distance between us.

I wouldn't get sucked into her beauty and supposed innocence. Not again.

"Is everything okay?" she asked with pinched brows until she glanced down at her phone in my hand. "Is that my phone?"

"Yeah," I said. "It is."

"Why?" She wiped her hair from her face and adjusted herself to a seated position. "Were you on my phone?"

I stared at the picture of Alek and Liz and turned the screen towards her.

"Do you know who they are?"

She frowned and shook her head. "No. Should I?"

Adelaide took the picture with Alek's back to her, but she should have still been able to recognize him. She was up close with him at the party.

Taking two long strides, I shoved the picture of my best friend and his wife into her face. "Don't fucking lie to me."

"Jake…" Her voice wobbled as her shallow breaths produced micro whimpers that thickened my cock, but turned my fist hard as stone.

Don't touch her.

Don't touch her.

"I don't—"

"Once a liar, always a liar, they say." I stepped away from her and squeezed her phone, willing it to disintegrate into dust in my hands. If it wasn't visible anymore…

Maybe if the evidence didn't exist, I wouldn't feel like she ripped my insides out and splayed them out on this coffee table.

"Jake, let me—"

"What's the real reason we met Adelaide?" I asked, pausing my wrathful march across the room. "Why were you really at the club that night? *Hmm?* Was it really your birthday?"

Of course it was her birthday. Her background check proved as much, but she couldn't possibly bet on me being there and letting her in. Did she orchestrate the event in the back of the club so I'd come to her rescue?

That would be some elaborate plan that relied on a lot of luck instead of strategy.

Adelaide tried getting Merlin and me to meet her for her birthday, and I agreed, but I'd gotten sidetracked with paperwork at the office. Then an incident at the club needed my attention, and I needed to take care of it since Alek passed it on to me while he took care of Liz. I didn't expect to get so busy I'd forget to ask for a meetup location.

She jumped from the couch, then held her head and wobbled. "Of course it was. You know that."

I took one step forward to catch her if she fell.

Bravo.

She played her innocence like a fiddle and had me dancing to her tune.

I took two more steps and pressed my finger into her chest. "Don't play dumb with me, little girl. I'll destroy everything you've ever dreamed of. I'll eviscerate wants and desires you haven't even thought of yet. And just when you think it's all over, you'll look to the future, but there'll be nothing but a black hole before you."

My stomach pinched as the hate spewed without a filter, but she did this to me. She turned the simplest emotion and amplified it to the extreme. How could I think straight with her in the room?

She shook her head, her mouth gaping, and I walked away from her, putting distance between us. I paced her apartment—her phone still clenched in my fist.

I'd bought this place for her. Searched high and low to fulfill her dreams, and this was the outcome.

A deceitful swindler.

"You're scaring me, Jake." She held her hands up between us. "Let me explain."

"Yes. How about you explain your little plan to infiltrate my life, hack my company, and make a killing off mine and my employee's backs?" I paused, waiting for her to deny my accusation, accept it, smile, frown, give me something, anything.

She stood like a statue carved by David himself.

"Bravo." I clapped. "You're a piece of shit just like the rest of those low-life hackers you associate yourself with."

My veins bulged against my skin as my conflicted emotions battled about. I couldn't look at her face without seeing my future with her, the things I wanted to do *with* her. Now all I saw were the things I wanted to do *to* her, and that scared the shit out of me.

"Jake, I wanted to tell you—" She stepped closer, her hand reached out for me.

"Don't fucking touch me. You don't have the right to come near me anymore."

"But Jake..." Tears slipped down her cheeks, the same tears I'd lapped up earlier in the night. These waterworks were for me, but not mine. Nothing of hers was mine anymore.

I'd relinquished my claim on her and set fire to her existence.

She grabbed my hand, and my vision bled until a fog settled over me, and I responded without a thought.

My fingers gripped her fragile throat as I drove her backward, slamming her back against the wall. Her skull hit the drywall, rattling the dishes in the cupboards. She hissed out a strangled cry, her eyes wide like a frightened doe as a generic framed picture teetered and fell off the hook. The malodorous vibration of glass shattering against the floor spread across the room, causing a cataclysmic shift around us.

"You mean nothing to me." I seethed, spittle bursting through my teeth. "You don't exist."

"I'm sorry." She shook her head, her face burning crimson as the veins bulged in her throat against my tight grip. Her fingers clawed into my hard grasp as she choked out, "Don't say that. Please."

"I hope your unhappiness chokes the life from you."

"Let me... e-explain." Her strangled voice tore my conscience in two.

On the one hand, it turned my dick into a fucking rock, and on the other, it ground my nerves, freeing my rage.

"I wouldn't trust a word you say."

Adelaide clawed at my forearms, her nails drawing tiny beads of ruby liquid against my inked skin. Her grip loosened its hold on my wrist, and her eyes rolled.

It wouldn't take much more to end it all, right here and now, but that'd be too easy. I released my grip on her throat and let her drop to her ass on the floor. Her hands held her throat as she wheezed.

"Jake... please." A fit of coughs pulled her to her side. "Stop."

"You don't deserve my mercy, but remember, I gave it to you." I bent down on one knee as I dropped her phone beside her and pushed a lock of her hair from her face so she could see me. "I'll only say this once, so listen and listen well. If you come around me, my company... or hell, anyone I care about. I'll destroy your life and the lives of everyone you've ever loved until the only thing left..."

She turned her face from me, but I snatched her chin and turned her gaze, forcing her to look into my eyes. "Until the only thing left is to draw the jagged blade across your throat." I freed her jaw as another tear slipped down her face. "And if you think your friends will get away with it, think again. I'll come after them too. Just you watch."

I stood and grabbed my things, pausing to take in her shaking frame curled up on the floor.

Maybe I'd taken it too far, but so had she.

I slammed the door behind me, leaving her a sobbing mess and my guts torn to shreds.

Adelaide

2

"I'm sorry," I cried, my compressed voice no higher than a whisper.

He'd taken my heart and stomped on it, digging his heel into it for good measure until it shattered. Each piece sharpened by his hatred, cruel words, and murderous rage.

His reaction to my betrayal was all that I'd feared and more. After a night of bliss and visceral contentment, I'd woken to hell's fire released upon me with a vengeance.

As soon as he showed me the picture I'd taken a few weeks ago, I knew the fantastical moment I'd spun up in my mind had come crashing down, making my stomach twist into knots.

A barking, raspy cough escaped my throat. I rubbed my neck again, willing my heart to cease beating.

He'd turned on me so fast, like a starving dog on his owner.

I braced my weight on my hands and knees, then rose to my feet and wiped the tears from my face.

What if he came back? I glanced at the door and quickly locked the deadbolt. Not that it mattered. He had the key.

I needed to get out of here before he finished what he started.

He hadn't strangled me for long before I'd lost consciousness for a moment.

When I'd discerned what had happened, I was on the floor, my ass aching from the fall.

He didn't care enough to catch me.

And why would he?

I was the enemy now.

He hated me.

"Oh my God." I put my hand over my mouth and pinched my eyes closed.

He hated me.

As much as I told myself this day would come, a part of me prayed it never did. Although I'd prepared for it, I never expected such a violent reaction from someone who made me feel I was worth the effort.

I never expected him to lay hands on me the way he did.

The things he said.

The hateful things.

He threatened to kill my friends and me—

Would he follow through? Could he possibly do something like that, or was it something he said in the heat of the moment?

I picked up the broken picture frame of a cow licking her nose with her tongue. The shattered glass stayed in the confines of the frame, but when I put it on the counter, the micro scratches became visible.

Tears flooded my lids again, but I brushed them away and walked toward the couch.

We'd sat there moments ago.

He held me in his arms and told me I was his. I didn't want that before. I wanted him to let me go, so *this*... So *this* wouldn't happen..

But he also told me he'd never hurt me. He told me he wouldn't let me go.

Some part of me thought that would be my saving grace, but it wasn't. Not even close.

Now he'd vowed to destroy everyone I've ever known.

The white walls bore down on me like giants looming over ants. My breath caught in my chest, constricting it until I couldn't suck in a single breath.

My hand slammed against the imposing fortress around me as I collapsed to my knees, my stomach churning.

Not again.

Not again.

I stood and ran into the bathroom.

My stomach cramped, and I heaved forward, emptying its entirety into the toilet.

Crawling to the counter, I used it to steady myself on my feet, then brushed my teeth, my gaunt face staring back at me in the mirror. My pale skin and dark circles under my eyes only added to my misery.

A door slammed, and I jumped.

I peered out the bathroom door, down the hall, and to the front. The deadbolt hadn't moved from its locked position, and there wasn't a noise to be heard inside the apartment.

The tremor in my hands lessened as the threat dissipated. Running my toothbrush under the faucet, I tossed it onto the counter and grabbed my hand with my other, willing the remaining shakes to stop.

Once they calmed, I rinsed my mouth with water, then went into my room for clothes, needing more than a t-shirt and panties if I wanted to go home.

That's all he wanted me in, and I was okay with it. It made his touch against my skin effortless.

Now, his touch hurt.

I dug into my dresser, moving as fast as my pained stomach would allow to find something to cover my lower half. It was only a two-mile walk home.

Black sweats with a drawstring and elastic around the ankles sat in the back of the drawer. These would do. I'd blend into the night, and so long as I stayed on the sidewalk, that wouldn't be an issue.

I slipped on the sweats and grabbed a long sleeve because even though the sun caused sweat to drip from your pores, the night made you vibrate with chattering teeth.

I sat on the couch, turned the TV off, and slipped on my shoes. My phone lay on the ground where he tossed it in front of my face near the kitchen, and the blanket we'd shared lay crumpled on the couch.

An unexpected urge to clean things up slapped me across the face like an icy hand of reason.

I darted for my phone, tucked it into my bag, and bolted out the door, not bothering to lock up behind me.

If people wanted to take what was there, they could have it. I wouldn't be coming back.

It was half-past midnight, and this part of the city was asleep, unlike downtown. Not even the crickets chirped.

My feet hit the pavement, my gaze darting over my shoulder every ten paces. My heart shuddered inside my chest, my breaths rapid and achy, and the hairs on my neck rose to attention. There were eyes everywhere, yet nowhere.

Street lights illuminated the tar every twenty steps.

I counted them.

Each time I hit twenty, the light consumed me, and a heaviness slipped off my shoulders, but the moment I stepped away from it, the burden of night crept back in and weighed me down.

I quickened my pace, challenging myself to lessen the distance between—my heels hitting the cement with deafening thuds.

Two steps, and I was back in the dark. I clutched my bag tighter, keeping the tears from my eyes as the haunting darkness in his gaze plagued me.

My skin crawled and tingled like tiny ants making their march across my body. With tense muscles, I continued on the sidewalk, praying my house would spring up.

Blackness swept over the trees, streets, and upcoming yards. A dog barked in the distance, and the pungent scent of dewy grass hit my nose.

"Not far," I whispered as a vehicle turned down the street. Their headlights momentarily blinded me as they passed by.

My hands shook as the big black truck revved his diesel engine behind me. Even though he'd driven away, my raw nerves fired off until every part of my body shuddered.

One mile down and another to go. Sweat dribbled down my spine despite the chill on my cheeks and nose.

Ten more steps until the light.

Nine.

Eight.

A cat meandered across the street ahead, pausing in the center with no sense of self-preservation.

They had to know that it was a dangerous place to be hanging out, right? Like I knew that walking in the dark was a stupid idea, yet I did it anyway.

The roar of the diesel engine came up behind me.

I didn't have to look over my shoulder to know it wasn't normal. My pulse swooshed in my ears, and my heart picked up the tempo.

A car door shut, followed by heavy footfalls against the cement, approaching me from behind.

Shit.

Oh my God.

I grabbed my purse and tucked it tighter into my body as I quickened my pace, my thighs burning from the abuse. The footsteps behind me echoed down the barren street in time with my own.

Glancing over my shoulder, I did a double take as my heart stopped dead in my chest. A man with wide shoulders and tapered waist cast a shadow into the street like the Iron Giant, and he was heading this way—his shoulders swinging to and fro.

If he got hold of me... I didn't stand a chance, and Jake's threats would come to fruition.

I needed a means of escape. My heart thudded in my chest, exhausted from the terror and paranoia as my eyes darted all around.

The Iron Giant's footsteps grew closer, and the sight over my shoulder drove my heart into my stomach.

Run.

My feet hit the asphalt without a second thought, and he and the truck responded in kind.

The distant roar of the diesel engine became a monster about to lash out at me as my feet hit the middle of the road.

Another long stride.

"Ahh," I cried out as a truck collided with my shoulder, my world spinning around me. The collision twisted my body around, my feet tripping over themselves until I hurtled into the curb, my hip taking the brunt of the impact.

My hands burned as they skidded against the pitted cement. A keen-edged bolt of agony tore at my bones, sending an electrical zap to my toes.

Boots.

Running.

Closer.

I pushed myself to my feet in time for the Giant to hit the street. His face glowed a demonic maroon as the truck's brake lights cast shadows around the darkened street.

The red lights vanished into the night as I limped toward Miss. Lavender's yard, followed by squealing tires.

Home. It was so tangible I could feel the doorknob in my hands. But that's all I'd get is a distant memory if I didn't hightail it out of here.

I jumped over Miss Lavender's wooden fence and lumbered across her backyard. My feet hit landmines of empty pots and bricks like a bull's horns in a China shop.

A hoarse, deep voice called out as I hit the shadows on her back fence, and I peered around.

Where did he go?

My ragged breaths filled the air as I hoisted myself over Mr. Belvedere's chain-link fence, my heavy sweats catching at the twist on top. I tilted head first toward the ground, my pants pulling away from my body until the material gave way with a tear, sending me plummeting to the ground as if someone reinstated gravity without warning.

"*Owowow*," I whispered, shaking out my wrist. A faint ringing in my ear caught my attention, freeing space from this nightmare for a moment. I pulled in a ragged breath, staunching it just before capacity as the stitch in my side ripped a gasp from my lips.

Where did they go?

Miss. Lavender's yard remained shrouded in darkness. Not a single moving object flitted across her yard.

They wouldn't have given up so easily? Would they have?

I scooted my back to Mister Belvedere's brick home and caught my breath, listening to the surrounding nothingness. Not even a distant rumble from the man's truck. It was like I'd hallucinated it all. But the ache in my shoulder divulged a secret no one knew yet...

Someone had tried to kidnap me... or worse.

Shivers broke through my skin as chilled air slipped through the tattered hole in my pants, thrusting me back into the here and now. How long had I been sitting here?

My heart still raced, my breaths steady, but my mind had calmed only a fraction. Enough for me to picture the yards it would take for me to get home. I bounced my finger in front of me in the unique pattern it'd take, the neighbors' names on my reticent lips.

A zinging ache rushed down my thigh as I hoisted myself to my feet. The adrenaline hadn't given up the reins yet, and it still hurt to move.

I groaned, using the brick wall for support as I steadied myself and walked through the front gate, peering down the street in both directions the closer I came to the front of the home.

Nothing.

No engine.

No footsteps.

The thick air around me set forth a beat of death. These were either my last moments or ones I'd remember for the rest of my days.

I limped across the street, opening the fence to Mrs. Gracens' yard, then to the next, and then another until I toppled over into my backyard, my body aching, lungs gasping for air.

My heavy feet and cramping thighs slowed me down as I slugged through my father's damp grass, safety holding me in its fragile arms. I dug out my key as I avoided my father's sprinkler system and walked around to the front door.

How had I made it home when it felt like such an insurmountable task? Did they determine I wasn't worth the effort? Were they just a bunch of drunk idiots looking for a good time?

I waddled up the stairs and slipped my key into the lock, praying they forgot about the chain as a pair of headlights illuminated the porch.

My heart sunk into my stomach, and my fingers slackened on everything in my hands, dropping them to the porch as the engine's rumble reverberated around me. How did they know where I lived?

The big black truck with the menacing lights and oversized tires revved its engine two houses down, placed strategically to see me approaching from all sides.

How was that possible? Who were they?

"Daddy!" my voice broke as I pounded my fists on the door. "Daddy, open up, please!"

I turned over my shoulder as the revving stopped, and I found a scene straight out of a horror movie. The broad, beefy man stood at the end of my driveway with a scowl on his face and a wide stance.

He took a step forward, drawing a high-pitched scream from the bottom of my lungs, shattering the tranquility of the night. I jumped over the side railing, my feet sliding on the wet grass, and set off the sprinkler as I rounded the corner.

There was no way I'd jump back through people's yards, so I dropped into my window well and laid on my back, my knees tucked up to my chin.

Don't make a sound.

The sprinklers stopped, allowing my thudding heartbeat to bleed into my ears with enough force to transitorily deafen me.

A fresh stream of water hit the side of the house with the telltale *chink, chink, chink* as the impact sprinkler started again.

I pinched my eyes closed and held my breath, praying they couldn't see me in the dark.

A steel grip grabbed my arms and pulled me into the air as I screamed, "Let me go!" I dug my nails into the man's meaty arms around my chest, causing him to squeeze like a boa constrictor until my screams were nothing more than a wheezy breath.

The hulking Goliath waddled as I kicked his shins, the spray of water hitting my face, causing my lungs to seize. Water shot up my nose and down my throat, burning my sinuses and eyes.

I hacked and coughed as he stepped into my driveway and suddenly stopped.

"There's a shotgun pointed at the back of your skull. I suggest you let go of my daughter."

Certain sounds in this world strike fear without hesitation, and one of those is a shell being racked into the chamber of a pump-action shotgun.

"Daddy," I wheezed.

The man's thick arms dropped me to the ground, my hands and knees smarting as I crawled toward my father, standing on the porch wearing nothing but his boxers and a double-barreled shotgun.

I sucked in air through my waterlogged lungs as the Hulk put his hands in the air and slowly backed away.

"Adelaide, get inside."

"You're fucked now, you asshole."

I grabbed the railing as the man turned tail and ran off down the driveway, the end of my father's gun trailing after him.

"Come on." My father shifted his gun to one hand and helped me stand on my shaky feet as he kept his eyes on the man. "Get up. Now. Inside."

I stood and wrapped my arms around him, a sob breaking through in a whoosh. "Daddy, I was so scared."

"Linda, call the—"

"I did. They're on their way."

He shut the door, bolted it, and then wrapped his arm around my shivering shoulders. "What happened?"

Where do I begin?

"Jesus, Chris. She's shaking," Mom said as she wrapped a thin shawl around my shoulders.

"Jake and I got into a fight, and I left." My teeth chattered, breaking up words as I stuttered. "These guys started chasing me when I got halfway home." I pulled the shawl tighter around me. "I thought they were drunk and looking for trouble, but they..." I trailed off, not wanting to speak the obvious out loud, but they needed to know. "These guys knew where I lived and were waiting for me."

"He let you walk home alone?"

"He left too, Dad."

A sliver of pain shot through my temple, turning my head hot and itchy as I defended him. He didn't deserve my defense, but I couldn't have my father thinking it was his fault this had happened.

"The police are here, Chris," my mother said, taking me in her arms as my father raced to his bedroom.

"Sheriff's department," they announced as a knock sounded at the door.

Their lights turned the living room into a disco of blue and red flashing lights, dancing across the walls, ceiling, and furniture.

My mother opened the door with me wrapped around her waist. "Thank you for coming."

The rest of the night was a blur as they interviewed both my father and me—my mother hadn't come out fast enough to see the man holding me. She'd only heard my frantic pleas at the door and woke my father.

It was now three A.M., and the last of the investigators shut the door, my eyelids drooping and losing the battle to stay awake. My hands shook, and my knee bobbed up and down as my adrenaline crashed—the nausea worsened.

"Why don't you get some rest, sweetie?" My mother kissed my forehead and hugged me as I winced in silence. I didn't want her to worry more than she already had.

I gathered my things my father had collected from the door and nodded. "Thanks, Dad."

"I don't know how you find yourself in these situations, Adelaide."

"Me either."

Shrugging, I made my way downstairs, shutting the door behind me—my bedroom window staring at me like a glowing furnace in the basement. I rushed forward and slammed the curtains closed.

I'd been right there. So close to safety, but yet impossible to hold.

I kicked off my shoes, stripped off my damp clothes, climbed onto my bare mattress, and tucked my hands under my pillow.

Sleep, take me... I don't want to be here right now.

Jake

3

"**A**gain."

"Come on, Jake," Scott said with beads of sweat dribbling down his reddened face. "I think we're done."

I exhaled, dropped my stance, and held my hand for a power shake. "All right."

We'd grappled for the last four hours, turning our years of Krav Maga practice into a well-trained, choreographed battle.

We'd worked on our hand-to-hand techniques for three straight days as I toiled through the shit going on in my head.

It all made sense to me now. How her behavior changed when she couldn't get into my server. Then she blamed it on me like it was my fault this relationship didn't work out.

The nerve she had to try to manipulate me.

"Anytime but tomorrow. My kid's little league soccer game is two hours away, and we won't be back until late." He wiped the sweat from his brow. "Can you believe they make us travel that far?"

I shook my head. "I know they did that in high school, but eight-year-old's too?"

"Yeah. It's no wonder parents can't put their kids in sports."

He grabbed his gym gear and headed for the showers.

"I'll catch you later."

Normally, I'd shower at the gym, my bag ready in my trunk, but today I had an important meeting with Adelaide's parents that I didn't want to miss and a handoff for the SAMs.

When I stopped by a few days ago, Chris wasn't home, but I put together a time where we could sit down and discuss what their precious daughter had been up to—a time when she wouldn't be there, of course.

I unlocked my car as I walked out of the studio, tossed my bag in the back seat, and headed home with that woman invading my thoughts. She'd been on my mind every second of every day since she'd penetrated my life. It didn't bother me, but now it felt like a persistent earworm that wouldn't go away no matter what I did.

Switching on a tech podcast as I drove home, I tuned in to their monotonous voices talking about the latest and greatest software for business. It gave me something to focus on that wasn't a redhead with freckles to die for.

I pulled into my driveway; time flying by faster than I'd like to admit, and glowered as I parked and climbed out of my car. My sore muscles screamed as I walked down the steps to the lower half of my split-level home and stripped my clothes off my sweaty body.

Shivers trailed up and down my legs as the cool water hit me from all angles when I stepped into the shower. My tense shoulders slackened as the heat came through, pounding into them like an overdue massage.

Shit.

I'd need a massage after the days I'd spent beating my sparring partner. Scott didn't deserve some of the moves I'd pulled on him, but it was my only means of getting out my frustrations without causing someone serious damage.

It gave me the patience and methodical movements I needed when all I wanted was to give into the reckless side she'd dug out of me. Like strangling her... again.

I hated that I'd done that to her. The fear in her eyes when she looked at me still haunts me, but I couldn't bring myself to apologize.

And why the hell should I?

After what she did to me, throttling her for thirty seconds was a fair take away.

I scrubbed my body, wiping away the day's sweat and hard work, then rinsed—the water hitting the ground with emphatic smacks like it'd been thrown with force towards the tile. I stepped out of the shower and wrapped a towel around my waist.

Everything in my house held memories of her, right down to my goddamn closet when I'd gotten her some clothes the first night we met.

Or was that really the first time? Had she stalked me like she did Alek? I didn't look far enough back to see if there were any pictures of me. I'd gotten too hung up on the first picture.

What benefit would it be to follow them? And the look in her eyes when I confronted her about them seemed authentic. For a split second, she'd convinced me she had no idea who they were.

"*Ugh*," I groaned as I slapped the top of my head and drew my palms down my face. "Stop thinking about her."

No matter what I did to pull her from my memories, she'd stuck there.

I threw on a pair of jeans and a t-shirt, not bothering to see what it said, then a pair of socks with black shoes. I didn't even bother styling my hair, I just shoved my fingers through the wet strands, pushing them over to the side, and called it good.

My kitchen.

God, even my kitchen.

I couldn't walk in here without seeing her sitting at my damn table with Becca, enjoying breakfast with us. Pulling out a box of leftovers, I flipped the lid and dug into the cold steak.

Protein after a workout was the best way for me to sustain my stomach. Otherwise, I'd make the terrible mistake of filling up on pizza, and two hours later, I'd be starving like a homeless person. And that reminded me.

I pulled out my phone and called Becca.

"Blackstone Tech, this is Becca—"

"It's me," I said, cutting off her speech. "I need you to talk to accounting about donating to a different homeless outreach. The last one had some bad press about mishandled funds. I don't want that bouncing back on us."

"Okay. Anything else?"

"No. Thanks."

"You're welcome."

Hanging up, I took the last chunk out of my steak, threw the bone in the trash, along with the container, then set it to compact.

The motor whirred as I washed my hands, then snatched my keys and walked back out into my garage.

Adelaide declared war the moment she came after me, then made it a slaughterhouse when she tried to take me for fifteen million.

I'd make her see the error of her ways... the hard way.

Adelaide

4

I dug into the pile of clothes next to my backpack, searching for a pair of clean panties, but came up empty-handed. "Dammit." I slapped my thigh with an exasperated sigh.

I'd run out of clean clothes and sanity, and I was not looking forward to venturing out to gather more—clothes, not sanity.

That ship had long since sailed.

It'd been two days since I left my parent's home to hide out in this motel room with ratty curtains, mold in the shower, and grimy carpets. I'd slowly but surely rotted away with boredom while waiting for Rachel, my go-to girl, to create my new IDs.

Between the guy who tried to kidnap me, some bizarre note that showed up at my parent's home, and Jake, I'd decided it was probably best I left. I couldn't put my parents in any more danger. If something happened to them, I'd never forgive myself.

And because of that, I'd sat in this dingy motel room, taking small hacking jobs that paid for the room—A senior wanting to change his final grade and a girl wanting to see if her boyfriend had cheated on her.

Simple tasks that paid well and took little concentration. Because my ability to sit on a task for long had gone out the window—along with the mini bar and two boxes of Saltines. It was the only thing I could stomach.

The stress burned my insides with nausea until it forced me to make several trips to the bathroom. I guessed the liquor didn't help matters much either. Of course, I was out of that now, too, so that left me dealing with my feelings stone-cold sober, which was just unacceptable.

I peeked out the window that overlooked the parking lot. Pushing aside the shabby flower curtain that hadn't been cleaned since the early two thousands, I confirmed the regulars were here. No stragglers or anyone sitting by and watching.

It had taken me three hours to get to this motel because I'd taken two buses, five separate taxis, and an Uber after hiding in an alleyway for thirty minutes.

Logging into my Uber app, I requested a ride, telling him to park on the street, not in the parking lot, then gathered my dirty clothes around the room. I tossed every scrap of clothing I had into my bag, which wasn't much, and zipped it up, then waited.

Ten minutes passed, then another five, until the small blue four-door sedan I'd reserved pulled into a space close to my room.

Why can't anyone listen to instructions these days?

I sighed and snagged the old-fashioned key off the little entertainment center—if it could be called that—then hyped myself up.

It wouldn't be long. I'd just go inside, drop off my clothes, then pick up new ones.

Peeking my head out of the door, I peered left, then right.

Clear.

Slipping a thin piece of thread between the door frame and the door, I shut it. It was a neat little trick I'd picked up from all my spare time. It assured me that if anyone were to walk into my motel room, I'd know about it.

I rushed to the Uber, keeping my face down, and slid into the back seat, my backpack held tight against my chest like a teddy bear.

"All set?"

"Yes," I said to the brown-haired man as I clicked my seatbelt into place.

He drove off as I stared at the window, wishing I had the guts to tell him off for not listening. But what purpose would that serve? It would just create more waves in this ocean I was drowning in. And what was that saying? 'Don't bite the hand?' The last thing I needed was for him to leave me on the side of the road and at the mercy of those people.

Whoever those people were.

I'd watched the police department handle this case with bumbling hands and no interviews. They had gotten nowhere in the investigation, which grated on my nerves.

So I did a little investigating of my own, searching for black trucks registered in this county. I got a hit of over sixty-thousand matching that description with nothing to narrow it down.

"Just drop me off on the corner, and I'll walk the rest of the way," I said as he crept up to the stop sign. He paused, waiting some untold amount of time, then turned right. "This will do. Right here." I pointed to the curb, and he pulled over. "Thank you."

"Have a good day."

I snorted. Yeah. I haven't had a good day in a long while. Not since...

He was too painful to think about.

It wasn't love.

He was just a guy who made me feel good.

That's what I kept telling myself because I'd fucked things up, and there was no going back.

"Can you wait for me? I won't be long, but I need a ride back."

He nodded. "You'll get charged per minute."

"That's fine." Grabbing my things, I got out of the car. "I'll be right back."

I rounded the corner and stopped dead in my tracks. My skin flushed as my pulse whooshed in my ears, building pressure in my skull. I wasn't ready for this, but I had no other choice. I could walk in there and ignore him. No one said I needed to speak or even acknowledge his existence.

Could I do that? Probably not. I'm sure I'd cave at the moment I saw his ice-cold blue eyes.

What was he doing here? Was he looking for me? Did he want to talk? There wasn't any data I could provide him about what had happened to his company. Holeo had blocked me from the chat room and personally.

I'd tried telling the team about Jake's knowledge, but Holeo made that next to impossible. Instead, I privately messaged them individually without a single response in return.

My automatic footfalls brought me closer to his car parked on the side of the road like he used to do when he'd pick me up or drop me off.

I shook my hands out and diverted my gaze away from his car as though it helped create a new reality where he wasn't really here, and I wasn't about to interact with him.

Oh my God. What if he's telling Mom and Dad what had happened? What if...

I rushed up the driveway, ready to end his tattling when the front door opened, and he walked out with possibly the worst timing of the century.

Jake's smile slid from his face. His piercing blue eyes struck every nerve in my body as he smirked.

"Adelaide."

My hand went to my throat and his gaze followed as it settled around my neck. The slimy grin he'd made faltered for a fraction of a second as if he felt remorse over what he'd done to me.

"What are you doing here?" I swallowed... hard. "What do you want?"

He tucked his hands in his pockets and walked down the steps towards me. I skirted around him and took a step backward, my arms tightening around my backpack.

"I was just having a little chat with your parents."

"About what?"

He tipped his head forward and pulled his brows together. "I think you know," he said with a flint of anger rippling across his face. "They are pretty upset about everything that's transpired, Adelaide."

Jake stepped towards me, and I took another step back, my heel hitting the edge of the porch stairs, sending me off kilter. I took another step, my other heel tripping over the same brick of cement.

My equilibrium tilted as my hand reached for the railing to catch my fall. Jake's muscular arm wrapped around my waist, his scent engulfing me before my ass even touched the edge of the steps.

"Watch what you're doing," he said, pulling me upright.

"I'm..." I sucked in a steady stream of air with a hint of Jake's cologne riding on it. Shivers shook my arms as his heat pressed against me. It would only take a slight shift forward, and my lips would touch his scented neck. What's wrong with me? I pushed against him, swallowing my desire for him down into my fluttering stomach. "I'm fine."

"Could've fooled me." He kept his firm hold on me. "You seem nervous?"

His head dipped down as if battling the same desire as me. But that wasn't possible, not after what happened.

I backed away, but he walked with me, his grip tight. "Why wouldn't I be after what you did to me? You tried to kill me, then sent your freaks after me." I shoved him hard. "I have every right to be scared."

That wasn't exactly fair. I hadn't suspected him since that first night, but he had me a flustered mess, and it just came rushing out.

He frowned and pulled away from me, planting his hand on his hip. "Okay, for one, I didn't try to kill you. If I had, you'd be dead. And two, what do you mean I sent someone after you?"

I shook my head and spun on my heel, walking up the porch with careful steps. "Forget it."

"Tell me, Adelaide." I glanced over my shoulder as he pointed his finger to the ground, demanding my cooperation. "What do you mean? Did someone come after you?"

I walked inside and shut the door, but before it latched, he slammed his hand against the surface.

"Just leave me alone," I whispered, afraid my parents might hear.

Jake stepped inside and shut the door behind him as I sped through the kitchen where my parents stood discussing something.

"Adelaide?" my mother said, putting her cup down on the counter. "Jake?"

"What's going on?" my dad asked.

"It's okay, Mr. and Mrs. Leaver. Adelaide and I are just discussing the damages." He followed me towards the stairs, and my heart jumped into my throat.

They weren't going to say anything? Or stop him from pursuing me?

Snorting, I bolted down the stairs. If I could get behind my bedroom door, I'd be safe there.

Jake rushed after me, close on my heels. By the time I'd gotten to the bottom step, I'd become winded and almost sleepy.

I'd only grown weaker since that night. With the alcohol, puking, and saltines as my only source of sustenance, there wasn't much to keep me nourished.

Jake shut the door behind us and turned the lock—the click a resounding nail in my coffin.

"Leave," I panted.

"I think you know how this is gonna go."

We've been here before. He was persistent, stubborn as a fucking mule, and eventually got what he wanted. And that was when I was at full strength. There was no way I could have battled him now.

"I don't have time for this."

I dropped my backpack and dumped my dirty clothes into the hamper, then hit my closet and dresser, repacking my bag as he stood in the center of my room, his fists on his hips.

The sheets and comforter I'd left on the floor for the last two and a half weeks were gone. Mom must have picked them up when she came in to feed Fruity.

That left my room feeling as bare as my mattress.

"Where are you going?"

I snorted again. "Like I'm going to tell you." I walked around him, shoving a pair of socks into the front pack. He gripped my arm, his fingers digging hard into my flesh.

"I'm not playing this fucking game with you, Adelaide," he seethed. The same frightening look he had that night shined in his eyes now, sending prickling shivers up my spine. "Tell me what's happened and where you're going."

"Why do you care? You threatened to destroy me and everyone I've ever loved. Shouldn't you be happy? Your plan is coming to fruition, and you haven't even lifted a finger." I pulled on my arm, but he squeezed harder. "Let me go."

"If anyone is going to ruin your life, it'll be me."

"Oh, so it's not because you care, but because you want first dibs?" He may have infuriated me, but there was a smidgen of hope raised inside of me when he asked about my safety, only for him to dash it with his hatefulness. My eyes burned as tears threatened to make an appearance. "Let me go, and I'll disappear from your life just like you want."

"And who said I wanted that?"

I pushed my arm up between us, rotated the direction of my elbow to the outside of his grip, and plunged it down. The self-defense move twisted his wrist and caused pressure against his thumb, forcing him to relinquish his hold. It was the move I'd learned the last two days watching YouTube videos.

"I believe you said I didn't exist anymore. Was that before or after you choked me into unconsciousness? I don't remember. The night's a little fuzzy." I zipped up my backpack and waltzed into the bathroom. "So let me go, and you'll never have to think about me again."

I dipped into the cabinet below, searching for another tube of traveling toothpaste.

"It's a little premature for that, isn't it?"

I looked up at him with a glare.

Jake leaned against my doorway, his arms crossed as he stared at something on the counter.

A white box sat on the countertop with two pink lines staring at me. My eyes bugged out of their sockets as I grabbed the unopened box and threw it under the sink.

"It's not mine. It's Monica's."

"You expect me to fall for that?"

"Believe what you want."

He bent down beside me, his elbows resting on his knees, the new heart tattoo visible on his finger. "I want to be there when you take that test in two weeks."

"Two weeks? I won't be here..." I hung my head.

Shit.

I'd be out of his life whether he liked it or not.

Besides, what was the significance of two weeks? Was there something else he had in store for me?

His fists clenched. "You will be here. I'll make sure of it." He stood, towering over me. "Don't even think about disappearing. I'll find you, Adelaide."

Jake turned on his heel, leaving me on the bathroom floor.

"What are you going to do to me?"

"It's not what I'm going to do to you. It's what I've already done. I'm warning you," he pointed his finger at me. "Don't make things harder than they need to be."

And with that, he unlocked my bedroom door and walked out.

What had he done? And what would he do if I didn't stick around?

My mind reeled with every possible terrifying scenario as I squeezed the toothpaste.

Shaking myself free of the imaginary glimpse of my future, I grabbed the pregnancy test in one hand and toothpaste in the other, then shoved them into my pack.

The image with two pink lines stared at me, its advertisement not appealing to me. I looked back at the bathroom, then back at the package.

I could take the test and then be on my way. It was probably just an over-abundance of stress that caused the symptoms.

Only one way to find out?

I took the box back into the bathroom and locked the door behind me, taking no chances that he could return and find me in a compromising situation.

Double checking the lock, I sighed with relief, then tore open the box. The small white rectangular plastic test sat on my counter with a results box and this tiny as sin space where I was supposed to put my pee.

How the hell was I supposed to aim for that? I wasn't a man.

I read over the instructions and found the pipette included that I'd missed.

A cup... I needed a cup. Oh, Lord. This turned out to be more than I'd bargained for.

I dipped down below the cupboard and, with shaking hands, pulled out a roll of paper Dixie cups I used for mouthwash, then picked one with pretty carnations and sat over the toilet, my bladder freezing.

Didn't the manufacturers understand it wasn't normal to pee when your hand was in the way? Everything seized up.

After sitting for a good forty seconds, convincing myself this was totally fine, I filled the cup, then put it on the counter and wiped.

My stomach twisted in knots, making the bile rise in my throat. I'd need some anti-anxiety medication after everything was said and done.

"Adelaide," my mother said from my bathroom door. "Are you in there?"

Shit. "I'll be right out," I said, scrambling to hide the evidence. My hand brushed against the cup, and the contents dumped into the sink. "*No. No. No.*" I whispered.

"Is everything okay?"

"Yeah, I just..." Lost my opportunity to cleanse my mind of worry. "Spilled my foundation."

"Okay, well, you have a visitor."

I groaned. "Coming."

"When you're done, your father and I need to talk to you."

A 'family meeting,' as Monica called it. I wonder how *her* 'meeting' went? I hadn't heard from her since she'd forced me to buy the damn test. Then everything hit the fan, and she became an afterthought.

"Okay," I grumbled.

I gathered the test, resolving to take it later when my bladder filled back up. When my bedroom door clicked shut, I exited my bathroom and stuffed everything back inside my backpack, then zipped it up.

Glancing down at my dirty sweats, I carefully pulled them off and stripped my shirt over my head.

A deep purple bruise covered my hip bone like a bullseye where I'd fallen. It matched the one on my shoulder where the truck mirror hit me. I closed my eyes and winced as I lifted my arms above my head and slipped on a loose t-shirt, followed by sweats.

After tying my shoes, I grabbed my backpack and slunk out my bedroom door, but not before giving Fruity a few bloodworms and saying goodbye.

"He's on the porch. I didn't want him coming inside, given everything that's happened," my mom said as I hit the top of the steps.

"Okay."

I stepped outside and stared at a man in his mid-thirties. He stood with his hands tucked into his pants pockets, his gaze tipped to the floor, which had his flaxen hair hanging in front of his face in natural waves. It was a hairstyle I hadn't seen since my mother showed me a CD of Hanson.

"Can I help you?"

The man looked at me with sky-blue eyes. His bushy brows pushed together when he saw me. "I didn't expect you to be so pretty."

I raised a brow and adjusted my pack. "Um... thanks? I think."

A thin mustache covered a portion of his cupid's bow, accenting his upper lip as he smiled, sending chills running up my spine.

"Who are you?"

He walked towards me with his hand out. I stared at him as if he had leprosy, then put his hand down when I didn't take it. "I'm Franklin." He tucked his hand back into his pocket.

"I don't know a Franklin." I shouldered past him and down the porch.

"You know me as ButCrysis."

Adelaide

5

"You have some nerve," I murmured as I turned on my heel and poked his chest with my finger. "You're lucky I don't break your fucking nose, you bully."

He put his hands up. "I'm sorry. I suffer from inadequacy stemming from a poor childhood, and it causes me to be hateful to the people who I like but don't return the affection," he said with a smirk.

I scoffed. "Is that what your therapist told you?" I rolled my eyes and dropped my finger. "How did you find me, anyway?"

He shook his head and bowed his hands to his sides as he shrugged his shoulders. "Not that hard, really."

Goddammit.

I waited for him to explain. Instead, he placed his hands in his pockets and rocked on his heels.

Helpful.

Really helpful.

"What do you want?" I looked around him, checking for a black truck, then continued walking to my waiting Uber around the corner.

"To warn you."

"About what exactly?" I grabbed his shirt by the collar and pulled him into my neighbor's yard, behind the six-foot hedges bordering the front yard. "Why?"

"Things went wild in the last few weeks, but you weren't there. Holeo said it was because you resigned but wouldn't say why, and then things went dark."

"Dark?"

"He went into hiding. We thought maybe you went with him since it was such perfect timing, but then Skipper died, and Torpedo... he's in critical condition... Shot in his own home. Can you believe that?"

My heart leaped, spiking the pressure in my brain. "How do you know that?" *Weren't we an anonymous group of hackers?*

"It's all over the news." He raised his shoulders as though I should pay more attention to the workings going on in the world. "Why did you start asking questions?"

The news? But how...

"What does it matter? I asked Holeo a few things, and he gave me an answer."

I glanced around the hedge, keeping an eye out for anything suspicious. Eyes were everywhere, and they raised the hairs on the back of my neck, setting my senses aflame.

"Why do you keep looking around?"

"Franklin... Crysis. Whoever you are, I need to leave."

He grabbed my elbow. "Wait."

"Make it quick," I said, shaking him off. If I didn't hurry, my Uber would disappear, then I'd be stuck... again.

"What do you know about Sev Shun?"

I choked. "Come again?"

"That's who you're running from, isn't it?"

I faltered as my heart raced. "That's not possible. We haven't even hit them yet."

He shook his head, my paranoia bleeding into him as he looked around. "That's what I thought. But Holeo had a different agenda... a personal vendetta."

"What for?"

Franklin sighed and pulled out his phone, showing me a newspaper article.

A high school IT team went to Mexico City, Mexico, for a hack-a-thon. While they were there, a bomb exploded, killing three of their classmates and two Mexican students. No one was arrested or came forward to take responsibility. The Mexican government assumed the cartel was behind it, catching innocent civilians in their retaliation. It wasn't the first time that had happened.

"Where does Black Dog come into all of this?"

"Black Dog? *Ah. Right.*" He faltered, and I gave him a guarded look. "They were the ones responsible."

"And how do you know that?"

"A picture from an article, I think Ye—Holeo said." He planted his feet wide, his arms crossing over his chest.

"How did he know for sure it was them?"

"This soldier had a black tribal band around his forearm. Two of them. He recognized..."

Why did that sound so familiar?

"You okay? You look a little pale."

"I'm pretty sure I've seen the guy you've just described." I shook my head and stepped away as he reached for my shoulder. "You didn't come here to warn me, did you?"

"No." He shoved his hand back into his pocket. "I came to see if you knew where Holeo is. He's the only one that can fix this."

I shook my head. "I have no clue. My life is in shambles because of him."

Like how I destroyed everything good with Jake, my parents now think I'm a lowlife living off of take-aways.

"He did a lot of people dirty."

"I guess that means everyone gets caught up in his mess." My stomach tilted as I backed away from him, looking all around me. "What about my parents?"

"They'll get caught in the crossfire."

I sucked in a staggered breath. The thought of someone hurting my parents because of me rocked my stomach. My plan to leave just accelerated to tonight.

"So you don't know where Holeo is then?"

I shook my head and turned, speed walking down the sidewalk away from him as thoughts of escape worked through my mind like a tired CPU.

"Good luck," he hollered after me.

Rounding the corner where I'd left my Uber driver, my shoulder deflated. I'd taken too long, and he was gone.

Shit.

Pulling out my phone, I scheduled a new one to take me to the motel. I still had my laptop and gear there, and once I checked out, I had one more pit stop before leaving this place for good.

My heart sank as I found Rachel in my contacts and dialed. I'd never get to say goodbye to my parents. Not in person, anyway. I'd have to call them from a secure location to let them know I was okay, but I couldn't risk going back there. This was it for me.

"Rachel here."

"I need it today."

"Meet me at ten tonight."

The phone call ended, and I put it back in my pocket. After tonight, I'd be known as Felicity.

After standing for ten minutes, a car pulled up with an Uber sticker in the back, and I tucked my head inside.

"Going to the Burlton Motel?" he said, confirming my destination.

"That's me."

I slid into the back seat and hugged my backpack again, only this time it was filled with fresh clothes and less odor. The driver drove off after I clipped my belt. Again, I stared out the window, making sure they didn't follow me, making sure Jake was nowhere to be found.

The driver turned onto Burlton Street. "Just park right here."

He stopped the car alongside the curb and the driver, in his mid-twenties, turned around. "Here you go."

Grabbing my bag, I opened the door, then froze when I spotted a blue four-door sedan parked two spaces off to the right from my motel room door. A man wearing black khakis and a matching shirt pushed the driver against his car.

"Shit." I ducked into the backseat, shutting the door. "Drive, please. Drive away."

"You have to start a new ride."

"Fuck." Next time I'm using a taxi service. I dug into my pocket with shaking hands and peeked back out the window.

A man holding my laptop bag in one hand and my gear bag in another turned his massive shoulders as he exited my room.

The Iron Giant.

I started a new ride, putting in the last address I remembered.

"Thanks." He put the car in drive and drove away as I sat back up, the man speaking to another equally large man with two black bands tattooed on his arm.

Son of a bitch.

Crysis... Franklin told me the truth.

"Fuck." I kicked the passenger chair in front of me.

"Hey. Don't do that shit."

I closed my eyes and shook my head. "Sorry. Sorry, I'm just..." *In a boatload of trouble.*

"Don't do that again."

"I won't."

I won't.

Tears pooled in my eyes, and my heart thundered in my chest. This was it. Everything I'd ever known was over–gone. Forever and never to be seen again. I'd never see my parents, Jake, or Monica.

I scrolled through my pictures on my phone, pausing at the image Jake yelled at me for. I recognized the man now and often stared at it these last two days. But it was an innocent picture taken at the wrong place at the wrong time.

"We're here."

"Thanks." I tucked my phone away, exited the vehicle toward the sidewalk, and walked inside the building. The door made an obnoxious ding, the one where if I had to hear it all day, it'd drive me insane.

"Hi, do you have an appointment?" the receptionist, with tattoos and a septum piercing, asked.

"Um.. No. It's kind of a last-minute thing. Can I talk to Janelle?"

"Sure, she's not with anyone right now."

I walked around the booth and found her staring over her tablet with a stencil in one hand, tapping against her lip, and her other holding her head as her elbow rested on the desk. "Janelle?"

She looked up at me with surprise. "Adelaide? What can I do for you?"

"I wanted to apologize."

She smiled. "You came all this way to apologize in person?" She put her stencil down. "For what, exactly?"

"For acting like a teenager." I winced.

Since I *was* a teenager, it was hardly an apology, but I needed to say it. To clear my mind, especially since Jake set things straight.

Janelle laughed and nodded. "I get it. I tried to make you jealous, but it backfired."

"Why would you do that?"

She twisted in her barstool chair and turned off her tablet. "Do you know why Jake got his tattoo?"

"No." I shook my head. "He didn't tell me." *Not that I asked.*

"He did it for you."

I snorted and rolled my eyes. "He might be getting *that* removed." The thought pained me.

"Have a seat." She pointed to the chair Jake had occupied when we were here. "Why don't you tell me why you're really here?"

I rolled my lips and wrung my hands together in my lap. "I wanted to match his tattoo, but with a twist."

A smile slipped across her lips. "So you want a queen of hearts?" Janelle rolled her chair closer to me and grabbed my left hand. "In the same place?"

I nodded.

If I couldn't have Jake, I'd have a tattoo to remind me of him—to remind me to never let my fear take away my happiness.

"I've got time. Want to do it now?"

"I'd love that, thank you. I have to leave town, and I wanted someone who understood the style."

"Sure. Give me a few to print the image."

"You have it ready?"

She smiled, and it wrinkled the corners of her eyes. "Jake thought you'd get one eventually, so he paid for it in advance, and I made the stencil."

"He..." I stuttered. "He did?" I lowered my gaze to the ground, and she patted my hand.

"I'll be right back."

I nodded and rubbed my eyes, trying with all my might not to let the tears fall, but it didn't work. They dripped down my face, landing on my pants with a splash.

"Here you go." Janelle thrust a box of tissues in my direction.

"Thanks."

I wiped my eyes and put my hand in hers, allowing her to manipulate it around and side-to-side.

"How does this look?"

The bluish outline with a large Q and a heart below with a small crown tipped on the right swell of the heart stained my finger. "I love it."

"It's going to hurt, you know?"

"That's okay."

"You ready?"

I nodded, wiped my eyes, and laid my head on the cushioned bed.

The buzzing noise, accompanied by a sharp pinch, had me flinching from her grasp.

"Are you okay?"

"Yeah." I nodded, swallowing down the pain.

"Are you going somewhere?"

I glanced up at her and caught her gaze flitting back up from my bag.

"North, I think." She returned her attention to the small tattoo while I tip-toed around her question. "I just need to get away for a little while. Self-care. You know?"

"I get that. What will you and Jake do?"

I sighed. "He doesn't know."

Jake and I fell hard, and it was the happiest few weeks of my life, but that was all it was.

I closed my eyes and hid my face in my elbow while she worked her needles back and forth and side to side. I flinched, winced, and nearly pulled my hand out of her grasp again.

How did Jake get this done all over his body?

"Did you do his reaper tattoo?"

"Yep. And his friends' too."

"They have the same one?"

Janelle pulled away, wiping my finger clean. "Yes." She put her machine down. "They're a tight little trio."

I bet they were.

"Thank you, Janelle. You didn't have to do that after how I treated you."

"I told you. All is forgiven." She wrapped my finger in the same material she did his, then handed me an instructional guide. "You never said where you were going."

"Somewhere far away from here."

"He'll find you, you know." She braced her hands on her spread thighs covered in faded black jeans with stress tears and chains.

"That's what he said." I grabbed my bag and walked away. "Thanks again."

"Good luck." She hollered. "You're gonna need it."

That was the second time I'd heard that today. Maybe they weren't wrong. Maybe I needed all the luck I could get.

6

"There was something odd about that guy, Tonk." It was as if the devil sat behind his glazed-over empty eyes.

Typically, I stayed in the back with my computer, but Liz went into labor, forcing us to do this transaction without Alek.

"I agree."

At least the devil recognized his minions.

Christopher Doyle spoke very little and came alone.

In all the years of acting as a broker for the criminal underworld, we'd never had a single person show up without bodyguards, which unnerved me.

"Be prepared to hear this shit on the news. I'm telling you now."

"Don't grow a conscience. It doesn't suit you."

I laughed. Ironic since I'm the only one that *had* one.

We left the abandoned warehouse as my phone rang in my pocket.

"See ya," I waved to Tonk as he got in his truck and sped away.

I pulled out my phone.

"Janelle, how are things?"

"Good. Good." She cleared her throat. "Listen, I thought you'd like to know…"

I hated when conversations started like this.

"Adelaide came in today. She was crying and mentioned leaving town. I think something might be wrong, and I thought you'd like to know."

I squeezed my phone, my heart zooming into overdrive as I flung my car door open. "She didn't say where?"

"No. Just that it was far away from here."

"Thanks, Janelle." I pulled the phone away and caught sight of my fresh tattoo. "Hey," I said, hoping she was still there as I placed it back up to my ear.

"Yeah?"

"Did she get it?"

"What do you think?"

A smile broke across my face until I scrubbed it free with my hand.

I hung up and pocketed my phone as I got into my car.

Adelaide had a head start, but I told her in all seriousness that I'd find her. She didn't want to listen.

I flipped through my phone, found an old contact, and dialed his number. He picked up on the third ring.

"Hey, I need a favor."

"Okay, I was just leaving work."

"Perfect. I need you to pull up a location for me."

I gave him Adelaide's phone number, wishing I'd been the creep Tonk was with Ivy, and put tracking software on her phone.

"I've sent it to your email. You should be getting it now."

My tablet and phone pinged with an incoming notification, and I opened it. It was a map of the south side, the bad part of town, worse than Azrael's territory, and on it was a blue dot moving down Carrington Street.

One of the worst streets in the city.

A tremor ripped through my body as the tendons in my neck tightened, sending a zinging pain into my chest and jaw.

"What are you doing down there, sweets?"

I plugged the address into my GPS and took off, hoping she didn't get stuck between rival gang members or some drug addict looking for a good time.

Adelaide

7

T he sun had dipped behind the tall derelict buildings with iron bars on the windows and trash littering the streets. The pungent stench of ammonia burned my nostrils, and a discernible moan echoed from an alley across the street.

I'd walked into Tent Alley. It wasn't an actual alleyway more of an abandoned section of the city, where gangbangers and homeless people ruled each other like a lawless province.

But that's how Rachel stayed off the radar. Cops didn't come down here. The murder rate on this street was higher than in the entire city.

Ahead of me on the narrow backstreet was a green dumpster overflowing with rancid trash, boxes littering the ground along the brick walls, and rusted fire escapes above me. You'd have a better chance at survival if you battled the fire than stepped onto one of those rickety things.

A man sat at the doorway in the middle of the alley, next to a one-step porch. He wore a holey gray long-sleeved shirt that reminded me of something out of the Matrix and jeans covered in soot or oil. His beanie hat covered fake dreadlocks mixed with vibrant colors of orange and red, and his two-week-old beard could've used a comb-through.

If it had been my first time here, he'd convince me wholeheartedly that he was a tweaker, but it was the smell that gave him away. Citrus and cedarwood, an expensive brand of cologne that no tweaker could ever afford.

"Frodo," I said, nodding to the bodyguard.

"Who are you today?" His gruff voice rattled around like stones in a blender.

"That's classified, hobbit." I smiled.

His name wasn't really Frodo, but Rodolfo. I'd made the mistake the first time I met him, and it became our little inside joke.

"She's upstairs."

"Thank you."

I pulled open the rusted metal door that towered over my head by a good two feet. Its antiquated hinges cried out for oil.

"You should really get that fixed."

"It's a cheap alarm."

Valid point. I walked inside, letting the door close behind me with a deafening thud, then took the steps on the right to the second floor.

"Rachel," I said, pulling her beaded door to the side with a huff. "Get yourself an elevator, please?"

She laughed as I bent over and rested my hands on my knees.

"Stop eating pizza and Oreos."

"That's sacrilegious. How could you say such treacherous things?"

I leaned against her desk and dropped my backpack from my bruised shoulder.

"Got your stuff, but it's extra for rush order."

I nodded and handed her the cash after digging it out of my bag at my feet. I'd taken a hefty cash advance from Miranda's credit card before tossing it and started on Felicity's.

"Girl. You know better than to be walking around with that much green on you."

"I'm desperate." I shrugged.

"Got yourself into some trouble?"

I nodded again.

"That explains the splotchy black hair you got going on."

After leaving the tattoo parlor, I stopped at CVS, picked up some hair dye, and made a mess of their bathroom sink. It wasn't like I had a choice. Red heads stuck out, but the problem with red... it didn't like to grab the color, especially while using over-the-counter products. "I went with the darkest color I could find."

"Give me a sec." She tossed her head in the direction of her hall. "I'll go get it."

Rachel, a woman in her fifties with half pink, half blue curls, dipped her head as she walked through the beaded curtain separating this room from the next. Last time it was a curtain, and the time before that, a door.

She liked to change things up, give it more of a homey feel with each transition. This time, lava lamps line the wall on a shelf, casting moving shadows up and down like hungry blobs seeking escape. Her shag rug turned red from its previous white... at least I think it was. It'd been six months since I'd been here last.

"Here you go," she said as she swiped the beads away, walking back in.

She handed me a bundle of IDs wrapped in a thick tan rubber band. "Thank you." I tapped them against my hand, then shook them out as they hit my fresh tattoo. "Ow."

"Is it the jail kind of trouble or the regular rebellious variety?"

"The kind that kills."

"Damn. Stay safe, *Felicity*," she said with a wink. "Here, give this to Rodolfo." She handed me fifty bucks. "Tell him I want it with spicy peppers and anchovies." Then handed me a switchblade as I grimaced at the thought of little dead fish with their eyes baked into their skulls. "And you keep this."

I gave her a tight-lipped smile. "Thanks for everything, Rachel."

She nodded, and I turned, bouncing down the metal stairs with a metallic *clank* on each step. Pushing open the back door, I looked in both directions, left to the back of the alley... *clear*. Right to the street... *Odd*. A parked car with its lights off sat across the street where the illumination of street lamps didn't touch it. The sun had made its way down, so not even shadows walked the land, making the vehicle appear black in color and impossible to ID.

"Hey, Frodo," I said, keeping the car in my periphery. Any movement, and I was out of here like a rabbit fleeing from a wolf. "When did that car get here?"

"The one behind you?"

"Yeah."

"Just pulled up."

I spun my lip ring. "You have another way outta here?"

"Behind me, through the hall, at the end, take a right. It'll end with glass doors to the other alley. They here for you?"

"Hard to tell." I handed him the cash and looked back at the car. "She said spicy peppers and anchovies."

"She's got the strangest tastes."

"Whatever it is, I'm glad I'm not here to smell it."

I slapped his open hand, fist bumped him, and then opened the door. Casting a glare toward the vehicle, I darted inside and followed his instructions.

"You okay?" Rachel asked as she came down the stairs.

"Just gonna take the scenic route."

I continued running down the hall and paused before turning the corner. I took out my phone and smashed it against the brick wall. They couldn't use that to find me now. Turning the corner, I darted down the hall and slammed the glass door open into an alley on the other side of the building, my ribs aching, my hips sore and throbbing.

"Hey, pretty lady," a man cat-called me as I bolted to the right in the opposite direction.

When I hit the end of the alley and turned left to another alley, I froze.

"Shit." He never told me about this.

Two industrial garbage bins blocked my path. They sat in front of a chain-link fence with razor wire over the top.

What the fuck are they trying to keep out... *or in?*

"Here, kitty, kitty."

The man waddled closer. Days old liquor and a musk that only became that potent after weeks of not showering hit my nose from a faint breeze, causing me to gag as I jumped on top of the closed dumpster.

"Stay back, or I'll make you wish you never laid eyes on me," I snarled. More than likely, he'd overpower me, and we both end up smelling like last week's garbage.

Taking my chances on the other side, I laid my bag over the razor wire, then carefully slipped over as the homeless man slithered up to where I'd been standing.

"You're going to die over there," he mumbled.

I jerked my bag off the wire before my feet hit the black ground with a thud. "I'd die over *there* too."

It was darker over here like someone had snuffed out the light.

I jumped as the bottle I'd kicked skittered across the rough asphalt and collided with something metallic that clanged with an echo. Pulling my bag closer to my chest, I looked back to the fence I'd crawled over and watched the homeless man weave back and forth, watching me with vested interest and a raised brow.

Forcing myself to move, I walked toward the end of the alleyway where the streets came alive, and light touched the sidewalk.

My shoulders sagged as I stepped out through a storm of collected fear and started my short walk to the bus station.

There were two places I'd had in mind when I first chose to leave three days ago. Montreal and the furthest point north in Maine.

Montreal won the toss-up.

The only issue was getting there. Planes were quick, but there were cameras everywhere. Trains were another one of those... *eh, maybe*, options. Downside, it had predictable routes and stops. But buses... I could get off anywhere for a potty break and never get back on. No one would ever know.

When I reached the bus station, sweat dripped from my hairline, and with each breath I took, the stitch in my side ripped down to my limping leg.

"Hi, where would you like to go?" Wanda said, her name tag attached to the breast pocket of her white polo.

"I need one ticket to Montreal."

She gave me the total and asked if I had any luggage. I paid in cash, and she handed me my ticket.

"Is there a store here?"

"Right around the corner." She pointed. "It's next to the food mart."

"Thanks."

I took my ticket and followed her direction to the store where they had burners next to neck pillows and tech magazines that only someone like me would read.

"How much are these?" I asked, holding up the smartphone without a price tag. The elderly cashier with a bushy mustache that would make Tom Selleck jealous squinted and placed his glasses from around his neck onto the bridge of his nose.

"Hundred-thirty."

I grabbed it and a box of saltines, then checked out as he eyed my wad of cash. I'm sure many strange people came through here, but none as crazy as me to pay with a roll of twenties.

"Is there a bathroom around here?"

"Closed for maintenance. You'll have to catch it at the next one."

I sighed and nodded, tucking my cash back into my side pouch, then walked back into the main lobby and took a seat against the far wall where I had a view of the door and a charging port.

"Bus twenty, departing for Montreal, is now boarding," a voice screeched through the overhead speakers.

"Shit." I tucked my phone into my pocket and grabbed my bag, looking around for anyone suspicious, then headed out and stood in line with my ticket in hand.

I stared at the oversized Prevost and imagined it taking me to a new land I'd never seen before.

Alone.

A tear rolled down my cheek, and I stifled the rest, causing a painful lump under my chin.

I shuffled forward as the ticket master tore tickets, letting one person on at a time.

It wasn't fair that we didn't even have a fair chance, but that's what I got for thinking I could make the world a better place. Maybe that was God's way of teaching me not to play judge and juror.

I sniffled and handed him my ticket. He took it and ripped a piece off with a barcode, then let me board.

My hips bumped each seat as I walked by, as though I played bumper cars with my sides. It jostled my belly until a cyclone formed in the pit of my stomach. Finding my seat, I plopped my ass next to the window and held my backpack to my chest like it was my lifeline.

And in a way, it was.

It had my money, IDs, and clothes stuffed into a tiny carry on. This was all that I owned now.

My broken reflection hit me in the window as I squinted through it, but the bright lights inside contrasted the darkness outside, making it near impossible to see...

Until I found him running into the station and looking around with his hands clenched by his sides.

"Last call for Montreal."

He turned his gaze this way, and I swore for a split second he saw me. Jake walked my way with determination in his step as I slunk into my seat, hoping he couldn't see me. The bus doors screeched closed, and an unexpected exhale breezed past my teeth.

A man slipped into the seat next to me, his tight khakis forming around his thick muscular thighs. His hand rested on them, giving me a view of the silver ring overshadowing his middle finger.

"I've always wanted to go to Montreal."

Jake

8

I sat in my car, watching her pass cash to the homeless man by the door, when she bolted back inside the building and sent an icy glare my way.

Adelaide played with fire, but she was afraid of getting burned. Her wide, darkening gaze said as much when I'd wrapped my hands around her fragile throat. An act I still hadn't come to terms with.

I jumped from my car, reluctant to leave it on the road in this part of town, and raced down the alleyway, making it to the thick metal door where the drug dealer stood.

"Got a meetin'?"

He put his hand on my chest as I reached for the handle. I grabbed his thumb and pulled it to the side with a sickening crack, eliciting a high-pitched scream from a man you'd never expect could utter such a noise.

The man bent at the knee as he recoiled from the agony his face mirrored.

"Where did she go?"

"I'm not tellin' you."

My stomach rocked as I pressed my fist into his chest and rushed him backward, slamming his back against the crumbling brick wall. My knee crashed into his groin, and a low, guttural cry erupted. I released my hold on his hand, grabbed his shoulders, and pulled his chest down into my knee, brutalizing the impact.

One. Two. Three times. My knee slammed into the hardness that made up his sternum and ribcage until he collapsed to the ground, holding his chest. I dropped onto him, straddling his hips with my thighs, and crossed my arms over his throat until my forearms pressed into his jugular, staunching blood flow to his brain.

If years of Krav Maga taught me anything, it was 'brutality.'

The man's eyelids fluttered, the whites of his eyes overpowering the color as they rolled into his skull. I held him a few seconds longer for good measure, then stood, wiping my hands of debris, and bolted through the door.

What the fuck was she doing here? Buying drugs? That wasn't the Adelaide I knew. But then again, did I *really* know her at all?

The musty interior split off into two sections as I stepped inside. One going up and the other going down. If she was as smart as I thought, she wouldn't run upstairs and risk cornering herself.

I took the stairs down, rushing around the corner to the left, where remnants of her phone lay broken on the floor.

So she *was* here. But how was I going to find her now?

Dammit.

"Who the fuck are you?"

A man stepped out of a room as I turned. His three times too large Snoop Dogg t-shirt hung mid-thigh, covering up the chain that no doubt attached to his belt buckle and wallet.

"Mind your business."

"This hallway *is* my business."

I picked up her phone and put it in my pocket.

"Whose shit you stealin', boy?"

"Boy," I laughed. I was at least five years older than him and more filled out than his scrawny ass could dream of.

Running my hand down my jaw, I smiled. "Go back into your apartment."

"Handover what you just put in your pocket, and I'll be on my way." He put his hand out and walked towards me, his feet wide to hold his pants around his ass as his inseam dropped to his knees.

"Don't even think about putting your hands on me," I warned.

He laughed. "You hear him, Rachel?"

A woman in her late fifties with wild-colored hair and a pistol pointing my way stepped out of the room.

Well, this just got interesting.

"I did. You heard him, mister. Give him what you put in your pocket."

"I'm good."

If I ran back to where I came from, I'd need to take them both out before she squeezed the trigger... highly unlikely. If I bolted around the corner and ran toward the glass door I saw there, I'd have to make it through before she shot me in the back. Again... *unlikely.*

The kid took two more steps my way, his hand held out.

"Have it your way."

I grabbed his arm and jerked, pulling him into me as my other ripped the chain from his hip. He spun his back to my chest as I wrapped the metal links around his throat. She'd have to shoot my human shield to get to me.

"Put the gun down, and he'll live," I said as I backed around the corner toward the door.

"You're gonna kill him."

"Only if you don't put that gun down."

I tucked my body tight against his, making my target area smaller.

"You're who she's running from, aren't you?"

The mention of Adelaide, even without her name being drawn out, caused me to pause.

"You don't know what you're talking about." The boy in my grasp sputtered, his face taking on a purplish-reddish hue. "Your boy here doesn't have much time."

I tipped my head, catching the whites of his eyes when he tipped his body to the side. His elbow struck my brow with a deadening thud, causing my teeth to jar together and a bone-splitting ache to spread like lightning across my face.

My mistake.

I stepped back, keeping hold of the chain until my butt hit the glass door and a warm trickle rippled down my cheek.

"Maybe I'll kill him on principle now." I jerked the chain tighter, spittle spewing from his lips as he gasped.

"All right, fine." She lowered her gun, one hand out in surrender as she squatted.

"Kick it over and be quick."

She slid it over, and I stopped it with my foot. Tucking the toe of my shoe underneath it, I gave it a jerk and sent it flying into the air, catching it mid-flight. I shoved the man into her and charged, slamming the butt of the pistol into her forehead as she put her hands out to catch him. They tumbled to the ground, Rachel out cold, and the boy holding his throat and coughing.

"Next time, listen." I pocketed the magazine, including the bullet in the chamber, and tossed the handgun to the ground. "Let's see if you've learned your lesson. Okay?"

Dipping down, I fisted his shirt and pulled him up as he held his bruised throat.

"Tell me where she went."

"Who?" He crossed his arms across his face as I raised my fist.

"The girl who was just here."

He shook his head. I pulled back and railed my fist into his nose. Blood burst to the sides in fragmented droplets until it ran a steady stream down his cheeks.

"Try again."

"I-I don't know. I was inside until I saw you run by."

I raised my bloodied fist again.

"I'm telling the truth," he said, his voice rising like a prepubescent boy. His fingers shook in front of his face, vibrating with fear and adrenaline.

"Where does this alley lead?"

He shook his head, and I rattled him back and forth until he spoke.

"Jesus, okay. Boston St. It leads to Boston St."

"That wasn't so hard, was it?" I said, lightly slapping his bloody cheek, then dropping him onto the ground. "Next time, keep your pants around your waist. You'll have better luck."

I rushed down the hall, past the woman, and back out to where I'd come. The dealer lay on the ground, his eyes closed, his breathing steady.

Boston St. was two blocks over and not too far from the bus station. If she wanted to leave, I bet that's where she was heading. I jogged across the street and slid into my car—the light illuminating the blood creeping down my jaw.

Grabbing a napkin, I dabbed at the wound as I pulled out with squealing tires. A car behind me blared their horn as I winced, my fingers pressing into the cut on my brow.

Don't even think about it, Adelaide. I warned you.

I fucking warned you.

Two blocks and three pissed-off cars later, I parked along the curb and ran inside the station, searching for her.

Where the hell did you go?

A woman with blonde hair in a halter-top, a man with a beard, and a family of three. None of who fit her description or the clothes she'd worn today.

"Last call for Montreal."

If she got on one of these buses, I'd hunt each one of them down until I found her. I didn't care if she went kicking and screaming. I'd pull her by her hair if I had to.

A line of people shuffled onto a bus, the lights inside illuminating most of the people already seated or walking down the aisle.

My spine tingled as I searched each seat as I walked toward it. The last man stepping aboard and the doors closing.

Blonde.

Blonde.

Black.

Brown.

Blonde.

I worked my way back through the passengers until I'd exhausted my options.

"Shit."

I walked back inside and around to the bathrooms with caution tape, crossing them off, then into the little store. She'd broken her phone on purpose, but she'd need another one. I'd put everything I own on her, buying one before she left.

"Have you seen this girl?" I asked the cashier with spiked red-tipped hair.

"I just started the till for the night." He eyed me, his gaze settling on the stinging cut on my brow. "I have a first aid kit." He pointed to the wound. "If you need it."

I shook my head and tucked my phone back into my pocket as the bus to Montreal pulled away from the curb.

My stomach sank as I watched it drive away. Did I miss something? I could follow it, but if she weren't on it, I'd waste an entire night hunting it down.

Irritation and indecision tore me in two until I walked toward the ticket station and cut in line.

"Sir, I'm gonna have to ask you to get in the back of the line."

I pulled out my phone and showed her a picture as the man I'd shoved out of the way backed up. "Have you seen her tonight?"

"Sir, please."

Placing my phone on the counter, I pulled out my wallet and fished out two-one-hundred-dollar bills, then slid them in her direction.

"Have you seen this *girl* tonight?"

Her gaze dropped to the green pressed between my finger and the white speckled countertop. "I can't give you that information."

"You can. It doesn't violate any privacy policies." I slid the money forward, tempting her. "Have you *seen* her?"

She looked around and flicked her tongue out, wetting her bottom lip. "Yes, but she had black hair."

"Good." I tossed another hundred down and slid it closer. "Where did she go?"

She shook her head, but before she could open her mouth and give me some moralistic excuse, I cut her off. "The more questions you answer, the more money I put down. But if you don't answer it, I'll take it all away."

The woman swallowed, her throat bobbing.

"I could lose my job," she said, leaning in.

I dragged the money towards me slowly, but her hand came down on mine.

"Wait. What's her name? Since you're *family*, I can tell you."

She'd use her fake ID, or maybe she wanted me to think she would, so she'd use her real one. My pulse settled in my temples as if I played 3D chess with real-life consequences.

"Miranda."

The woman turned to her computer and typed in the name. "We don't have a Miranda."

I dragged in a ragged breath, my non-violent options dwindling.

"What bus did this girl get on?"

Her eyes darted to the man standing beside me. I turned my gaze towards him as he inched closer.

"Do not make me cause a scene."

The man's face blanched as his eyes bugged, and he took two healthy steps back.

"More." I motioned him backward.

I turned my attention to the woman. "Where did she go," I skimmed her nametag, "Wanda?"

"Bus twenty for Montreal."

"The one that just left?"

She nodded.

I released the money on the counter, rewarding her for her defective morals, and walked away.

You won this round, Adelaide, but I'll be there waiting for you.

I picked up a route pamphlet and tucked it into my car.

Adelaide

9

"Oh God," I grumbled as the bus bounced over the never-ending potholes in the road. My stomach roiled, and no matter how much my belly piqued from hunger, I couldn't force myself to reach into my backpack and pull out the salted crackers.

If only I could sleep away the nausea. But Berat, the man beside me, droned on nonstop in an indecipherable accent about his experience in Fallujah during the Afghan war, drawing irritation to the tip of my tongue and unease down to my toes.

I thought Fallujah was in Iraq?

Couldn't he let me sleep? Wasn't there some bus etiquette or something—like don't talk after ten?

We'd traveled for over two hours—my eyelids drooping as I stared at my reflection in the window with each passing street lamp until the driver made an announcement, and we came to a stop.

"We are taking a ten-minute restroom break. Please be back on the bus with your ticket stubs in hand. If you are not back in time, we will leave without you."

Superb. I'd had to pee since before we left.

He opened the doors with a horrendous screech, signaling my ten-minute escape from war stories.

Berat stepped back, obliging me, and I took it with a hurried step, slipping my bag over my shoulder. Most stayed in their seats, their eyes closed, one or two snoring as I passed by.

Lucky bastards.

The pressure in my bladder pressed against my pubic bone with each step, making me grateful I'd worn sweats instead of the jean shorts I'd wanted.

"Going to the bathroom?" he asked as we stepped into the empty station, his cardamom cologne sticking to my clothes like a putrid skunk.

"Yes," I said, drawing out the word with annoyance.

"Me too. Those bathrooms on the bus are dirtier than..."

"Listen," I said, the words spewing out without a second thought. "Just leave me alone."

My stomach flip-flopped as Berat's brows furrowed together, his eyes turning icy. There were people around, and if he did anything stupid, there'd be witnesses.

I picked up the pace, eyes focused on the women's bathroom. His booted footsteps echoed into the rafters a fair distance behind me. I hope he took the hint and left me alone.

Hell, if he found another seat for the next thirty-five hours, that'd be even better.

A light wood door appeared in a shallow cut-out along the wall, and I slunk inside, turning my gaze over my shoulder. He'd gone hopefully to the bathroom, as he said before.

The freshly cleaned bathroom wiped away some of the heebie-jeebies as I chose a stall and relieved myself, then washed my hands next to a woman with a crying baby.

I gave her a sympathetic smile and walked out, only for it to falter when I saw Berat standing with his foot propped up against the wall, a lighter flicking in his hand.

Why can't he just go away?

"I'm just going to sit for a second... *alone*," I said, explaining myself to a man who clearly wasn't very good at taking social cues.

He nodded, his finger jerking over the lighter, igniting it for a split second, then doing it again.

My hands shook as I brushed past him, my grip on my backpack cramping my palm. The cool night air hit my lungs with a hint of fresh rain in the distance and a momentary sense of freedom.

Even though I'd wept for everything and everyone I'd ever known, this was a new start for me, and nothing could stop me from starting over.

I sat down on the bench and pulled my new phone out of my backpack, and powered it up for the first time—the screen reflecting movement too late for me to respond.

A spice-tainted hand curled over my lips, sealing the breath inside my chest, and dragged me against him.

"Don't make this harder than it needs to be," he urged before switching to a language I couldn't understand. My sneakers scuffed on the uneven tarmac as he dragged me into the shadows behind the vacated buses.

My muffled screams caught in his hard, sweaty palm as he hauled me behind the furthest bus to a camouflaged car waiting in the distance. My fingers dug into his arms without deterring his efforts—my heart and mind running wild.

I slammed my heel down onto his toe. My scream broke free as his fingers slipped past my lips and into my mouth, his salty dew touching my tongue. I bit down on his finger, my teeth hitting solid bone.

He howled and slapped me over the head. As I continued twisting my heel into his toe, another man opened the trunk.

"She's just a little girl, Berat. Put her ass in the trunk."

Berat picked me up with a growl and dumped me over his shoulder, my bag falling to the ground.

"Help!" I beat against his solid back. "Someone help me!"

"Hey, this doesn't concern you," the other man said as Berat shoved me into the trunk and closed me in.

Suffocating darkness enclosed around me with a faint red gleam from the taillight and a yellow tab glowing on the trunk door.

A heavy thud hit the ground outside the car, a grunt, and a meaty slap followed by a crack like someone had broken a stalk of celery in my ear, causing a shudder to muddy my already sensitive gut.

The car rocked as a large object collided with it not once but twice until his groans echoed in my shadowy coffin.

What was happening? I covered my mouth as I held my breath, listening to the chaos ensuing all around me. My body jumped with another grunt and thud. A man cried out in agony as my shaking fingers looped around the glowing tab and pulled.

I flung my legs over the edge of the trunk and ran as two men grappled on the ground.

"Adelaide, wait."

Jake?

Jake's voice broke through the chaos as I ran, never looking back. How did he find me? Was it he who hired these men?

"Adelaide. Stop."

My heart quivered in my chest—torn between what I should and shouldn't do.

I wiped the confusion from my mind as something banged against metal as it did before, causing me to pause and turn around.

A man kneeled on the ground, his head bent back at an awkward angle as Jake stood above him.

"Berat?" I whispered, squinting into the darkness.

Jake held Berat's other arm stretched out to the side and when he glanced in my direction, he plunged his knee into Berat's elbow, causing him to shriek.

I stumbled backward as Jake turned and walked toward me.

Oh my God.

I covered my mouth, my scream snagging in my throat like ice shards clawing their way up. I shook my head as microscopic black pins flooded my vision, my pulse pounding in my head.

Who? What... The stationary buses drew in closer as Jake took long strides toward me.

Run.

The door wasn't far.

I spun on my heel and raced toward the lit covered waiting area.

Arms wrapped around me the moment my foot hit the sidewalk, and I screamed, my fear ricocheting off the brick building.

My hip burned in agony as his hand hit my bruise, bringing me close to my knees. Jake slipped his hand over my mouth, muffling my cries, and spun us into the darkness away from the prying eyes of a passenger exiting the bathroom.

"Stop fucking moving," he growled, and I chilled. "It's me, sweets."

I didn't care if it was the Pope himself. I couldn't trust him, even if he saved my life back there. I kicked out, my feet coming up into the air as I drove my elbow back, nailing him in the ribs.

He grunted, bringing a satisfied smile beneath his hand.

"Stop fighting me, or I won't hesitate to put you back in the trunk."

His hand slipped up, stifling the air I sucked in through my nose, causing my lungs to burn for oxygen.

I pulled at his hand and wrist, prying his palm away from my mouth by his two fingers, allowing me to gulp in mouthfuls of air with a gasp.

"Relax," he purred. "I'm not gonna hurt you."

Not going to hurt me? How could he say that when he already had? How could he expect me to comply after all of this? His contradictory statements didn't bring me peace. They confused me until my world spun on its axis, and fear chilled me to the bone.

I couldn't trust him, could I? I nodded, showing him I'd comply.

Jake pulled his hands from my body, leaving my mind to pirouette with rejection. "We need to get out of here."

His bleeding brow left a crimson watery trail down his cheek and throat, and what looked to be a forming bruise on his cheekbone. An errant tear trickled down my face, mimicking the blood on his.

"I'm sorry, Jake." I gripped his shirt in both of my hands. "Don't let them kill me. Please? I didn't know." I shook my head, my cheeks now stained.

Jake wrapped his arm around my bruised shoulder and pulled me against him, causing me to wince.

"Did they hurt you?"

"No."

"Okay." He nodded. "My car is over here," he said, pointing through the station.

"Did you kill them?"

He sighed. "Adelaide, if I killed them, I wouldn't be in such a hurry to get out of here." He tossed my bag into my chest and grabbed my elbow as I flung it over my shoulder. "Now, let's go."

"I can't leave with you," I said, stopping in my tracks. "They'll kill me... us."

"If you don't move, they won't get the chance." He gripped my arm harder and led me through the station, with a few eyes following us. When we got to his car, he opened the passenger door and shoved me inside—my ass sitting on something hard and long.

He did it again, threatening to end my life as though he were ordering breakfast. It'd be the last time he sliced my heart open as if I were some science project in a lab where he could look at me with disdain and apathy.

I dug into my pocket as he rounded the car and pulled out the switchblade I'd forgotten about as he sat down in the driver's seat.

"Sorry." I flicked it open and pointed the sharp end in his direction. "I really am, but don't make me use this on you." Opening the car door, I slipped out. "I can't have you involved. These people are dangerous." *And it'd kill me if anything happened to you, no matter how cruel you are to me—no matter how much you* hate *me.*

He sighed as I shut the door, his shoulders sagging. I stepped back as his door opened, and he made his way around the car, his gaze fixed on the blade angled at him. "Really?" He pointed to the offending weapon.

"Just let me go." I bit back the never-ending tears burning my eyes. "I don't want them to kill you, too."

"They may kill me," he said, stepping forward. "But you know who won't?"

I swiped the blade in front of me. "Who?"

"Stupid little girls who think they can pull a knife on me." He held out his hand as he advanced on me, forcing me back toward the curb. "Give me the knife, Adelaide."

Another strategic cut into my beating heart. Tears blurred my vision before rolling down my cheek. He might as well have left me to them. What purpose did he have in saving me? Why was he here right now if he held nothing but disdain for me? "Please back up." I swung the knife side-to-side. "Don't make me hurt you, Jake. I love you too much."

"You love me?" he asked, his feet planted on the ground. "Then give me the knife, Adelaide."

Taking another step back, I shook my head. "You don't get to save me, Jake. You can't use my feelings for you and twist them against me."

I shouldn't have divulged my fucked up feelings, but I thought maybe he'd understand if I did this out of love for him, he'd let me go. He'd let me put distance between us to keep him safe. Despite everything he'd said to me, despite the look in his eye when he nearly choked the life from me, I'd still chosen to protect him.

What a maddening epiphany.

"Give. Me. The. Fucking. Knife. Adelaide," he said through gritted teeth.

"I can't."

"You can. Now stop playing games." He advanced, resuming the chase, and I stepped back, my heel kicking the curb behind me.

His car dipped from view as I went hurtling toward the ground.

Jake reached out, his hand gripping the knife's sharp blade, his fingers grazing my hand. "God dammit," he hissed as the blade slipped through his palm.

My ass hit the cement with a pained thud.

Jake bounced back, holding his hand against his thigh as his palm turned red.

The blood rushed from my face as sanguine fluid slipped to the ground. "I'm sorry," I said, gasping, my mouth gaping at the sight.

He growled and lunged forward, plucking the knife from my fist with his bleeding hand, then hauled me up from the ground as though I were a mere child.

My ribs worked double time as my chest throbbed violently. "I-I..." I shook my head. "I didn't want to hurt you. I swear."

He closed the knife, tucking the blade into the metal, and pocketed it. "A little late for that, don't you think?" Jake pulled me back to his car, my escape attempt foiled by carelessness.

He tossed me inside again and buckled me in, assuring an extra step if I tried to escape again, then slammed the door shut. Jake rushed to his trunk and rummaged around inside before hurling it shut. When he slipped into the driver's seat, he tossed a first aid kit on the console and wrapped his hand in a cloth, disrupting the deluge of blood spilling down to the tips of his fingers.

My head wobbled as the car spun all around me, sending my stomach on a tilt-a-whirl along with it. I tipped my head back and fanned my face, beckoning for a reprieve. "I think I'm going to pass out."

"Put your head between your knees."

I fanned harder against the stagnant air. "What?" I said breathlessly. "How will that help?"

He squeezed the towel around his hand and opened the first aid kit. "It pushes blood into the brain and prevents passing out," he said, ripping a piece of tape with his teeth and securing it around his hand. "If you're gonna puke, turn your head sideways, so you don't aspirate."

"Why do you care?"

I whimpered, tucking my head down as he said, "I don't."

He closed the box and tossed it into the backseat.

His admission singed my heart strings until it floated freely in my chest, knocking around forcibly against my ribs.

Jake started the car and threw it into drive while I kept my forehead on my knees.

I couldn't expect him to reciprocate or tell me he loved me just the same, not after what had happened between us. But for him to flat out declare he didn't care about me deflated even the slightest hope I'd had.

But how could he be so hateful? This wasn't the man he'd shown me all this time. The man who waited at my door for me to come out—who took me on my first date and took care of his sister.

Who was he?

"You aren't the person I thought you were."

"That makes two of us."

"No." I rocked my head against my knees. "Everything you experienced with me was one-hundred percent me."

He scoffed. "Sorry, I must've missed the part when you told me how you wanted to blackmail me for fifteen million."

My head shot up from his ridiculous accusation. "I didn't do that. I wish you'd believe me."

"Put your head down." He turned the corner.

"I can't. Your driving makes me sick even when I watch the road, much less when I don't."

The bus station disappeared into the darkness, but what bothered me the most was my lost opportunity to start a new life. That bus was my only means of keeping my family alive, and now Jake held me hostage and forced me to return when distance was the cure for this calamitous disease.

And for what? So he could return me to my parents so I could see the devastation on their faces? Or so he could take me to the police and make me fess up to a crime I never wanted to be part of.

"What did you really tell my parents?"

"I told them what happened."

I whimpered. "Why would you do that?"

"Because, Adelaide. You tried to fuck me over, so why wouldn't I fuck you right back?"

"But I didn't." I shook my head, laying my hand on his. "You have to believe me. I never would've allowed that... for anyone, not just you."

He jerked away from me. "Right. Because you have morals."

"We all have our lines we've drawn in the sand."

He squeezed his leather steering wheel, making it groan, then flipped the music on.

Abrasive, acid burned vocals flooded the small space between us until I pushed the volume button, turning off the music.

"Don't." He slapped my hand like a contrary child, then turned it back on.

I leaned back in my seat, folding my shaking arms over my chest, and huffed. The lightheadedness diminished with anti-climatic ease, making me wish I had passed out. Maybe I'd take him up on his offer if he forced me to listen to this shit music for the next two hours.

"Where are you taking me?" I said, louder than the music.

"Some place no one will find you."

My heart vaulted in my chest, causing a wave of heat and pressure up to my head. "Come again?"

What did...

No.

I grabbed the door handle and yanked, but with the automatic locks engaged, they didn't open. How fast were we going down the freeway? If I tucked and rolled, would I be able to walk away, or would it kill me?

"Adelaide, chill."

I flipped the lock, erasing the graphic mental images of my battered body in the middle of the road, my arm bent at a horrid angle and my vacant eyes staring up at my soul staring down, and opened the door. Tires rolling along the asphalt at breakneck speeds rode the seventy-mile-an-hour winds blasting through the cracked door.

A semi's horn blared behind us as I stuck my head out and watched the broken white lines pass as one solid streak.

I took a deep breath.
My thumb on my belt buckle.
Click.

Adelaide

10

"**A**delaide!"

My torso vaulted to the side, my shirt tight against my throat as he fisted the material with deathly white knuckles, the door closed with my hand still wrapped firmly around it. A gasp breezed past my lips as the car skimmed three lanes and came to a screeching halt on the side of the freeway.

Jake turned off the music, making our exasperated breaths a chaotic chorus surrounding us. He released my shirt and wrapped his bandaged hand around the back of my neck, pulling me close. "You pull that shit again, and I'll take away your hesitation."

My breath hitched as a strangled cry erupted from my throat.

I almost died.

What the hell was I thinking?

"I'm trying to help you, dammit." He jerked me closer like he used to do when he wanted to kiss me and stared at me with wild eyes flaming with rage. *Or was it concern?*

"You don't want to help me. You said so yourself." I swiped his damaged hand off of me, a quiver of turbulent lightning striking through me and down to my toes.

And now he wanted to take me to a place no one would ever find me? Was I just supposed to shrug and comply with such a ridiculous notion?

I shrugged out of the seat belt and bolted from the car. My shirt ripped through his fingers with the popping of threads, the collar burning my throat from the friction.

"Get back in the fucking car!" His thunderous voice sent my feet moving faster into the woods, my hip snagging on bruised flesh with each stroke.

Twigs snapped, echoing their fractured cries around me as he rushed after me. "Adelaide, would you fucking stop?"

His furious shouts urged me forward until he twisted me around by the arm, pinning me against a tree. Its bark pressed into my skin, reminiscent of the time he'd taken me in public. When he cared enough to search for me.

"You aren't going anywhere. I told you that."

"Jake. Please. Just—"

His body pressed into mine, his heat flaming my skin with lust and repudiated desire. I shouldn't have felt that way about him now. He should have repulsed me as *I* did him.

"Why can't you listen?" His tone grew cold and quiet, sending ice down the fine hairs on my arm, hardening my nipples.

I shook my head, and his bloodied hand gripped my jaw, his fingers digging into my cheeks.

"You're so fucking stubborn, and it's only gonna get you killed. You know that?"

His gaze bounced from my lips to my eyes, up and down, side to side, until his lips slammed against mine in a virulent turn of tongues, lips, and teeth. Our torrid bodies melded together as one until he ripped himself from me like a blast of cold water on two mating dogs.

"That'll never happen again."

I gasped, the breath sucked from my lungs as a cruel, twisted reality settled in.

Jake dragged me back with his bitter, unfeeling grasp and threw me into the car. I sank down on myself. The driver's door rocked the vehicle as he closed it.

"There are consequences to your actions in the real world, Adelaide. This isn't a game. There are no reset buttons." He pulled onto the freeway after a semi carrying a trailer full of logs passed by. "You don't respawn, and your stupidity affects the people around you."

"I know that."

"Then act like it." He flipped the music back on.

"I'm trying. Okay. I am."

He kept his gaze toward the bleak highway, his torso leaning forward as if waiting for me to try again.

I sniffled and wiped the tears off my cheeks.

I'd ruined everything, and *he* ruined my escape. The longer I stuck around, the worse things became, and the harder it was to face the fact that life would never be the same.

My vision shifted, and the glare of oncoming traffic smeared across my sight. I choked. Pressing my hand to my heavy chest, I worked my shoulders up and down like a manual pump, expecting it to draw oxygen into my lungs.

"Jake," I wheezed. "I can't breathe."

"Put your head between your knees."

"Is that your solution for everything?" I snapped, pulling in the air like a leaking window whistling in a storm. "It won't help."

Jake grabbed the back of my head and shoved me to my knees. "Stay there."

I wrapped my hands around his, threaded through my hair, and closed my eyes, soaking in his warmth. For just a moment, he rubbed his thumb against the dip between my skull and my neck in a soothing motion until he ripped his hand away, leaving me empty again.

The pounding in my chest subsided as I raised my head and leaned against the side of the car. My lids bobbed up and down as exhaustion sunk its meaty claws into my conscience and loosened my tense muscles. The soft sway of the car along the smooth road rocked my body into unconsciousness.

The car rolled to a stop, and I jerked up, my hands lashing out in front of me with a gasp.

"Where are we?" I asked as Jake punched in a code that opened a big black iron gate before us.

"Some place safe."

"Safe for *who*?"

He drove through at a snail's pace, the jitters inside my stomach sparking with each passing moment until he parked next to a truck and turned it off.

"Get out."

Jake exited the car and walked around to my side, but I hit the lock button, sealing myself inside.

It's not like the place he'd taken me to looked like a prison. In fact, it was a beautiful, modern home. But he never answered my simple question, and that caused the distrust to erupt like a volcano.

I wasn't getting out of this vehicle. Not willingly.

He slapped a hand against the tinted window, and I jumped. "What is with you women locking me out of my own car?"

How many women had done that? What gave them a reason to fear him?

Jake hit the button on the fob, unlocking the door, but I quickly locked it again.

A guttural blast of irritation had him clenching his hand into a solid fist when he moved to the back door and wrapped his hand around the handle.

Jake pressed the fob and jerked on the door. It opened with ease, almost as if he'd choreographed the move. He climbed on his hands and knees inside the backseat and reached for me. I lurched forward, avoiding his touch, and tumbled out of the car door, scrambling across the grass to the pool.

A man in jeans and a naked chest with a ghastly demon tattooed down his sternum stepped out from the pool house, wiping his hands on a red and white cloth. Or was it a white cloth with red on it?

I screamed and slid onto my hands as I changed course and headed for the towering cemented fence—three feet too high for me to jump over.

"Adelaide, stop this bullshit now."

"I've got her," the man said.

"Don't fucking hurt her, Tonk."

That was Tonk? The man from the awards ceremony?

I didn't get a good look at his face in the dark, but how was it someone looked bigger without clothes on than with?

"You mean you didn't bring her here for me?"

"She's already scared. Stop trying to make it worse."

I raced behind the pool house, searching for another gate, then turned right and slammed into a solid smooth mass.

"*Ahh*!" My voice broke as it hit glass-shattering decibels.

"You made this too easy," he said, his baritone voice resonating in my chest. "Want to try again?" Jake wrapped his arms around my upper torso and hauled my feet off the ground as his friend watched.

"I'm having a serious case of déjà vu," Tonk said to Jake as they assembled back where we'd started.

What did that mean? Had they done this before—taken someone against their will?

"Let. Me. Go." I kicked his shins, but Jake stood stolid.

"Again. Making things harder on yourself."

Tonk disappeared into the pool house and walked back out with a syringe in his hand.

Jake sat down on the ground with his arms tight around my body, then pinned my legs beneath his, immobilizing my struggles. "It'll only hurt for a second," he whispered in my ear.

"Jake, don't do this," I screamed and thrashed around as a sharp pinch hit my thigh. Jake's arms around me loosened, and he let me go.

"That's better. I like them compliant," Tonk said.

"Meet my serial killer friend, Adelaide."

"You told her that?"

"It started out as a joke."

He released his hold on me as my heart lodged in my throat, his voice warping into some out-of-this-world dialect.

Started as a joke? Did that mean it wasn't?

I wrapped my deadening fingers in his shirt and fell against him. "I said... was sorry." My words slurred as my tongue sat like a bar of lead in my mouth.

The green earth below smudged into textured lines on a soiled canvas. I crawled off his lap. The pricks of luscious grass stabbed into my hands like shards of glass—the sensation contradicting the pillows beneath my knees.

What did he give me?

I crawled until my hands slipped across the textured tile, and the shimmer of aquamarine water glistened in the near distance.

The moon's bright reflected light sent wild ripples dancing against the cemented bottom, luring me into their whimsical pattern. I touched the warm liquid, its essence smoothing over my fingertips yet offering me no comfort. My eyelids pulled down as if the weight of the world was pressed upon me.

I fell to my belly, dragging myself closer to the ledge.

"Let's go, sweets."

Jake grabbed my shoulder and rolled me over, his brows creating lines on his forehead. Picking me up, he cradled me against his chest, my dead arms hanging at my sides, no longer functioning.

"How much did you give her?"

"Enough."

Jake presented me to the demon with glowing eyes tearing out of his friend's chest, and I was powerless to his will.

11

Tonk set up a cot for her while I sat on the floor, holding her in my arms. Her pomegranate scent stirred abhorrent feelings inside of me as I stared at her fresh tattoo.

Even after laying hands on her, threatening her more times than I cared to admit, and letting her think I'd turned her parents against her, she still professed her love and got a matching tattoo.

A tattoo she had no intention of me ever seeing and a love she had no intention of sharing.

The thought stuck in my gut like a hot poker, bubbling my blood from the inside out.

But could I blame her? *No.*

Even if she had shared it without pointing a knife at me, I still didn't want to hear her confessions. She probably said it to manipulate me into letting her go.

But there was this niggling in the back of my mind that had me questioning everything I'd discovered about her. What if she'd told me the truth? Would it be so hard to believe that she didn't know who I was? Or who Alek was when she took the picture?

Yes. Of course it was.

She had to know. Two plus two equals four. *There are no coincidences.*

But how did she know I'd be at the club that night?

The conflicting back-and-forth thoughts filled my mind with rebellious doubt and anger, and it surged like a flash flood. I wanted to slap her away, hug her, shake her until she confessed, and wipe away her tears.

I moved her splotchy black hair away from her face and peered down at her placid features. She looked so different with it colored. I missed her red hair. It added to her spitfire personality. It acted as a warning to anyone who pushed her in the wrong direction. Couple that with her nineteen-year-old spirit, and you had a recipe for unpredictability and drama.

"What are you going to do with her?" Tonk said, standing in the doorway to the soundproof room.

"I don't know yet."

"Well, how long are you planning on keeping her here?"

"I don't know yet."

"Hmm."

"Who do you have next door?" I moved to my knees and shuffled her to the bed, and set her down.

"Kathy."

"And who is that?"

"A woman I pulled off the street."

I shook my head. "Any particular reason?"

"She has five counts of child abuse and is a habitual drug user."

"Working through your mommy issues?"

He chortled. "My parental issues are dead and buried at the bottom of a well."

I smiled, wishing my problems were so easily handled with a bullet to someone's brains.

Adelaide's chest moved up and down in a steady rhythm as I moved my hand down to her belly.

Was there something there that would tether her to me forever? Would that be so bad? It was what I wanted, but not anymore. Not after what had come to light.

This was what happened when you acted impulsively. She drove my recklessness into new heights, and now look...

Her shirt rode up, exposing her belly and a purple, ugly mark marring her skin. I pushed it higher, then dipped my fingers into her sweats and pulled. A deep, angry bruise covered her hip.

The inside resembled that of a galaxy with its swirls of purples, blacks, and specks of white scattered throughout—all the places the blood didn't touch. The outside branched into yellows and greens, and that's where the ugliness lay.

What the hell happened to her?

Anger sliced through me as I thought of those men who put their hands on her.

Didn't I say I relinquished my claim on her? Three days ago, I couldn't imagine being here—protecting her, bringing her to the basement.

I was *supposed* to be mad at her—I *was* mad at her.

No. I *am* mad at her. And mad didn't seem like the appropriate word for this situation.

There was no forgetting what she'd done, but that didn't mean I wanted her to die, especially after this...

My hand slipped back over her belly, feeling the thump of her pulse beneath my touch.

What the hell had we gotten ourselves into?

What drove me to the point of madness that I'd come inside her?

And after how I treated her, it wouldn't surprise me if she never told me she had my child growing inside of her.

Her smooth skin dipped as I moved my thumb back and forth, caressing her abdomen, my head tilting to the side as I stood mesmerized by her exquisiteness.

"Clean your hand before it gets infected, and I have to use my favorite bone saw," Tonk said, jolting me out of my hypnotic state.

I sucked in a breath, forgetting about a world made up of just Adelaide and me.

"You're morbid." I turned my rag-covered hand over, examining my blood-stained fingers. "I'll be fine."

"I wasn't asking."

Pulling Adelaide's shirt back over her torso, I laid her hand over her belly and stood. "How long will that keep her out?"

"Depends on her metabolism, but I'd say around twelve hours, maybe longer."

Enough time for me to figure out what was going on and let her parents know she was okay. Lord knows she didn't have the courtesy of saying anything to them.

I walked away from her with trepidation.

After everything that she'd done—the scheming, conniving little bitch—I still wanted to protect her. In fact, I saw myself doing anything to keep her safe.

Why?

What was so special about her that I'd erase my rules for life?

Loyalty was essential.

But I'd lay down everything for her?

Again, *why?*

"Make sure you lock the door. She'll try to escape the moment she wakes up."

A sly grin tipped Tonk's lips.

"She's mine," I growled at my friend, with a visceral reaction to protect her like a beast. "So don't touch her."

His grin vanished. "I have no interest in her," he said, shutting the door and locking her inside.

I nodded, shaking out my stinging hand.

It was an oversight and a stupid mistake when I reached for her, but I couldn't let her fall with the knife in her hands. She was too nervous and shaking it back and forth erratically. Knowing her, she'd end up accidentally killing herself with it.

"Twelve hours, then?"

He nodded.

That's enough time to fix up my hand and figure out who the hell those people were.

"I might need stitches."

"Kit's in the back," he said, fingering through a metal tray beside the door to Kathy's room.

He picked up a straight blade used for shaving and ran his thumb across the sharp end. "Sometimes, it's the simplest thing that causes the most amount of pain."

He glanced back at me after a passing of silence and placed the knife back down on the tray.

"How poetic."

He scoffed, and we crossed the hall into an open room filled with medical supplies. He didn't want his 'patients' to have an untimely death.

"Liz had her baby," he said, the random bit of information given unsolicited.

"What was it?"

"A girl. Hannah."

"She named her after his mother?"

"Mmm-hmm."

They'd had a rough beginning, but eventually, she came around, fell in love, and got married. Now they had a baby, and I can't say I envied them.

"What will happen to this place now?"

"They're selling it. I've started construction on my property for a new facility."

I sat down in the chair, placed my hand on the table, and started unwinding the makeshift bandage.

"And you feel comfortable with all of that around, Ivy?"

"It'll be nowhere near her."

"Does she know?"

"That I kill people?"

I nodded. "Yeah."

"She does."

I raised a brow and winced, pressing my fingertips to the cut there, then peeled away the towel from my hand.

"And she's okay with all of that?"

He sighed, his shoulders dropping slightly as he put the kit on the table.

"She is." He tore open the new package of gauze and doused my hand in cool iodine.

"I hope you know what you're doing."

He shook his head. "It's my first time."

"Oh, look, Tonk has jokes. Hilarious, man."

Tonk grunted, sounding similar to laughter, then patted my palm dry with clean gauze.

"Looks like you only need a stitch or two. Or I can put a liquid stitch on it."

"Yeah, let's go with the painless version."

Tonk pinched the skin together while I skimmed over my phone, hoping answers would pop up at me.

"How good are your interrogation skills without hurting people?"

I knew nothing of the men who wanted to take her, and until she woke up, my searching would end in nothing but a wild goose chase.

Adelaide knew them. She knew their motives and what they wanted. I was sure of it. That's why she ran. Wasn't it? If she didn't give me the information I needed, I'd feed her to the wolf until she did.

Adelaide

12

A spiteful ache pinched my belly, followed by a rumbling mimicking a groan from my lips. My head pounded with each heartbeat as though I'd kicked one too many back. I needed water.

I stretched, relishing the sweet burn in my muscles.

Flashes of Jake pinning me down to the ground, his friend injecting me with some sort of cocktail.

After that... nothing.

My heart vaulted in my chest, and I opened my eyes.

Open...

I exhaled, deflating my chest as my breath left my body.

"Open."

Wake up.

I drew my hand down my face and gasped. "What's going on?" I was awake, but the room was pitch-black.

Where was I?

Where had Jake taken me?

Was I buried alive?

I sniffed the air... Clean. No repugnant iron or mildew stench in the air.

"Jake?" my voice shook, laced with weakness and vibrating with my increased pulse.

How long had I been out?

How long had he kept me here?

My chest tightened as a bright, knifelike pain hit me centermass and held me captive in the nothingness before me.

"Jake?" I called out again, this time desperation moving my legs.

I sat on the makeshift bed, metal bars making up the frame digging into the backs of my thighs. My hip ached as I stood, my shoulder throbbing and the pounding in my head worsening.

I put my hands out in front of me and scuffed my feet against the cemented flooring until my hands touched a padded wall.

No-no-no-no.

Am I in a mental institute? Did he have me committed? How?

My chin trembled as I cried out, slamming my fists against the wall with a muffled thud.

He'd never hear me.

I was alone.

In a box where I couldn't see, and the only sound around me was my labored breaths and tinnitus ringing in my ears.

My lungs burned from the constant rush of oxygen, setting fire to them with each expansion.

I tilted sideways, my head swimming.

How did my head spin when I couldn't even see which side was up and which was down? I slunk to my butt and wiped my hands through my hair. This was it. I'd lose my mind if he didn't come for me.

Is that what he wanted?

I got up and walked the perimeter, my hands moving up and down the walls until my feet struck the bed.

Where was the door?

Where was the fucking door?

Tears soaked my cheeks as I bit my lip, fighting the fierce concentration of pain in my chest, and picked up another lap around the room until I stumbled upon the cot again.

I never knew darkness could be so asphyxiating. It stole the breath from my lungs and set my heart on a rampage in my chest.

It was thick like fog, infiltrating my lungs and taking over, preventing me from pulling in a lungful.

How was this possible?

What did I get myself into?

As I slid down the cornered wall of my prison, I gripped my chest and drew my knees up, wrapping my arms around them for comfort. I closed my eyes and took a staggered breath.

"He'll come for me." He always did. *He wouldn't leave me here.*

I leaned my head against the padded wall and focused on my breathing, letting the calm take over my insides like a black leech crawling through my bloodstream.

A muffled metallic jiggle had me tuning my other senses to the impending threat. I tilted my head, listening for anything.

Another rattle and my body congealed.

There wasn't a calming inside of me anymore. Instead, I shivered, my teeth rattling as my thighs shook with violent tremors that radiated through my body as a ripple effect.

What if it was Jake?

Intense bright light burst through my lids like a fiery orange sunrise, threatening to blind me with its awe.

My eyes flew open when the wall beside me scuffed against the cold, hard floor, swinging toward me until it touched my toes, pinning me in.

"Where did she go?" Jake said.

My mouth gaped open as I tried answering him, but nothing escaped my lips until the door moved away with a vacuum effect, pulling stray hairs into my face.

"She's here," Tonk said.

Tonk's broad, muscular shoulders stood above me, his feet placed wide with one hand on the door, the other beside him, his fingers moving in an up and down pattern.

"Shit, Adelaide?"

Jake shoved his friend out of the way and wrapped his arms around me, but my body refused to move.

"How long have you been awake?"

I jerked my head to the side.

How was I supposed to know? He'd left me in my own personal dark hell.

Jake tucked his arms under my knees and around my back, lifting me up against his chest, and walked me back toward the cot I'd run into so many times.

He was going to leave me again?

I wrapped my arms around his neck and pulled him to a stop.

"Don't leave me."

Don't leave me.

"I'm not going anywhere."

My chest deflated as I bit back my sob.

"You need to have lights in here," Jake said.

I buried my face in his neck, breathing in his rich, woody scent, letting my memories take me to a time with Jake between my thighs or our first date eating Mexican food.

"That defeats the purpose of sensory isolation."

"Come on, sweets."

He dropped my legs, settling my feet on the ground while keeping his arm around my waist, and led me out of the padded room into a brightly lit hallway with closed doors lining the length of it.

"What is this place?"

"A safe place for *you*."

I shook my head, squeezing his waist tight. "There are no safe places anymore."

"Now that you're awake, why don't you sit down and tell me about who it was that tried to take you?"

My stomach popped and gurgled as my foot hit the first stair. "Can we eat first?"

He nodded. "I'm sure you're starving."

My mouth watered at the thought of food, anything really, but I needed it with cheese. "Jake?"

"What?"

We walked past the pool, through the sliding glass doors, and into the kitchen. Jake pulled out a barstool at the kitchen island and sat me down.

"Thank you."

"What do you want to eat?"

"Do you have cheese?"

I leaned my elbows on the counter while Tonk took a seat next to me and stared.

Stared wasn't the correct word.

Observed, studied, inspected. His gaze roamed over my body with intense scrutiny and only stopped when a woman with ebony hair walked around the corner.

"I couldn't find the towels..." Her voice trailed off as she spotted me. She stopped abruptly, keeping herself a fair distance away. "Oh, hi."

Scars traveled up and down her arms and thighs in some brutal form of torture.

Did this man do that to her?

Tonk spun off his chair and walked towards her, moving her out of the room with an unexpected delicate touch.

"Who was that?"

"Ivy."

"Did he do that to her?"

He was a killer, right? That's what Jake said right before he let his friend stick me with a needle filled with some sort of sedative.

Jake dropped the jar of pickles onto the counter, causing me to jump in my seat, followed by bread, mayonnaise, and cheese—three different flavors.

"It's best you don't say that shit out loud. I can't protect you from him if you do."

I swallowed hard and grabbed the package of American cheese.

The processed yellow stuff was my favorite. When I was a kid and even recently I'd grab a slice of bread, slap a rubber square on it, and pop it in the microwave until it melted to perfection.

I snatched the bread, my stomach eating itself away, and shoved a piece in my mouth as I made three cheese and bread slices.

"Is that all you're having?"

I nodded, my stomach aching with hunger.

I put the slices in the microwave for fifteen seconds, watching the edges bubble.

"You should eat some protein."

"Cheese has protein."

I pulled the hot slice out and replaced it with another one.

"Not that kind."

"Why do you care?"

"Call it a vested interest."

"Well, don't worry about me. I'll get out of your hair." I took a bite of the folded cheesy bread when he grabbed my arm and stepped in really close, his breath moving my hair.

"If you think about taking off again, I'll lock you back in that room." He pulled me away from my food dinging in the microwave and forced me to sit back on my stool. "Now tell me about who's after you."

I shoved the next bite into my mouth, then another and another, until I'd devoured the whole thing, then pulled the sandwich toward me he'd pulled out of the microwave. "Do you have any juice?"

He dipped into the fridge and poured me a glass of orange juice. "Who's Black Dog?"

I stopped chewing, my stomach sinking like a heavy rock to the bottom of the lake.

"Where did you hear that name?"

"Your little chat group." He placed his hands on the edge of the counter and leaned like he did that night at the bar when we'd first met.

I sucked in a deep breath. "You may know them as Sev Shun." I gulped the juice he handed to me, then bit into the next sandwich.

"Sev Shun... I know that name." He popped the juice back into the fridge after pouring himself a glass.

"Who's house is this?"

"My friend, but you should know that already seeing as you stalked them."

I rolled my eyes and took another bite. "I never followed them," I said, talking around my food. "You assumed I did."

"And with good reason, Adelaide."

I slowed my chewing and put my food down, lowering my gaze to the countertops. I rubbed my hands together, removing the bits of bread stuck to my fingertips.

"You know, had I known any of this when I'd started, I would've gone to the ends of the world to make sure you knew."

"Knew what?"

"That they targeted your company."

My stomach knotted, and I rubbed my hand over my mouth, the rest of my food no longer interesting me.

"You mean when *you* targeted my company? Don't distance yourself from them. You're just as guilty as they are."

"Which is exactly why, when I found out, I quit. Holeo ghosted me. He blocked me from the groups and him. In fact, once I found out, he placed ransomware on the server—"

"I'm not interested," he snapped.

I'd wanted to tell him everything, like I needed air to survive, but fear had held me back. And now that he knew and hated me, I had nothing to lose.

"Just listen to me, Jake."

"I don't want to hear it. No matter what you say, I'll never trust you again."

"So why? Why are you helping me then? I don't get it."

"I told you. I have a vested interest."

I picked up the remains of my food, no longer interested in eating, and tossed it into the trash. "Mind sharing what this 'agenda' of yours is?"

"Tell me about Sev Shun."

I scoffed. Of course, the only person allowed to ask questions was him.

"Black Dog. They are an Armenian mercenary company based out of Turkey. You worked on something for them a while back, testing out their computer systems."

"How do you know that?"

I shook my head. "Because Holeo told me. But I didn't know who you were then. This was eight months ago."

"Just tell me why they're after you."

I sighed. "I think because Holeo went after them, making it personal. That's what Franklin told me." I shrugged.

"And how do you know he's not behind it?"

I snorted. "Because he's a six-foot nerd who has social anxiety like me. People like us don't go around killing people with military precision."

"Speak for yourself," Tonk said as he walked back in with random wet spots all over his shirt.

Jake glared at his friend. "And why do they want you dead?"

Shaking my head, I pinched off a piece of bread and nibbled on it. "I don't know. Probably because we were going to expose them."

"And who is Holeo?" Jake put the bread and cheese into the fridge, except the pickles. I grabbed them and dug in, popping a spear into my mouth.

"He's the lead. He gave us directives, and we followed his instructions. These guys are serious, Jake." I sucked off the juice from the pickle, then finished chewing. "They've already killed Skipper and shot Torpedo. He's in the hospital fighting for his life."

"Then there's hope," Tonk said, chiming in.

"For what? That they'll miss?"

"That they'll let you live."

"And how do you come by that?"

I twisted the lid back on the jar and tore a napkin off the roll, wiping my lips dry.

"They left this Torpedo guy alive."

"He's in the ICU, and I don't think they meant to."

Tonk laughed. "They didn't mess up. They sent a message. My guess is he was the first. And once this Holeo guy didn't stop, they went after the second, killing him."

"If that was true, then they won't stop until I'm dead."

My skin warmed and beaded with sweat as I pictured my gruesome death.

"I wouldn't. If you didn't listen to the first warning, I'd make sure you'd never make that mistake again."

I thought he was supposed to be security? Who the hell was this guy, and why did he have a basement like that?

"But I stopped. Well before anything happened..." I gave Jake the side eye, his gaze cast down toward my hand where someone had removed the plastic over my fresh tattoo. "How did you know where I was?" I said, hiding my finger under my other hand.

"I told you I'd find you."

"But how?"

"It's easy to find someone," Tonk said. "A bit time-consuming, but not diffi-cult."

I snorted.

Tell that to all the missing persons cases that went unsolved every year.

I'd done all the right things, yet they popped up like shadows everywhere.

"If that's true, then let me leave. They'll come after me, and you'll get caught in the crossfire."

I jumped from my seat, and Jake rounded the island with unnatural speed and grabbed hold of my shoulders. I shied away, wincing as his fingers dug into my bruise, the agony buckling my knees. "Ahh."

Jake's brows pulled together as he dropped his hand from my shoulder, then pulled my shirt away from my wound.

"I thought you said he didn't hurt you?"

"He didn't." I shrugged him off and adjusted my shirt, so it sat straight again. "That was from the truck four days ago."

"You didn't feel the need to mention this?"

"In case you've forgotten," I said, backing away from him. "We aren't exactly on speaking terms. Remember?" I cocked my head to the side. "Or did that slip your mind?"

He reached out for me again, but I dodged his touch. "You won't win this fight without me."

I rolled my eyes. "Seems like I won't win at all if what Tonk says is true."

"Don't call me Tonk. It's Randall."

"Fine... Randall."

Just let me vanish into thin air so I can pretend this never happened. I'd go skiing in the mountains or hide in the snow of Montreal. Maybe I'd go to Florida and swim with the manatees.

Either way, I couldn't sit here explaining my situation to Jake. Not because I didn't want to be near him, but because the longer I was, the more desperate the situation became.

But maybe he was right, and I stood a chance at survival with him. Because if it wasn't for him, I'd be in the trunk of some car, waiting for them to dig my grave.

Jake

13

It'd taken me seven whole days and nights filled with emails and phone calls that ended up filtering into a generic voicemail until they made contact. All the while, she'd complained endlessly because I'd cut her off from civilization and electronics.

"I'm leaving," I said, catching her reflected gaze on the TV.

She hadn't moved from that seat all day aside from digging into the fridge and eating me out of house and home. For a woman as thin as she was, she sure could eat.

Adelaide twisted in place on the leather couch, her elbow resting on the back, her chin on her arm. "Where are you going?"

"I have some errands to run." A meeting I'd worked tirelessly to make. "Don't leave the house. Don't go snooping. I've locked my computer, so don't even try to get on the internet, and the house arms the moment I drive away. I'll know if you even think about opening a window or door."

"Yes, Daddy." She snarled. "Why can't I go?" Her frown turned into a pout. "I've been stuck in this house for days now."

I could wipe the frown off her face if I bent her backward over the couch and slipped my cock into her mouth. Taking one step forward, then two, I paused, clenching my fist.

It wouldn't take much for me to fulfill that fantasy.

"Do as you're told. I won't be long."

I stepped back, putting distance between us, then grabbed my keys from the hook and pocketed the cool, thick key fob.

"What if something happens? I won't have any way to contact someone."

"The alarm will do it for you. You can hit *panic* on the panel, and they'll send the police, or when the alarm goes off, they'll call the police automatically."

She sunk back into the couch with an irritated grunt and crossed her arms under her breasts, propping them up into delicious pillows I wanted to take a bite out of.

Goddammit.

"Don't do anything stupid." I walked into the garage and slammed the door behind me.

I wouldn't allow my dick to lead me around. I had more self-control than that.

So why was it so difficult to stay mad at her?

Sliding into my car, I backed down my driveway, then took off to a discreet meeting location my team had used before. I glanced at the manila folder sitting in the seat beside me with my terms printed inside. If they didn't accept them, there was no telling what our next steps would be, other than I wouldn't allow them to have her.

Not when there was a potential... My car erupted with ringing and announced the caller.

"Tonk. I'm on my way."

"We're positioned. I brought everyone."

And no doubt they had done the same.

It was precautionary.

People were less likely to draw their weapon as a show of force if they knew the opposition had them, too. It's why mass shooters chose targets with the knowledge they wouldn't get fired on.

Cowards.

"I won't ask you how you feel about this..."

"Not good."

I chuckled low and quiet—the motion setting me back in my seat as I switched hands on the steering wheel, then shook out my healing, but still injured, hand.

"Dealing with any sort of mercenary is a risk."

They all lived by their own code, like pirates. Although, I'd say pirates were a bit more lawless than mercenaries. At least they followed their leader and didn't run mutinies.

"I'm pulling up."

Driving through the security gate, I found the empty hanger which housed an old millionaire's plane who'd left for a lengthy vacation.

There were three large black trucks parked in front of the wide-open hangar, and next to that was Tonk's vehicle. I pulled in beside his.

Stepping out with my folder in hand, a murmur of chatter filtered through the building where I was headed.

I counted sixteen men, all dressed in swat attire.

"Seems a bit excessive for a peace talk," I said as I walked through the doors towards their huddle.

"You can never be too cautious."

His underlying accent would deceive even the most well-spoken American. In fact, you wouldn't know where to place it. He could've passed for a tanned Jersey native, minus the obnoxious attitude some had.

"Sarkis?"

"Yes."

"Let's get started."

"Awful lot of work for a girl."

"Here," I said, handing him the folder. "This outlines the terms of our deal."

The men laughed as Sarkis took it.

"You want to contract our negotiation, so we don't kill your girlfriend?"

I shook my head. "I said outline, not a contract. That way, there's no confusion about what I'm asking of you."

"You're not really in the position to be asking for anything, especially after you broke Berat's arm and sliced the throat of one of my new operatives. He'll live, by the way."

I gritted my teeth and squeezed my fist, popping my knuckles with the pressure. "I know. That's why I cut the side of his neck and not his jugular."

"Where is my compensation for my two men you put out of commission?"

"I didn't know what was going on at the time, and they didn't bother to share when they shoved her in the trunk. So I took matters into my own hands." I paused and opened my copy of the deal. "Now, we both want something, and I'm willing to do whatever means necessary to make sure that happens."

"And what is it you can offer me?"

"A trade."

He laughed again, turning to the blond man at his side. "And here I thought you were here to protect her. What do you want in exchange?"

"Not her." I shook my head. "The leader of Cryptonic."

"And what makes you think we need your help?" He stepped forward, the paper by his side.

"If you knew how to find him. You would've already. Am I wrong?"

He scratched his chin, then cleared his throat. "Go on?"

"With me on your side, along with my tools, I can find him."

"And then what?"

"I'll hand him over, ensure Adelaide never touches your company again, and in exchange, you leave her be."

He passed the paper to the blond beside him, who opened the manila folder and examined the contents. His men spread out across the hanger as if they prepared for something, their itchy trigger fingers tucked inside the trigger guard.

My muscles hardened in place, setting my fists like stone.

If this was it, and they opened fire, it guaranteed me a dirt nap. I imagined that's why they didn't bother patting me down.

Armenians were a fierce breed who believed death with purpose was the only way to go. Not all, but most. When you dealt with people who weren't afraid of death but more or less welcomed it, it was hard to intimidate them or make an accurate reactive assessment.

"Offer us something else," the blond man said.

"And who are you?"

"Yervant."

"Well, Yervant, this is my offer."

Yervant and Sarkis glanced at one another, then back to me. "We want discounted prices on weapons and anything else you can get."

I scoffed and rubbed my jaw. "I'm a broker. We don't make the prices; the seller does. We just bring the seller and buyer together."

"Make an exception," Sarkis said.

I shook my head. "You don't understand." Pinpricks scattered up my spine. What he was asking of me was impossible. "I don't have control over the prices. They aren't my weapons."

"Then no deal."

"Over guns?" I frowned. "I'm willing to get two hackers threatening to expose your entire outfit, and you want to toss that out for guns?"

"We'll find them, eventually. Something tells me we just have to follow you home," Sarkis said.

His threat landed like a sucker punch, and I broke.

I lunged at him, ripping the terms out of his hand, and fisted his bullet-proof vest. The clicking of gunmetal taking position and hitting shoulders as they braced for the kick of their automatic weapons stilled the air with growing hostility.

"Do not threaten *me* or *her*—"

"We outnumber you, Jake Murray," he sneered. "You'll die before your pistol leaves your belt."

I returned his smile with a sneer. "Who said I'd be the one killing you?" I shoved him backward and picked up the terms scattered on the floor. "You've entered my home stadium, and I hold the upper hand, Sarkis."

"I don't understand these American terms."

"It means you walked into *my* territory where *I* have all the manpower. If I wanted to, I could kill you here and now, but I'm choosing to let you live and work with me."

Sarkis and Yervant glanced around. "I don't believe you."

"You don't have to."

"You must be crazy if you think this is all of us. She'd be dead by morning if you did that."

"We'll see."

I had my contingency plans set in motion. Alek wasn't here for a reason. One being his new baby, but the other because I needed someone to take Adelaide away if things went south. He'd lock her in the highest tower where not even God himself could see. I didn't care if she lived the rest of her days in Hell. At least she'd be safe.

"Fine. You have a deal, but if you don't deliver, we *will* reign unholy terror down around you and yours."

I didn't doubt it.

Yervant gestured to his team for them to put their weapons down, alleviating the vile vibration inside of me.

"Deal."

"Now leave my city."

Sarkis turned to his men and waved them forward, saying a word in a language I didn't recognize—most likely Armenian. His men followed him to the hangar with hungry scowls.

They were bloodthirsty, but they hadn't gotten their fix. If I played my cards right, they never would, not with *Adelaide or me.*

"Good luck," Yervant said as he walked past me.

"Luck has nothing to do with it."

I'd already started the process. Using a logger vulnerability, it monitored the comings and goings of a chat group Holeo liked to frequent before he disappeared.

The men got into their vehicles and drove away as I called to Tonk. "Clear."

"What kind of watch would I be if I didn't know that before you?" he said from behind me.

Tonk stood tall, his sniper rifle resting over his shoulder like it wasn't a large piece of killing equipment.

"True."

I rubbed my jaw, my other placed on my hip, taking up space around me.

"You sure this will work?"

"It has to."

"And if it doesn't?"

Then we're on the run?

"I don't know."

They were strong, yes, but we had the numbers in spades. And who knew if they were the leader or just the spokesperson?

Better to know thy enemy.

"Guess we better get started."

"There is no *we*. This is my fight."

Tonk scoffed and brought his rifle down across his body, making it land in his other hand. "We're brothers. This is *our* fight."

I nodded. "I have things moving, just waiting for him to pop up so we can get him. I *have* to go to the memorial in two days. Becca won't allow me to miss it."

"We'll have things covered on our end here."

"Roger dodger. Can we get a sandwich, or do you still have a little Kathy problem to deal with?"

"That little fighter was my most expensive experiment to date."

Expensive? "Do I want to know?"

"Probably not."

Adelaide

14

A week of The Office reruns, and my mind had officially combusted. I needed something to do, something to concentrate on, and sitting in front of the TV wasn't it. He could've taken me out on his errands two days ago and let me pick up some more clothes, but no. He'd left me behind to twiddle my thumbs... and worry.

Which brought me to my other stressor, the unused pregnancy test in my backpack that I'd been living out of. Washing clothes every two days was a bitch.

I'd put it off, finding it easy to slip into the bathroom and take it, but did I really want to find out if I was pregnant only for me to wind up dead?

Nah.

Ignorance was bliss, and I'd ride that train for as long as I could.

"Are you ready?" Jake said from a fair distance behind me.

Jake had spent most of his days locked away somewhere, 'working.' And all his nights with his arms wrapped around me as we slept, even though there were guest rooms, and the couch, he refused to let me out of his sight. He said it was easier to keep me safe that way.

If I was honest with myself, which doesn't happen often, I didn't care where I slept or how, so long as he was with me. I relished every moment with him because when this was all over, I knew deep down into my dying soul I'd never feel him around me again. And he solidified that when the sun rose in the morning. He'd go back to his cold self, kicking me out of his room and banishing me to the living room.

"I asked you a question."

I jerked. My gaze twisted away from his sculpted frame. "Huh?"

"Are you ready?"

"Ready for what..." I glanced down at my wrinkled shirt and two-day-old sweats. Not to mention my disheveled ponytail. "The drive-through?"

"We're getting on a plane."

"A plane?"

Where exactly are we supposed to be going? And how the hell was I supposed to be ready when this was the first I'd heard of it?

"Yes, get your stuff."

"You mean the backpack I'm living out of? Yeah, got it." I turned off the TV and dropped the remote on the coffee table. "And where exactly are we going?"

"Jake? I'm here."

Becca walked through the front door with two suitcases dragging behind her. "Becca?"

What was she doing here? And where the hell were we going that she needed that much stuff?

"Hi, Adelaide. Are you watching the house or something while we're gone?"

I scoffed, which made her brows twitch.

"She's coming with us."

"And where are we going exactly?" I asked again.

Becca's face turned down, and her gaze disappeared behind her lashes. Did I say something wrong?

"Adelaide, now."

Jake snapped his fingers at me like I was a dog, which made me want to bury my knuckles in his jaw.

"Don't do that," I gritted out.

"The jet is waiting for us. I don't have time for your stubborn attitude."

Standing, I made my way to the laundry room. "I don't think wanting to know where we're going is called an 'attitude,' but whatever." I grabbed my bag sitting on top of the machine and stomped back toward him.

I shoved my shoes on over my thin socks with Koi fish printed on them. My body tilted, and I hopped, trying to stay on my feet. I hopped again, and my eyes widened as I tilted towards the stairs.

My pulse spiked as my face rushed to meet the edge of the stairs, my wicked fingers refusing to release my damned shoe. Strong arms wrapped around my waist, and jerked me, making my vision run in reverse until the ending scene was his chest in my face, his spicy cologne intoxicating me.

I glanced up and shrunk in on myself. His profound gaze swirled wild strands of desire around my heart, tugging hard to let me know it was there. His brows softened. I froze in his arms, afraid that if I moved a fraction of an inch in any direction, he'd release me.

I was a fool who loved a man who wanted nothing to do with me. What was it they say? 'You always want something you can't have.' That was it. Although, I'd say my love for him blossomed well before I found out I couldn't have him.

"*Ahem*. I'm just going to put my suitcases in the car," Becca said from behind us.

Jake quickly released me like I'd been diagnosed with the bubonic plague. "Be more careful. We don't need you falling down the stairs."

"It'd be a simpler death than what they'd have in store for me," I mumbled under my breath as I sat on the floor and tied my shoe.

I didn't have a death wish. I loved my life and wanted to finish it out until I saw flying cars and virtual reality so real I could feel what I touched and tasted what I'd put in my mouth.

Fantasy, I know, but it's what I wanted.

"Stop talking like that."

He'd heard that?

"Right. The basement with your serial killer best friend."

He'd threatened it so many times now. It became an ongoing theme in our relationship.

Jake was the equivalent of a parent who made empty threats. Sure he'd put me in there before, but the look in his eyes when he found me shaking in the corner had me hoping he'd never do it again. So when I challenged him, I'd based it on that sole thought and hoped for the best.

I shook the thought off as I finished my other shoe, then followed him to the garage, where he threw my pack inside the trunk.

Becca sat in the back seat, her posture painfully straight while she worked her thumbs over her phone.

I got into the front passenger seat, wishing Jake had given me back my burner phone so I could talk to my parents or even Monica, but he'd refused. The only advanced piece of technology I could touch was his smart TV—which he'd disconnected from the internet.

I missed my mom and dad. What must they be thinking?

"Jake?"

"*Hmm?*" he hummed as he backed out of the driveway.

"Have you talked to my parents?"

"Yes, they know you're with me working off your debt."

"Her debt?"

I turned to Becca. "Yeah, your brother—"

"It's nothing," he said firmly.

"Okay," Becca said, drawing out the word, then returned to her phone.

Interesting.

He didn't tell her. I thought they shared everything.

We drove past Monica's house, and I sat upright in my seat, watching like a kid seeing Christmas lights for the first time.

Three moving trucks, two parked on the street and one parked in the driveway with movers shoving furniture wrapped in blankets into it.

"Did you know?"

He shook his head. "No. But the for sale sign has been there."

Poor Monica. What must she be going through?

I was fortunate enough to have parents that loved each other very much. Nothing impeded that. They always made time for each other and talked out their problems. I doubted Monica's parents ever did that.

Tears pooled in my eyes, blurring my vision, when I felt a tickling touch on my pinkie.

It was faint, but there was no mistaking it. Jake's arm rested on the center console beside me, his tattooed finger brushing mine with the faintest of touches.

I spun my lip ring with my tongue, sucking my lip into my mouth as I did. One moment he hated me, and the next, he acted like this—like he cared. I brushed my tears away with my right hand, not wanting to move the one he touched. It was a rare occurrence these days to experience such tenderness from him.

He drove down the freeway, his finger never leaving mine except to turn on the music, but he took up the same position as before. My breath stuck in my chest, and I averted my gaze out the window.

Tempting fate, I tucked my pinkie into his, our tattoos touching in a symbolic expression of the way my heart felt about him. His warm skin to my cool yet on fire hand.

I quietly sucked in a deep breath, only for it to rip from my chest when he tore his hand from mine and tucked it under his thigh, with his elbow still resting on the center console. I guess I'd crossed the line he'd already lingered over. Pulling my hand into my lap, I rubbed my pinkie, substituting his touch.

After a moment of silence and quiet humorous laughs from Becca, we drove through a security gate at a private airfield.

Well, he wasn't kidding when he said airplane. A big black lear-jet sat inside the hangar. Its size became more visible when he parked inside.

The pilot and a woman met him by his door, and the pilot opened it for him. "Good evening Mr. Murray."

"Everything ready?"

I got out of the car as one man with a captain's hat opened the door for Becca and the other with longish brown hair on top took the bags from the trunk.

"Yes, sir."

Jake left us and followed the pilot to the nose of the plane, then turned around and beckoned to the woman in a uniform. "Prudy, make sure they get situated, would you?"

"Yes, sir."

The blonde-haired stewardess walked toward Becca and me. "Right this way, please."

Her short hair exposed her long neck and round gold earrings as she walked in front of us.

"Hi, Prudy," Becca said. "How are the kids?"

"They are great. Thanks for asking..."

We stepped into the plane, and their conversation drifted to background noise.

The cream interior with black squares running down the aisle made me want to play hopscotch, even though it didn't resemble that at all. These were purely decorative. And seats so comfy they looked as though you could disappear between the creases.

"Wow."

"I know, right? I'll never get used to it," Becca said.

"Have a seat right here, please," Prudy said, pointing to a snug chair next to a couch with pillows and a blanket.

"I think I'll take this." I sat on the couch as Becca took the seat Prudy pointed to. "And a vodka tonic."

"She'll have water with lemon," Jake called from the entrance.

"I'll have a vodka tonic with lemon," I said, firmer this time.

"Prudy." Jake looked between us.

She nodded at Jake as she made her way past him and into the front of the plane while I glared at him.

He ducked as he entered the cabin, grabbed my arm and hauled me from my seat, and plopped me into a chair.

"Jake?" Becca said, alarmed.

"Stay out of it."

"No worries," I said as he buckled me in. "I'm used to his abuse these days."

Jake pulled the seatbelt tight across my lap, the veins in his forearms bulging as he squeezed the strap, making my mouth water.

"Watch your mouth," he seethed into my ear.

"I only speak the truth." I turned my head and gazed into his resentful blue eyes.

"Would that be the first time?"

I snarled and pushed him, but he didn't budge. "Leave me alone." I looked away from him, crossing my arms across my chest, his essence deceiving me.

Jake stepped back and took the seat across from me, then buckled himself in as Prudy walked towards me with my drink and a brown liquid in another cup, only his was glass with sharp cuts, like diamonds.

She handed me my drink with a lemon on the rim. I gave Jake a smug look, then took a sip. The smile fell from my lips from the lack of pleasurable burn.

"Water?"

"That's what I said." Jake took the drink she gave him and placed it in the cup holder running along the ridge of the plane.

"Prudy, a vodka tonic, please." I held out the cup in my hand. "I hate flying."

"You'll have the water. She won't get you anything else."

"You sure know how to make things dull, don't you?"

I plopped the water back on the tray, balanced in her palm, but kept the lemon, sucking on it with a puckered face.

Prudy walked away to the front of the plane while Jake glared.

"Watch it."

"Or what? *Hmm?*" I leaned forward, pulling the fruit from my lips with a slurp. "What are you going to do? Toss me from the plane?" I shrugged and licked my lips clean. "Please do."

"What's going on between you two?" Becca said, interrupting his death stare.

"Your brother has a hard time letting go." I leaned back in my chair as the airplane moved down the runway and picked up speed. My gaze never left his as he crossed his ankle over his knee and sipped on his liquor.

I never thought Jake could look at me as if I were the vilest human being on the face of the earth, but here we are, his gaze slicing my skin with each shift of his eyes.

His hatred of me didn't match the crime. Or maybe it did, and denial ran heavily in my veins.

"You're going to paint *me* as the bad guy?" he scoffed, putting his glass down as the tires lifted off the tarmac.

The plane shook as it rose into the air, my heart sinking in the opposite direction.

I gripped the armrests, digging my fingernails into the leather material, my stomach swirling with unease.

"Just take a deep breath," he said.

Oh, so now he wanted to offer me comfort when the liquor would've done it for him.

His hands slipped onto my knees and gripped them just in time for my screams to echo as the entire plane bounced in midair as if it hit a fucking pothole.

"Once we get to elevation, it'll be smooth. You'll never even know you're on a plane." He squeezed my knee a little tighter, his King of Hearts tattoo teasing the genuine pain in my heart.

I'd notice.

I'd notice that my feet weren't on the ground but rather, forty-thousand feet in the air. It made it worse that we were on a private aircraft. They typically flew ten thousand feet higher in the air to avoid all the commercial traffic.

I was amazed by the random tidbits of useless information I picked up as I skimmed the internet every day.

I counted down the time in my head. Seconds led to minutes, and minutes led to fragile peace. Did it say ten or fifteen minutes for a plane to hit altitude?

Either way, it was ten or fifteen minutes of Hell. Although, if I recalled correctly, no plane had ever crashed from turbulence alone.

What did Google know anyway?

I swiped his hand from my knee and glared at him.

How could he be nice to me one second and hateful the next?

"Don't touch me."

"That's not what you said before."

Another shudder rippled through the airplane, making everything rattle like it'd fall apart at the seams.

I closed my eyes and held on—a small whimper working its way out from between my lips.

"That was before you strangled me."

"What is she talking about?" Becca gasped from beside me, and I frowned.

Maybe she needed to hear what an absolute asshole her brother was... *is*.

She looked up to him like he hung the moon and stars, and he couldn't do any wrong. Maybe she needed to hear just how terrible he could be.

"Adelaide," Jake said through gritted teeth. "I thought you liked my hands around your throat?"

"Nice, bring up our sex life..." *or lack thereof,* "in front of your sister. Classy."

"Okay, this is getting a little too weird for me." Becca unbuckled and walked to the nose of the plane, leaving Jake and me to throw daggers with our gazes. "I'm going to go sit over there."

"You involve my sister in our shit, and I won't hesitate to show you just how capable of strangling you I am."

I leaned into him, my stomach swirling with nerves. If I puked on him, I'd hate myself more than I already did, but then again... it'd be hard to top that with a comeback.

"If you're afraid of your sister finding out, then maybe you shouldn't bring her around me." I swiped his drink out of the cup holder faster than he could react and downed the entire cup in two swallows.

He flipped the latch on his seatbelt and bolted towards me at the same time the dinging alert let us know it was safe to walk about the cabin. His seatbelt slammed against the wall and side of the seat with a terrifying clatter.

Jake wrapped his hand around my chin, digging his fingers into my cheeks until my soft inner flesh ground against my teeth. His other hand grabbed the cup from mine as he seethed above me.

"You have no sense of self-preservation, do you?"

"Jake, what are you doing?" Becca said, suddenly standing by our sides.

She put her hand on his wrist and took the cup I'd just downed, and tugged at him while I laughed.

His face contorted into a menacing snarl as he pushed my head into the seat and released my face, my stray hairs flying into my field of vision.

"I defended you, you know?" he started, pointing his finger at me.

I unbuckled my seatbelt, swiping my hair from my face, and shoved him as I stood.

"You didn't *defend* me."

Becca moved out of the way as I pushed him again. He grabbed my wrists before I made contact and spun me towards the couch, and shoved.

My ass landed on the soft surface with a shallow bounce. He leaned over me, and I swiped at him, his hands combating my flailing hits until he grabbed my arms and twisted them across my body, locking me in place.

"You're a fucking cunt, Adelaide."

His icy words froze me in place, my eyes brimming with tears. He'd said some pretty hateful things the night he'd found out, but for some reason, this cut so deep I could feel my soul leach out from the wound.

Jake wrapped his hand in my ponytail and tugged my head to the side, his face a hair's breadth away from mine. I caught Becca's horrified expression from my periphery, her hand covering her mouth.

"I fucking defended you to my *best* friends." His grip on my wrists tightened. "They told me there was something up, but I listened to my dick instead of my common sense." He moved in a little closer. "You were too good to be true, weren't you?" He shook me by the hair, his knees on either side of my thighs as he straddled me on the couch. "Weren't you?"

Jake

15

T ears welled in her eyes, but there was no fucking way I'd fall for them. Not after what she'd pulled.

She wanted a reaction from me. She provoked me until I burst. But now that she had my full attention, she cried.

How fitting.

"Answer me." I fisted her hair a little tighter.

"What we had was real." A tear slipped down her freckled cheek and hit the corner of her mouth, disappearing into the creases of her lips.

"Don't lie to me, Adelaide."

"I'm not," she whispered.

Where was the brat who just moments ago goaded me with laughter and smart-ass remarks?

"We were based on a lie and nothing more. You aren't real—to me or anyone else."

"Then why?" She struggled with my hold, her arms moving side to side in a seesaw motion. "Why are you protecting me?"

Adelaide pulled her head away from my tight grasp, despite the pain it caused her.

"I'm not protecting *you*."

"So what do you call keeping me hostage in your home for a week and ordering me around? A new kink of yours?" She struggled in my grasp, then grunted with frustration when I wouldn't give. "Get *off* of me."

"You're scaring her, Jake." Becca took a step toward us. "You're scaring *me*," she said, pleading with me from a safe distance.

Shit.

Talk about bad timing.

We were on our way to mourn our parents because of my unstable sister, who killed them and would've killed us too if we hadn't fled to the neighbors.

Now here I was, getting physical with Adelaide in front of her, no doubt making her anxiety flare.

I let go of Adelaide and held my hands out to show Becca I'd released her in a... stay of execution? Truce? Whatever it was, this wasn't over, but it was for now, for Becca's sake.

"You're lucky my sister doesn't know about you," I whispered in her ear. "She'd be heartbroken."

I climbed off her and took my seat next to the couch.

Adelaide sat frozen, but her eyes were wild, glancing all around her as though she were stuck in her own body.

What if what she said was true? What if what we had was real? How could that be? I'd have been a fool to fall for her siren's call again. Now that I knew how she worked and her goals, it should have been easy for me to resist.

Right?

Becca sat next to Adelaide and took her in her arms, but Adelaide kept her hands to her sides, her teary eyes staring at me as if I'd stomped on her heart and scared her to death in the process.

We only had a few more days until I forced her to take that pregnancy test. Then I'd either cut her loose or figure something else out. At least that's what I kept telling myself. I had given little thought to what that might be.

I opened and closed my fist as I stared at her red eyes and popping freckles. I'd come so close in the last week to breaking. To pulling her sullen ladened body into me and making her forget the reason for her fear and all the things I'd said to her.

But I knew better. At least, I thought I did.

"It'll be okay," Becca whispered to her.

Adelaide smiled at Becca. But just the slightest lift of her lips, nearly undetectable before she stood, grabbed her bag, and walked into the restroom with my glare tearing her down with each step until the door slammed closed.

My knee bobbed up and down as I waited for her to leave the bathroom. What trouble could she get into in there?

"What was that all about, Jake?"

I just shook my head. The words weren't important enough.

"Talk to me. This isn't like you."

"This is me," I snapped.

"No." She shook her head. "This isn't the brother I've known my whole life. Why are you acting like this?"

"Things have happened..." I plopped my hand down onto my bouncing knee and glanced back at the bathroom door. Why was she taking so long? "Things I don't want to discuss with you right now."

"It must be pretty serious for you to abuse her—"

"Abuse?" I scoffed. "I didn't abuse her. Don't let her get in your head."

Becca bolted to an upright position as I rubbed the tension from my temple.

"You put your hands on her, shoved her onto this couch, and pulled her hair as you held her down." Her hands writhed in her lap. "You abused her."

I ground my teeth. I'd never harm Adelaide. She wasn't hurt. I didn't leave a mark or draw blood. She was fine.

Right?

"Enough, Becca."

Just the allegation alone sent me spinning into a whirlwind of possibilities about myself that I never thought possible.

"I don't like this, Jake. Why is she coming with us? Tell me the real reason."

The real reason? I'd never given her a reason, to begin with.

Let's start with the fact that Adelaide was being hunted by mercenaries or how I was afraid the moment I turned my back... These conflicting thoughts and feelings weighed me down. On the one hand, I couldn't care less if they destroyed her—take her out back and put a bullet in her brain. I'd do it for them if I wasn't so torn. But with the same breath, I'd vow to protect her by any means necessary. It didn't make any sense.

"Adelaide isn't who she says she is."

The bathroom door opened, and she stepped out, wiping her mouth and the tears from her eyes as she took the seat closest to the bathroom.

A little piece of me drowned in her tears as they slipped down her freckled face.

What gives? It didn't bother me a moment ago.

Why now?

"Go talk to her and say you're sorry. There isn't anything she could've done that warrants you putting your hands on her like that."

Becca, you innocent fool.

I turned my head towards her while glaring out of the corner of my eyes. "Like I said, she isn't who you think she is."

Adelaide leaned over and placed her head between her knees as if the plane had taken a nosedive.

Her back expanded towards the ceiling as she inhaled shaking breaths.

My gaze dipped down to her thumb, caressing her tattoo.

If what she said was a lie, then why would she get the tattoo and then leave, knowing I'd never see it?

Was there some truth intertwined throughout all those lies? Or was she just in it for the long haul... like those method actors who ended up becoming the characters they played?

My brain couldn't handle the paranoia. I walked towards her, my chest aching to take away her pain and fear.

I'd done that to her, and it sucked even though I'd justified my actions a million times.

Had I gone too far?

I kneeled before her and placed my hands on her shoulders, then rubbed my fingers against the grooves of her spine.

"Don't touch me," she said, her voice muffled as she pressed tighter between her knees.

"I'm..." *How did I become the bad guy here?* "I'm sorry, sweets."

She sniffed but kept her head down, her thumb still caressing her tattoo.

"Why did you get that?" I asked, my curiosity eating me up inside.

She sniffed again and sat up slightly. Grabbing a tissue out of her pocket, she wiped her nose. "I wanted something to remind me of you."

A trophy... or was it something more?

"Why?"

"Because I love you, Jake. Even if I never get to hear you say it back, I wanted something that reminded me of a time you thought I was worth fighting for."

My heart stuck in my chest like my blood turned into sludgy mud.

"You don't love me."

Her hand covered mine that had slid from her back and landed on her knee when she sat. She lifted my hand and placed it on her chest.

"There's *nothing* in the world that I wouldn't do for you. If only you'd just *listen* to me."

I pulled my hand from hers, my mind at war with itself, and closed my eyes, exhaling through my nose.

"Okay."

She wiped her tears as I sat in the seat across from her.

"*Okay?*"

"Tell me your side."

Her teary eyes burned a fiery red from irritation. "Jake, I—"

"Excuse me, sir. We will be landing soon," Prudy said as the seatbelt sign illuminated again.

Not that I ever paid attention to it unless we flew through a storm.

Prudy walked towards my sister, who went back to her seat and read some self-help book.

"I joined Cryptonic when I was sixteen, nearing seventeen."

"The hacker's group you used to get into my company."

She nodded. "Yes." Adelaide tucked her tissue back into her pocket and buckled her seatbelt. "We started doing odds and ends jobs here and there. Nothing serious."

I held my hand up and crossed my ankle over my knee. "I don't want to hear about the beginning of your stupid little group. Just tell me when all of *this* started." I gestured between us both.

Turbulence struck, bouncing us in place, and her nails dug into the leather armrests.

"Holeo picked the target. He said this company tested Black Dog's systems. I didn't know this company. I didn't know you or anything about you."

"So you expect me to believe you hacked my company, talked to me on the internet, and dated me in real life without knowing there was a connection?"

"I never spoke to you on the internet." She shook her head, her brows drawn together as she chewed on her bottom lip.

"How do you think I found out who you were?"

"I thought you saw the picture on my phone. That's what I woke up to that night. You screaming in my face about a couple I took a picture of." She raised her shoulders, her palms upright. "I sent that picture to Monica, by the way. I told her how adorable they were, and I wished you, and I could have that."

I hung my head and nodded, rubbing my two fingers together. She couldn't have been so naïve.

"The code used on my server... I got it from someone I thought was my friend. *See*, she gave it to me when I was working on a project for my company. I never thought she'd use it against me. So imagine my surprise when I see it on my server."

"I don't..." She frowned. "I don't understand."

"Oh, come on, Pink Reaper." Her face blanched. "Don't you recognize your buddy, Merlin?"

Adelaide

16

*H*e *was Merlin?* The man I'd developed feelings for before meeting Jake? How was this possible?

How many similarities and coincidences had to occur before someone called it for what it was—divine intervention or someone had a hand in it?

No wonder he hated me.

"Merlin?"

Jake smirked, but it didn't meet his eyes. "You're good at that."

"At what?" I shook my head.

"Acting surprised."

"But..." My stomach lurched as the plane dropped a short distance.

I threw off my belt and bolted for the bathroom, making it in time to vomit into the stainless-steel toilet. The door banged open behind me, and Jake stood there, his legs spread in a wide stance to help him balance in the door frame as he held on.

"I hate flying." I grabbed a scrap of toilet paper and wiped my mouth before fully turning in his direction.

"I'm sure that's it," he said sardonically. He held his hand out, helping me to my feet. "You should buckle up, otherwise, your 'fear' of flying might just become real."

I snorted and rinsed my mouth out with the travel-size mouthwash from my pack. "My fear of flying is valid."

"The amount of people that die in plane crashes is negligent to those who die in car crashes."

"That's not a fair comparison."

"I'm not getting into a pissing match with you over statistics. Come sit down."

I held my stomach and followed him out, my hand sliding against the wall to steady me until I plunked down into my seat.

I'd stay as close as I could to the restroom just so I'd have some semblance of comfort because I refused to puke in a bag.

"Merlin?" I said again, not believing the name I'd spoken out loud.

Well, this wasn't fair, truly.

"Again, the act is remarkable."

"Believe me when I tell you, I'm just as shocked as you were."

"I don't."

"What do I have to do to convince you I had no plans against you?"

"Fool me once..."

"Will you quit that? Stop with the clipped retorts and bad attitude. You're starting to sound like—"

"You?" He looked out the window, his finger pushing the shade up more. "I've heard that before, too."

I watched him drown his thoughts in the disappearing clouds. "The night we met was the night we met. I didn't know you. I'd never seen you before, and I didn't know your name until the bouncer told me."

My stomach grumbled and clenched, so I wrapped my arms around my belly. "The night of your awards ceremony was the night I connected the dots."

He scowled but still refused to meet my eye, his knee bobbing up and down with pent up... emotion? Energy? Rage?

"I was there to cater. That much was true. Except, when Monica pulled up to your company, the company I didn't know you owned... I feel like this needs constant reiteration... I didn't know. I saw my opportunity to remove my code from the server you took offline."

He turned towards me and took a slow deep breath, his hand squeezed into a fist. The muscles along his sharp jawline bulged as he clenched his teeth.

The pilot made a clipped announcement I couldn't catch, but the flight attendant moved to the front of the plane and took a seat.

"Then your friend caught me. That was the night I learned about you and that your company was our... *their* target. That's when I decided it was better for me to end the relationship and quit the team."

He snapped the window shut with a loud clatter—causing me to jump—and leaned forward, resting his elbows on his knees, his head tipped towards the floor. "I remember. You blamed it on me—"

"I wanted to tell you, but they threatened me with the police, and I didn't want my parents to find out..." I rambled, my chin trembling. The heartache was still there, eating away at me like a vulture. "It was the hardest choice I had to make. I'd already developed feelings for you, but it was the right decision."

"No, the right decision would be to come clean."

"Right, so you could try to kill me in front of your friends and sister?" I tossed my hands in the air, forgetting about my upset stomach. Anger boiled just beneath the skin, heating me up from the inside out.

"I didn't *try* to kill you. I've told you this." He glanced up from the floor; his icy blue eyes stung with venom. "But if you want me to show you what that looks like, I'd be happy to."

I closed my eyes and pinched my lips together, my hand tucking under my thighs as I rested my head against the back of the seat.

The more hatred he spewed toward me, the more my heart crumbled. He wanted to hurt me, and with every vile thing he said, every action he took against me, he did just that.

I wanted to believe he still had feelings for me, and those feelings fought with his hatred. But it didn't matter because we were over. And all I'd have as a reminder of us were our tattoos.

"Now you know. I've given you the wholehearted truth. You can either choose to believe it or not. Either way, it doesn't matter. The outcome is the same. I'll be dead by the year's end."

A shitty reminder of the devil who lurked on the earth, but it was yet another truth I spat forth today. Black Dog would catch up with me, and when they did, I'd make sure I wasn't anywhere near Jake.

I couldn't let my poor choices affect those I cared about, not anymore.

"When we land, you'll stick close to me." He leaned over me, his scent filling my nostrils. "You won't say a word to anyone. If I catch one iota of an idea forming in that thick skull of yours," He grabbed the two ends of my seatbelt and tightened it across my lap. "I'll chain you up in the trunk for the duration of our visit. Understood?"

My brows pulled together as I winced from the tightness across my hip bone.

"Understood?" he repeated as the wheels touched down on the tarmac with a jarring bounce.

I cried out as everything seemed to creak and moan. The engines screamed, and an overbearing roaring resonated in my ears.

My fingernails dug into the backs of my thighs until we came to a stop.

"If you're going to puke again, do it before we leave the plane. We have a thirty-minute drive, and I'm not stopping."

I sucked in a breath and removed my hands from beneath my legs, my knuckles aching from the strain.

"Aren't you thoughtful?" I rolled my eyes and unbuckled my seatbelt as he stood.

"Not in the slightest."

He put his hand out to the side, not to help me stand, but in a silent way of telling me he was waiting for me to stand so he could follow me out.

I stood, grabbing my bag as I did, and stalked towards the front of the airplane where Becca waited for us.

Becca gave me that same look of sympathy she gave me the night of the award ceremony. *Pity.*

I chewed on my inner lip, my backpack hanging in front of my legs as I waited for Prudy to finish lowering the staircase, then followed Becca out once she did.

The sun hit my face, warming my skin, temporarily erasing my dismay until Jake clasped my elbow and dragged me towards a black SUV with an emblem of the letter 'B' in the center of the tires.

If I didn't know any better, I'd say that stood for Bentley because it was a sure cry different from his BMW.

Jake opened the back door, tossed me inside, and then snapped his fingers at Becca. "You take the front." He slammed the back door, then slid into the driver's seat.

God, he made me crazy.

Why did he have to be this way? Just be a regular guy who wanted nothing to do with me. Instead, this constant need to 'protect' me only prolonged the torture. It wrecked my mind with all sorts of possibilities I should have marked as impossible long ago.

Maybe it was him who was crazy, and he tried pulling me inside of his chaos with him. Misery loves company... right?

Becca shut her door and buckled herself in as Jake glanced at me in the rearview mirror.

"Buckled?"

I exhaled and drew the strap over my shoulder, clicking it into place.

A stickler for safety yet threatens to kill me. Make it make sense.

"Are you going to tell me where we're going now?" I asked as he drove away.

Becca turned in her seat and looked at Jake for him to answer, but he wasn't in the sharing mood.

"We are here to see our parents?"

"Your parents?" *Didn't he tell me they were dead?* "I thought—"

"They are," Jake said, placing his elbow on the console.

"Every year we visit their graves," Becca explained.

I tipped my head back in understanding and stared out the window, watching the cars zoom past us until he turned on his indicator and made a left-hand turn into a cemetery.

Cemeteries were the most depressing location in the history of the earth. It was a bubble encompassing pain and loss to suffocating levels—each stone a blatant reminder of lost loved ones and just how fragile life was.

I sat up in my seat as he pulled up behind another vehicle and parked behind a white Porsche.

A cemetery for the rich. Was there such a thing?

"Stay in the car, Adelaide."

"But it's hot."

"I'll leave the AC on."

I nodded, rubbing my sweaty hands together.

Stick close.

Stay here.

I'll protect you.

Do that again and I'll... Fill in some gruesome death detail.

He couldn't stay consistent even if he tried.

Jake and Becca left me in the car, its alarm alerting everyone within earshot that he'd taken the key fob, and walked a fair distance into the grass until they stopped at two headstones with a statue of a crying angel behind them.

I unbuckled my seat, keeping my eyes on them, and slid across the bench to the other door.

Jake looked back at the car as if he could see me ready to escape. I held my breath until he turned his attention back to his grieving sister, then slipped out of the vehicle and flung my backpack over my shoulder before shutting the door closed without so much as a sound.

God, I was such an asshole.

Here I was, escaping into the new city while he comforted his sister over their dead parents. But after what happened on the plane, it only solidified my plan to leave.

I bent over and ran, my depleted body huffing from exhaustion before I left the tombstone-laden grass, my mind running along with me at a thousand miles a minute.

How was I going to get money or a phone? Jake took my burner, fake ID, and credit cards. I had nothing but clothes in my bag.

My feet hit the concrete like ominous beats against time. It wouldn't take Jake long to find me on the main street, which meant the longer I stayed, the faster he'd find me and probably wring my neck for good this time.

I stopped at the light, waiting for a safe time to cross, my gaze catching every bit of movement around me with heightened paranoia. The street cleared, and I crossed, running towards the smell of charcoal and BBQ'd meat. Where there was food, there were people with their wallets out, money on tables, and chitter-chatter to break up someone's concentration.

The art of deception is distraction.

I walked three more blocks, my thighs shaking and ready to give up, threatening to leave me lying on the dirty sidewalk until I walked into a coffee shop with a logo of a broken cup and the words *'Break'* written in calligraphy on the door.

Dark roast and sweet cream hit my senses, making me groan as I looked around.

A man in a dress suit walked towards me with a paper cup full of coffee, a brown honeycombed sleeve wrapped around it to protect his hand from the heat, as he tucked his wallet into his inside coat pocket with the other.

"Shit," I said as I bounced into him, my hand sliding right into his coat and snatching his wallet with my free hand, then tucking it behind me. "I'm so sorry."

"Watch where you're going."

"You're right." I swiped my hand down his suit and tie, pretending to wipe the spilled coffee from his clothes. "I'm so sorry."

"Stop." He swiped my hands away. "Just forget it." The man glared at me, shook off his dripping hand, and grabbed some napkins from the dispenser before storming out.

I pulled his wallet open and picked out the ID. "Sorry, Clive Moran?" *What a weird name.* "Desperate times."

After emptying his wallet of three hundred dollars in cash and a visa, I dumped his wallet in the trash and left.

Well, that was easier than I thought.

"Excuse me," I said, stopping a woman in red high heels and a tight skirt. "Can you tell me where the closest store is?"

She smiled at me and pointed in the direction I was headed. "Just keep going that way," she said. Her high-pitched voice reminded me of the 90s TV show with the black-haired woman with an obnoxious laugh. "It'll be on this side of the street. It's small, but it has everything."

"Thank you."

I looked around, making sure Jake wasn't around in that ridiculously expensive car that stood out like a sore thumb.

Finding the store, *Reeds*, just where the woman said, I walked inside and headed straight for the electronic department. I grabbed myself a new burner phone, the most expensive ASUS laptop with a case they had, and a can of Rockstar energy drink.

Because why the fuck not?

I swiped the man's credit card in three separate transactions to avoid flagging it, then walked to a fast-food restaurant across the street and ordered three burgers and a large fry. I took a back seat with a wide vantage point, then bit into my fresh burger, ready to fire up the laptop and phone.

The bright orange and burned brown-colored benches sank under the pressure as I bent over, plugged my laptop into the outlet below the table, and pressed the power button.

It felt good to have a computer under my fingertips again, almost like a rush of drugs in my system. The withdrawals that developed during my week of 'celibacy' gripped me hard, forcing me to fill my time with TV as a hopeful distraction.

I took a bite of my burger and wiped the juices off my chin with a napkin.

A middle-aged man sat by himself, sipping his drink while staring out of the big windows we sat next to, overlooking the parking lot and main street.

By the time I set up my computer and logged onto the internet, my first burger was down and half my fries demolished, but my stomach still rumbled as though I couldn't get enough food in my belly. I started on the next burger and broke my phone out of the box.

Just like with the computer, a rush of endorphins formed a smile on my face as the smooth rectangle slid in my hands, the screen lighting up with the phone's logo.

I'd missed the permanent brick that led to our intellectual destruction.

Three people had come and gone, sitting in the same place the middle-aged man once occupied, and the sun had started its descent to the other side.

I'd applied for a cash app, taking a hefty advance on Felicity's new credit card, having memorized the number, and transferred it to the app.

Another burger down and my phone synced with my contacts and all of my passwords—it was as if I had never smashed my phone into the wall.

There was only one thing I needed to do, but I couldn't seem to press the button to do it.

My thumb hovered over the button, my nerves flying like butterflies in my belly.

Just do it...

I closed my eyes and hit the button, peeking through my lids when the ringing came over the speaker.

It's now or never.

"Hello?"

"Hi, Mom."

17

She'd cried on my shoulder as she always did when we visited, her nose stuffy, eyes red.

"I just wish they could see us now."

"I know."

What would they say if they were alive now, knowing the criminal I'd become—the hardened beast I'd contorted into? Would I be the person I am today if they hadn't *died*?

I glanced back at the car. Adelaide must be getting antsy, especially with nothing to occupy her racing mind.

"We need to get going, Becca." I rubbed her shoulder. "We'll come back tomorrow."

I'd booked us in at our usual hotel. Two rooms on the top floor with king-sized beds, a fully stocked mini-bar, and valet parking. And if I felt like dropping another ten grand a night, I could've had a butler. But I didn't have one at home, so why now?

Becca nodded and used her small packet of tissues to wipe her nose as we walked back to the car.

A tall man dressed in a suit with a girl touting dark hair gave me pause until recognition had me grinding my teeth.

Great.

Nico Moreno stalked forward, his hand out for a shake. "Strange seeing you here."

I threw my thumb over my shoulder. "Visiting the parents." I turned to Becca. "Why don't you go sit in the car?"

Becca nodded, making me miss Adelaide's smart-ass mouth that would have accompanied my request, which was odd because it'd done nothing but made me want to put her over my knee this last week.

I glanced at the window she sat at and squinted, trying to see her through the heavily tinted glass.

"My condolences," he said as Becca walked away.

"Is that your sister?" Charity, Nico's girlfriend and enforcer, asked.

"What are you guys doing here?" I asked, ignoring her. The less information Charity knew about my family, the better. Even though we'd been around each other for years, I'd kept my sister far away from anything criminal.

"Visiting my brother," she said.

We'd all shown up for her brother's funeral. The circumstances of his death fucking sucked and softened me just a little towards her.

"Jake," Becca said from the passenger's side as the door swung wide open. "What?"

"Wasn't Adelaide supposed to stay in the car?"

I spun on my heel, my jaw clenched, as I yanked open her door and found the bench seat empty, her backpack gone.

No trace of her.

"Goddammit!" I slammed the door shut and pressed my steady fist against the glass, sucking in a lungful of air through my nose.

"Adelaide?" Nico paused and stepped toward me. "That wouldn't be Adelaide Leaver, would it?"

I swung my gaze toward him. "Did you see her?"

"Not lately. The last I spoke to her was when I had her do a job for us." Nico tucked his hand in his pantsuit pocket. "What are *you* doing with her?"

"Two hackers together, Nico. I think that's obvious," Charity said.

I glared at her, then turned back to Nico. "That's one complicated story," I said. "Becca, get in the car."

If I had any chance of finding Adelaide before she made it to another bus or a fucking train this time, I'd need their knowledge of the area. It had changed too much since I was sixteen, and their connections would only make this faster.

"I see her disappearing act hasn't changed much," Nico said, drawing me out of my thoughts.

"What?"

"Well, the last time I had a job for her, she disappeared only to call me back with results ages later, then hung up. Are you having her look into your parents' death or something?"

I shook my head. Where the hell had he drawn that conclusion?

"No. That case is closed. Why would I have her do that?"

"Well, I thought because you had her access your parents' murder case at the police station."

My ears rang, and my limbs grew heavy by my sides. That conniving little shit.

"When was this?"

"I'm guessing he didn't know that, Nico."

"Oh gosh." He paused. "It's been a while."

The thudding in my chest quickly replaced the ringing in my ears, drowning out the high-pitched sound with the raging thump. I clenched my fist.

I should have been grateful she ran off, but I wasn't. There wasn't a part of my body that didn't want her dead now. I'd bury her right next to Charity's traitorous brother so they could spend eternity in Hell together.

"Help me find her," I said, grinding my teeth as if asking for help was the hardest thing I've had to do.

The sun dipped, casting ominous shadows across tombstones as far as the eye could see.

"Anything you need. Just let us know."

I nodded and pulled out my phone, showing him an updated picture of Adelaide with her black hair.

"Oh... that's Adelaide," Charity said, laughing as if there was a joke I didn't understand. "I saw her hobble off that way." She turned and pointed towards the road. "Like twenty or thirty minutes ago."

"Which direction?"

"Towards the road... I just said that... and pointed."

That's it, I'm swearing off women.

I clenched my teeth and sent the image to Nico. "I need everyone looking for her. Anyone you can spare. Get the word out."

"No problem," he said, tugging his phone out.

Charity's phone dinged in her pocket. "I'll send it to some people around," she said. "Do you want my dad to put out a *BOLO*?"

"No." I shook my head. "This needs discretion. There are mercenaries after her. But if they think she's taken off on me, our deal is over..."

"How does she have such enemies at her age?" Nico asked, shaking his head.

I scoffed. Because she's a hardheaded nineteen-year-old girl who thought she had the competence to piss people off and not face the repercussions.

"She got caught up in the wrong crowd."

"I'll talk to Max, and we'll get out there," Charity said, walking around the Porsche I should've recognized when we arrived.

"I need to drop Becca off at the hotel."

"Meet at our place when you're done," Nico said. "I'll send you the address."

"Thanks." I hopped into my rental and sped off backward, then switched it into drive and went around his car.

"What happened, Jake? Where did she go?"

I shook my head. "I don't know."

But when I find her, I'd make her regret ever looking in my direction.

Adelaide

18

B y the time I'd finished my phone call with my mother, the sun's rays filtered through the buildings onto the streets below. Her desultory cries wrecked me, making me beg for her forgiveness with everything I had until we'd both shed tears.

She'd never understand how much it killed me inside to hear her cry over me—for all the stress, worry, and heartache I'd caused. And a small part of me hated Jake for all of this. They never had to be involved.

Mom urged me to come home, saying we'd work it out, but she didn't know how much trouble I was really in. Besides, I couldn't continue sitting around Jake's home waiting for the other shoe to drop.

If I disappeared, everyone could get on with their lives and never have to worry about me again. But before I did that, I needed my parents to know how much I loved them, how sorry I was that I'd become such a shitty daughter and that I missed them so much.

Now, I wandered between rows of wrecked cars with my new laptop, burner phone, and two days' worth of clothing. I'd even bought a blanket for the night before I walked into the junkyard.

I'd do things differently this time.

As I rounded a smashed car, I shifted my laptop bag over my shoulder. I'd bought a blanket for the night because if I went to a hotel like I did last time, they'd find me. It was just my luck.

The long night would give me plenty of time to plan out my mode of transportation, which consisted of hitch-hiking, sleeping under overpasses or junkyards, and praying I didn't get swallowed up by a sicko with a fetish.

I squeezed past a blue Dodge Dakota with a busted window and smashed-in rear end, sitting next to a white Chevy truck, single cab, without an engine.

None of these would do.

One row away sat a white panel van, the ones everyone's parents warned us about, with no windows and a sliding door on the one side.

I wandered between the two rows with abject defeat weighing me down, my feet heavy as I clambered inside the dusty, decrepit vehicle with a metal grate blocking the front seats.

The blue cloth bench seat looked rather clean for who knows how long it sat here, but that didn't stop my skin from crawling as I sat down and dropped my backpack on one end where I laid my head.

Is this what my life had come to? Sleeping like a runaway teen?

I closed my eyes and frowned as I dug out my blanket and covered myself up. If I couldn't see where I laid down, maybe it'd slip my mind and allow me to get a few hours of rest.

That was until metal scraped against metal as it fell...

I froze; my heart slugged against my chest like the man who sucker punched me in the club. Metal ground against a hard object, intermingled with the cricket's stridulations, set me on edge.

I turned on my side and gripped my bag for comfort. Why didn't I pick up a knife at the store? Safety should have been a priority, but it came in last when you were desperate.

A train's horn blew in the distance as the movement crept closer—two long, one short, followed by another long.

Movement scampered across my periphery as I pulled my blanket close to my chin. My legs shook as the rhythmic hum from the train's wheels traveled through the air, settling around me. The scent of rotting foliage, and God knows what else, stung my nose.

Please don't let there be a dead body around here—or even someone alive, either.

"Ahh!"

I kicked my legs into the air, my blanket flying over my face, smothering me as if it had a mind of its own. I clawed at the possessed material in time to see a dirty orange cat rush after the white one whose tiny face had sat in the corner of the opened door like some ghostly peeping tom.

Their reverberating hisses and growls made them sound larger than life as they toppled under the vehicle, their bodies vibrating the floor beneath me as they wrestled.

Feral beings. What if they scratched me and I contracted rabies?

I sat up, grabbed the door, and slid it closed, leaving a gap for the gentle cool breeze to blow through.

Find a happy place.

I plopped back in place—the van swaying with the motion—and closed my eyes, letting my mind take me off to someplace sunny with smooth beaches and clear blue waters. I could sit on the beach with my laptop like Sandra Bullock in the movie The Net and work.

I rubbed my eyes with a heavy exhale. *I will not cry.*

That was the movie Jake and I would've watched if I hadn't eaten so much ice cream and nearly puked all over his floor.

We'd never get those moments back. The trust we'd had could never get rebuilt, and he certainly hated me, which twisted my gut until it ached.

I sniffled and curled into a ball, letting the darkness take me.

19

I 'd dropped Becca off eight hours ago and drove around town, scouring the city streets for her. Searching the closest bus and train stations. She was nowhere to be seen, and I was exhausted.

"Where the fuck are you, Adelaide?"

I brought my watch up and groaned. Three A.M. No wonder my body threatened to shut down on me. The adrenaline drove me into a hyper-focused state until it wore off, depleting me.

The longer she was out there, the higher the chance of her making a mistake and they not only going after her but coming after me. I made the deal with them, after all. So, it wasn't just her ass on the line...

My phone buzzed, and I silenced it after seeing a number I didn't recognize.

"She's really got under your skin," Charity said as I slapped the steering wheel, striking out on another dark alleyway.

Adelaide had me wandering the bad side of town not only once but twice, searching for her.

"Yes."

"What's her goal?"

"What do you mean?"

"What's her end goal? Why did she run away from you?"

I thought about it for a minute, thinking of all the reasons, excuses, and things she's said over the week. "She's scared."

Charity snorted. "Of you? I doubt that."

"No, not of me."

"Is she as paranoid as you?"

"I'm not paranoid."

She scoffed. "Okay. And my boots aren't black."

I ground my teeth. "Fine. Not as much, but I'm sure more so now."

"Then we need to scratch the typical places. She won't go there."

"I hadn't planned on it."

"So then, where should we look?"

I gripped the steering wheel and exhaled as I pulled over.

"If I knew where to look, I'd go there. But I don't. She's difficult to pinpoint. She's random and does shit without thinking sometimes."

Adelaide would like to think she'd made calculated decisions, but she was still a teenager who lacked life's experiences and made mistakes left and right.

That's how I'd found her before, and that's how I'd find her again.

"You don't have to come with me," I said, expecting her to be tired by now with constant yawning. "I'm sure you're tired."

"I'm a night owl, and any opportunity I can get to break some kneecaps, I'm on it like flies on shit."

"*Hmm.*" If I didn't find Adelaide soon, she'd get the opportunity.

"I might have an idea. There's this one guy I know who helps runaways cross borders. Maybe we can check him out. He could know of some hiding places."

"Call him. It's worth a shot."

There wasn't a place on this earth she could hide. I'd tear this city apart, the next, and the next, until I found her, even if it were her bones rotting in a shallow grave.

I'd find her.

Adelaide

20

The sun bled through the spider-webbed windshield, creating a prism effect across my sweating body.

How long had I slept?

My body ached despite waking up several times to the hard blowing wind and switching positions, then letting the soothing sway lull me back to sleep.

But now it was warm, way too warm, and the wind had calmed. Sometime into the night, I must've kicked my blanket off onto the filthy van floor.

A wave of warmth intermingled with a chill rolled up my spine and over my shoulders as I cranked my neck from side to side.

I swiped the bead of sweat from my brow as my stomach gurgled. Damn. I knew I should have bought snacks.

What time was it?

I couldn't have slept that long because I didn't feel rested or rejuvenated. Instead, I felt used, sluggish, and exhausted. I glanced down at my phone lying on the laptop bag.

"What?" That can't be right. It was eleven-forty-five. I'd slept all morning in this god-awful heat?

Another wave of sweaty chills rippled up my chest and into my throat. I needed to get out of this sauna. I shoved the blanket into my bag, grabbed my laptop, and pocketed my phone, doing an extra sweep of anything I might have missed before tugging on the sliding door.

My pulse shot up in my ears, my heart hammering against my breastbone. I jerked again, but it didn't budge.

I put my bags down, wrapped both hands around the metal door, and then tugged.

Nothing.

Shit. Shit. Shit.

Exhaling a puff of irritation, I turned toward the shut double doors at the rear, void of any windows, and shuffled the three steps to the rear.

A shiny metal bar for a handle held the key to my escape, yet when I tugged on it, the crumpled metal groaned but didn't budge.

Oh my God.

Sweat bloomed across my back and trickled down, collecting on the waist-band of my sweats. My throat constricted.

What if I didn't get out of here? No one would find me, and somehow those feral cats would find a way in here and eat my body. Or rats.

I cried out and banged on the back doors. "Help me, please! Someone!"

The thick air sat like syrup, slugging down my windpipe and pooling at the bottom of my terror-gripped lungs.

I moved back up to the middle and weaved my fingers into the rounded-dia-mond-shaped metal, which separated me from the front where the locks were and tugged. My shaky arms turned to Jello as I struggled, curving in the metal grate in the center, only for it to spring back to normal when I let it go.

"*Ahhh*!" I shook the grate and slapped it with my open hand. "Goddammit!"

I rushed to the back, my legs slick with perspiration in these heavy sweats, and laid on the floor, giving the back a solid kick like a battering ram.

Tiny sparks of light shimmered through with each kick but disappeared once the pressure released.

"Shit."

This wasn't right. I waved my hand in front of my face in a makeshift fan and slowly breathed out. A droplet of sweat raced down my temple to my cheek as I returned to the sliding door again.

"Someone help me!" I cried as I banged on the door. "I'm in here! I need help!"

The never-ending scurry and scuffles of cats all night sat in stark contrast to the silence outside of this door. A burdensome weight sank inside my chest, making the van shrink, the walls coming in closer and attacking me with their solid state.

I sat on the bench and covered my face with my dirty hands.

There was another option. But how much of an asshole would I have to be to make that phone call?

I didn't want to do it, but the van would only continue to bake in the sun as the heat progressed. If I didn't get out...

No. No. No.

I don't need anyone. I can figure it out on my own.

I dug out my phone. Thirty minutes had passed with me banging, tugging on doors, and screaming. Not one solution worked.

A ticklish sensation rolled down the back of my knee to my ankle.

There were no windows to open, no cross ventilation.

I was fucked.

"Just do it, Adelaide."

My fingers froze in the blazing heat as I sat on the bench I'd slept all night on just to avoid him. A clear drop of fluid landed on my screen, dripping from my brow.

Sitting a moment longer, I found his contact, thankful I'd transferred all my contacts into my phone at the restaurant, then pressed the little green button and braced myself for his unholy wrath.

The phone rang, then cut short and went to voicemail.

I spun my lip ring around, bouncing my sweating leg back and forth, then dialed again.

"Listen here, you fuckers—"

"Jake?" I said, panting into the phone with a sniveling cry of desperation that made me sick.

"Adelaide?" he said, surprised. "Adelaide, where are you?"

His dark velvet tenor, filled with worry, covered my concern with fictitious salvation.

"I n-need your help."

"Where are you?" he repeated. "What's wrong?"

"I don't know. I'm trapped inside a van, and it's getting really hot in here."

The air thinned out around me, making my head swim as my chest rose and fell far too fast.

"Calm down, sweets. Where do you think you are?"

"I'm..." I swallowed.

"Hold on. I'm going to put you on speaker. Tell Charity and Max where you were last."

I'd only heard of one Charity in my life, and my world wasn't so small that Jake could possibly be sitting with the Mafia's pretty little killer.

"In a junkyard. White van. No windows. Broken, but intact, front windshield."

"Which junkyard?" Charity said.

"I don't know. I wandered in during the night."

"Was it large or small?"

"Pretty big, I think. I got turned around a few times."

"There are four major wrecking yards here," Charity said. "We'll have to split up if we're going to find her."

"What's around you?" Max asked.

"Fucking vehicles. What the hell do you think is around me?"

"Well, at least you know we have time. She still has an attitude," Charity said.

My phone beeped in my ear, and I pulled it away, looking at the screen. "Fuck," I said, raising my voice with urgency.

"What is it? What's wrong?" Jake asked.

"My battery is going to die."

"Sit tight. We'll find you. Get off the phone. I'll call you if we get close."

"If?"

He had to find me. We still had years left of being angry with each other.

"When, Adelaide. I'll find you."

His disquieted tone sent my thoughts on a tailspin, and it only exacerbated my fear. If Jake was worried, then I had reason to panic.

"It's going to be ninety degrees today," a male said in the background.

I groaned, and pressing my head between my knees didn't help this time.

"Just try to stay still. Don't do anything strenuous. We'll find you, sweets."

A small smile tilted the corners of my lips. "Okay." A tear slipped down my cheek, and I brushed it away as if someone could witness my fragility. "I love you," I whispered before hanging up and putting my phone on the bench beside me.

I focused on my breathing, in and out, using a steady rhythm a meditator would be proud of.

This was a mistake.

Leaving him was a mistake when all he wanted to do was help me in his odd, roundabout way. And now...

Fear summoned panic, and panicking didn't help me. I stripped off my heavy sweats and grabbed my laptop with clammy hands.

Windows computers came with two games, Solitaire and Hearts.

A warm wave rushed over me, followed by a shiver of goosebumps. That's odd. My skin raised as the pressure sank into my chest.

Jake would find me.

He has to.

But what if he didn't? What if I became another dead body among many? Would the police be able to identify me even without an ID on me? Did I have dental records in the system?

How did that even work?

I have black hair now, not red. What if my parents came to identify me and didn't recognize me? I'll end up in an unmarked grave with the name Jane Doe number one-thousand or something.

Shit. This wasn't working.

I dropped my laptop back into my bag and rattled the door again, my head swimming as I stood. I didn't want to die here, not without knowing... Not with Jake believing me to be some piece of shit.

Jerking on the door, I pulled hard, my brain rattling inside my floating head, setting me off balance. I stumbled backward, tripping over my bag and landing on my ass in a near somersault.

Thunk.

A whimper hissed past my lips as my throbbing skull slid down the side of the van. A sharp nail-biting stab stung the back of my head, making my vision circle around like a merry-go-round.

I groaned as stars sparkled across my vision. I put my hand to the back of my head and winced when it slid through the slick warmth. Pulling away from the sensation, I jerked my hand away. Bright crimson covered my fingertips in a silky-smooth blanket of life.

That's not good.

Jake

21

"There are three major wrecking yards that are near here. Another one is further up north. But I doubt she went there," Luca said as he zoomed out of the city on his tablet.

"I would've gone here," Charity said, pointing to the one closest to the cemetery. "You don't have to go far, and it's the largest of the four."

My heart constricted. There was too much land to cover and very little time to find her before she died.

"Let's go. She was on foot," I said, pointing to the area Charity suggested. "She couldn't have gotten far since she didn't have money." That's probably why she slept in a junkyard rather than a hotel.

"I thought you said she didn't have a phone?" Max asked.

"She's resourceful. Maybe she stole it."

How was I supposed to know?

I spun on my heel and walked out to Luca's grand foyer with them following behind.

"Vito, take Max and go to the wreck yard on Coronado," Luca said. Vito nodded as we walked out the front door. "I'll take Nico to the one on Harrington."

"Charity and I will head to this one on Belvedere," I said, opening my car door and sliding inside before Charity could walk around the front. "Keep the lines open, and let me know if you hear anything."

I fired up my vehicle as Charity got inside and buckled, slamming it into Drive before she settled.

"Chill, Rambo."

"Rambo? Does it look like I'm fighting someone?"

"Rambo sounded better than Bob, so I went with it." She shrugged and paused. "We'll find her, don't worry."

"That's not what I'm worried about."

"You're afraid we won't make it in time?"

"A vehicle in this weather can easily climb upwards to one-hundred and thirty degrees. We could be too late."

"We'll find her." Charity dug her phone out of her pocket, punched something in, and then put it to her ear.

Of all the years I'd known Charity, back when she dated Alek and after, I'd never known her to exude sympathy. She was better at it than Tonk was, no matter how much he tried to work it out of her. So her uncharacteristic behavior had me shaken. Maybe her brother's death did something to her?

"Give me Dennis," she said.

I watched the road, glancing back at her as she waited for the man to pick up the phone.

"It's Charity. Grab a group of people and search for a white panel van with a shattered window. There's a girl inside." She tapped her finger against her thigh. "Dennis, do I look like a girl who wants the police involved?" She rolled her eyes and pointed to her phone. "Do you think you can do that, Dennis? Good. I'll be there in forty minutes. Call me when you find her." Charity's finger tapped away on her thigh. "Didn't I say no police? Well, if she's dead, she wouldn't need an ambulance, would she?"

She put her hand over the speaker and shook her head. "I swear to God these people..." Her hand slid away. "Yeah, I'm here. Hey, don't forget to bring some water. She's gonna be thirsty."

My brain rattled, desperate to hear the conversation brewing on the other end until she hung up with a scowl.

"He owns that yard. It'll buy us some time. I hope."

Thoughts about the crazy things I'd said to her beat against me, breaking me down until I felt just as worthless as I'd made her feel. I couldn't let my hatred be the last thing she'd heard from me. I wouldn't allow it.

But sometimes, she drove me stark raving mad, making me feel things I couldn't control, even though she tried to rob me and my company blind.

Even though she infiltrated my life and watched me.

Even though everything we had was a lie.

I needed her.

And that was a feeling—for some insane reason—only she could invoke.

I wasn't one to attach myself to someone, but with her... it was as if we were made for one another. We went together like wood and fire, and the moon and the stars. She was the sun, and my world revolved around her, even if I didn't want it to. Her gravitational pull had my mind stuck in a perpetual state of motion with nothing but *her* binding my thoughts.

She consumed me day and night. And no matter how much I tried to pull away from her, her hold on me was infinite.

I just hope there was a moment in time where I'd overcome her moment of deception and forgive her for it. Because as much as I hated to admit it, I needed her more than she'd ever need me.

Charity's phone rang, freezing my thundering heart in my chest.

"Yes," she answered. "You found it?"

I swung my gaze to her. What was he saying to her? I needed to know.

"Is she inside? You didn't get her out? What do you mean it's stuck? Well, keep trying. Cut it apart for all I care. No. We're almost there. Keep working at it. Yeah. Bye."

My frozen heart cracked with a deafening crash.

"How close are we?"

She glanced down at her phone. "Five more minutes."

I pressed on the gas, making it four, and skidded to a stop in the parking lot with gravel flying behind us like mini-missiles. By the time they'd found their target, pinging off of parked cars, I'd opened my door and ran through the opened gated entrance, leaving the car running and my door wide open.

Let the car run.

Let someone steal it.

I didn't give a shit.

All that mattered was finding Adelaide in time.

"You go left, I'll go right, and we'll meet in the middle at the end," Charity said before darting left, leaving me shaking my head with confusion as if she didn't just give explicit instructions to do the opposite.

I ran down a row of vehicles, striking out, then another and another. The blazing sun sat high in the sky, pelting down its hellacious intensity, which caused an endless array of mirages in the distance. This would be a comfortable day on any other day, but today it was like stepping through the gates of Hell.

A heatwave, they'd called it.

Humidity sent rivulets of sweat down my forehead and back. My shirt stuck to me like a second skin, and my jeans were no longer appropriate attire.

I ran my hand over a crumpled blue truck when my heart leaped. The tops of two men's heads one row over caught my periphery, along with their grunting and muffled speech.

There she was.

I raced around the vehicle as they lodged a crowbar into the side of the white panel van and wedged it back and forth, grunting with their efforts.

"Adelaide?" I called out, rushing towards them.

I beat my hands against the metal coffin until I reached the driver's side door and flung it open. "You can't get in that way," one man said. "And the locks are broken."

My guts twisted as I gawked at the solid steel wall towering halfway up with a metal grate attached to it and the ceiling.

"Adelaide?" I climbed inside and wrapped my fingers around the metal, looking in and all around. And once again, my heart plummeted as though I were on a never-ending ride of fear, sorrow, and shock.

She lay on the ground, her splotchy black hair matted with congealed blood, her face as white as a sheet of paper.

"Sweets?" I shook the metal grate, then slammed my shoulder into it, only making it bow and bounce back.

Her labored breaths tormented me as her chest rose and fell too fast. It was too fast. Her body was shutting down as the heat boiled her from the inside.

She didn't move.

I placed my back on the dash, resting my butt on the console, and kicked my feet into the grate. The center bowed, and a corner popped free. I gave it three more kicks, breaking one side off, but still not enough to climb through and get her out.

The men worked their crowbar, its metallic protests groaning along with their grunts, as I gave it two more swift, firm kicks. The metal shot off, flying into the empty cavity where she lay half dead.

"Adelaide?" I said, scrambling in a panic to get through the tight opening, ignoring the searing pain in my hand as I pressed my healing cut on the jagged metal. "Adelaide, come on." I fell through, landing next to her, and dragged her limp, exposed body onto my lap, tapping my palm against her cheek. "Open your eyes, baby."

"Hmm," she murmured, her weak grip wrapped around my wrist. Her eyelids fluttered open, just long enough for her eyes to connect with mine and my name to cross her dry lips with a crippled sigh. "Jake?" Her hand fell to her chest.

"Open this fucking door now!" I bellowed to the men on the other side. "Keep your eyes open, sweets." I tapped her cheek again. "Come on, Adelaide.

Not like this. Okay?" The weakness in my voice sickened me, but an all-consuming terror gripped me tight, stripping me free of my control. "Not like this."

"Did you find her?" Charity said from the other side.

"She's here," I said, banging on the sidewall. "Get us out of here."

Adelaide's pulse pounded against my fingertips, her cheeks a bright cherry red. Her skin was dry in stark contrast to her damp shirt.

The sliding door cracked as they wedged the crowbar further inside. It cracked wider, allowing a beam of sunlight to break through. Then wider and wider until it broke open with a slow roll.

A slight breeze caressed my soaked skin, bringing temporary relief from the baking temperatures inside the vehicle.

"We need a doctor. I think she has heat stroke."

"I'll call my doctor; he'll set up a team," Charity said.

That may be too late. "I don't think she'll make the forty-minute drive."

"You can take her to the hospital around the corner, but that might flag her."

I scooped Adelaide's limp body into my arms and held her to my chest as Charity picked up her belongings, then raced to my car. Where the hell did she find the money for a laptop and cell phone?

"Thanks for the fucking directions, Dennis. Really helpful," Charity said as she followed behind me.

"It's a junkyard, Charity. How do you give someone turn by turn out here?"

She mimicked him, but I tuned her out and slid Adelaide into the backseat of my rental.

"Drive, Charity." I slid in beside Adelaide and pulled her shirt off over her head. "Put the AC on full blast. We need to lower her temperature."

Charity adjusted the dials as I fanned Adelaide's face, then took off down the road toward the hospital.

Adelaide's chest lurched toward the ceiling as though someone had hit her with a thousand volts of electricity, then fell back to my lap. *What was that?* Her body did it again, coming alive with wild motions—her face turning a vibrant red.

"Sweets? What's wrong?" I tapped her cheek.

Her chest rose again, twisting at the waist, and she puked bile all over the carpeted floors.

"Go faster, Charity." I slammed my hand against the side of her chair. "*Fuck.*"

Her body shivered as goosebumps erupted across her skin, but she remained latent, her arms hanging limp beside her.

"I'm going as fast as I can," she said as she picked up her phone and made a call. "We've got her, but we need to hit Saint Mary's hospital. She's in rough shape."

My heart wrenched with agony as I watched her fragile body shiver. My gaze dipped down to her bruised hip, still marred with a ring of light yellow circling around dark green—like a halo of pain.

Bastards.

"Adelaide, open your eyes." *Just show me that bratty glare.* Something. I needed to see her agate gaze to know she'd be okay. "Don't do this."

My throat constricted when they remained closed, her limp body in my arms. The car came to a screeching halt in front of the emergency room sliding doors. Charity bolted inside as I pulled Adelaide out of the car. A team of nurses met me at the door with a gurney, where I placed her on the rolling bed.

"How long has she been like this?"

"She was stuck in a car all morning. I spoke to her forty minutes ago. When I found her, she was like this."

"Was she responsive?"

The doctor, a woman in her mid-forties, rubbed her gloved knuckle along Adelaide's breastbone, making her face flinch from the pain. That was a good sign, wasn't it? She was still reactive. That was good.

"I got her to open her eyes once. She vomited in the car on the way here."

"We have a head contusion and possible heat stroke," she said as they raced through double doors.

"Sir, I need you to stay here," a nurse said, breaking away from the team. "We'll come and get you when she's stable."

My feet quit moving as I threaded my fingers through my unruly hair and tugged. Everything inside of me wanted to tell her to go fuck herself. I needed to be beside her.

Do you have any idea who I am?

Instead, I obeyed. As if on autopilot, my body listened to her order without question, leaving me displaced outside of the double wooden doors with a sign etched across them.

Restricted area.

"Nico's on his way," Charity said as she tucked her phone into her back pocket. "It's going to take them a bit to get an assessment. Why don't you come sit down?"

I didn't want to sit. I needed to be there, holding her hand while they worked on her. She'd be uncomfortable and in pain.

The waiting room sat in one long oblong rectangle with white-tiled floors lining the walls and dark tiles in the center where the blue chairs sat side-by-side.

It sat empty, a wasted space which had seen more pain and heartache than anyone could ever know.

I took the closest chair to the doors she disappeared behind and rested my elbows on my knees.

My knee bounced, making it impossible to see straight as it jarred my entire body.

"I'm going to park the car. I'll be right back."

The sterile antiseptic room stung my nostrils as I scanned the area. *I can't be here. We shouldn't be here.* We should be in our hotel room eating room service while we both pretended to ignore one another. Instead, my entire world disappeared behind those doors, surrounded by strangers without me.

If she survived, my world would never be the same again. I'd never let her out of my sight. She'd be stuck with me forever.

If she didn't, that was it.

There'd be no peace in the world.

I'd burn it down.

Adelaide

22

"Can you hear me?"

White speckle paneled ceiling tiles met my vision, engulfing everything except my periphery.

"Hello?"

Bright lights stabbed my retinas with a red-hot poker, and my skin burned as the sheet rubbed against me. I rubbed my eyes, and something tugged my arm.

What the...

A sticky object clung to my chest like honey.

A sticker with wires?

Where was I?

I rotated my hand in front of my face and scowled. Clear tubing attached to a pink cap disappeared into my skin, followed by mounds of tape that stuck to me like it belonged there. The sticker on my chest irritated each movement, making my body vibrate with an undesirable itch.

What's that noise?

A strangled beeping bore down on me, and the more I panicked, the faster it berated me.

Where was I?

The room reeked of sterility and commercial cleaning products—not the good kind you get at home, like Fabuloso or Pine-Sol—like a crime scene stripped of evidence.

I tipped my head against my crinkling plastic-covered pillow. The wooden headboard attached to the wall behind me contained devices, dials, and things I didn't understand.

A hospital?

Right. That would explain the IV, but how?

My gaze moved across the room. A flat-screen TV attached to the wall sat above a long desk with a chair. To the left of that, a computer screen with a keyboard, most likely for the staff, and next to that, a blue couch with cream-colored flowers designed into the backrest.

Jake...

Jake, the man I loved with all my heart and soul, lay sprawled out on his side, covered in a white blanket. Dark circles pillowed under his eyes, his hair disheveled.

"He hasn't left your side," a voice whispered on my opposite side.

I jerked my head towards her, making the room spin.

A female nurse, wearing blue scrubs with a blonde bun, leaned over me and placed her chilly hands on my arm.

"Who are you?" I slunk away from her touch.

My heart rate rose, sending a furious beeping out into the quiet room, assaulting the silence.

"It's okay. I'm your nurse, Maddy," she said, rubbing my arm, sending ice shards of pain right up into my molars. "You're lucky, you know?" she smiled as she checked my IV and then wrapped a blood pressure cuff around my arm. "If he hadn't gotten you here when he did.." She leaned in close, eying Jake sleeping on the couch, then nodded. "You and your baby may not have made it." Her gaze rose to Jake sleeping on the couch.

My throat tightened. I must have heard her wrong.

How could she slam me with such life-altering news? I'd only just woken up since who knows how long—the beeping reflecting my ticking tempo.

The nurse tucked her hand into her shirt pocket and handed me a sonogram image. I blinked back my listless vision and stared at a small blob mixed in a sea of gray and black.

"I kept it for you so you could see when you woke up," she said as I studied the seven and a half week-old baby growing inside of me.

I shook my head and gave it back to her, my hands trembling. "Take it back. I don't want it."

Her brows furrowed. "I'm sorry, I thought you'd want to—"

"I do," I said. "I just don't have a place to put it, and he..." I glanced towards Jake, who stirred. "He doesn't know yet, does he?"

The nurse shook her head and stuffed the picture back into her pocket. "I understand." She smiled and finished recording my vitals. "The doctor didn't tell him if that's what you're worried about."

Yeah, I'm not sure if a surprise party is something he'd appreciate now. *Or ever.* The last thing I had in my mind was setting down a pee stick in front of him and saying, 'surprise, you're going to be a daddy. Now we can live happily ever after.'

That'll go down well.

"Thank you," I said, the exchange taking too much out of me.

Maddy laid her hand on my arm. "Is there anything I can get you?"

I shook my head, my lids doused with weights too heavy for me to lift.

"Get some rest. You've had a hard couple of days."

Days?

Baby?

My body sank into the bed until it swallowed me up in the darkness of dreams with veritable nightmares.

Adelaide

23

J ake sat on the couch as he talked on the phone, his rugged appearance a meager example of the hell he must've gone through in the last few days. "I need you to make sure she arrives," he said as I caught bits and pieces of his conversation with someone about Becca, who'd he sent home.

I'd ruined their visitation to their family's graves, leaving Becca to mourn their death alone while Jake sat by my side, making sure they took care of me when he should be with his sister, consoling her—a consequence of my selfish actions I hadn't thought through.

A nurse sporting gray scrubs and purple clogs walked in. "I think it's time to get you dressed." She rubbed the sanitizer she'd gotten at the door all over her hands. "How does that sound?"

I shook my head and whimpered as Jake stood from the couch and pocketed his phone. "I'll help her with that."

The headache assaulting my brain from it nearly frying had begun to wear off, but that didn't mean I could tolerate the loud noises.

One of the many doctors I'd gotten to know, Doctor Jennings, explained how my body would feel as though I'd bar hopped all night without drinking an ounce of water, but so long as blood work kept improving, it wouldn't last long. That was over twenty-four hours ago, and it had barely started waning.

He'd also promised Jake that if my neurologist signed off on the cognitive test I'd taken, and my blood work looked great, I could go home today. Which had me champing at the bit and begging for Tylenol.

I glanced back and forth between them. Would this be another thing Jake insisted on doing? Like when the nurse came in to give me a sponge bath the night, I'd first gained consciousness two days ago.

He was so close to being removed from the hospital until I'd stopped the argument, and he calmed down.

"It's okay. I can do it on my own," I said, swinging my legs over the edge of the bed and touching my socked feet to the floor.

I'd been able to get up and use the restroom all on my own, but that didn't stop Jake from walking around the bedside and gripping my elbow for support.

I wasn't weak or unable to stand. In fact, I felt almost normal, aside from the body aches and headache. Not to mention the massive bruise inside my thigh from the catheter they'd used to cool my blood. There was also the slight twinge of nausea, but now that I knew I was pregnant, I didn't expect that to go away anytime soon.

"Thank you," I said, glancing up at Jake. His tall, massive frame dwarfed the woman standing behind him.

"At least let me disconnect the IVs first," she said, coming around to his side with a tender smile that would disarm even the grumpiest of men.

I nodded and sat back down on the edge of the bed. She taped my port down while Jake watched with crossed arms.

"All set." She tucked her scissors back into her pocket, and picked up the wrappers, then tossed them in the bin. "Can I help you with anything?"

Shaking my head, I walked towards the bathroom, my hospital gown flapping behind me. "I'm good. Thank you."

A fresh pair of clothes lay on the sink, folded and ready for me. I sighed and ran my fingers over the soft fabric. I'd been in this itchy gown for too long and needed to feel normal again.

I shut the door behind me, but it swung back open with Jake standing in the open doorway.

"I'm going to step out and get your paperwork settled so we can go."

"But I thought you were going to help me get dressed?"

"Do you need my help?" He stepped into the bathroom and placed his hand on my hip, his fingers skimming the top of my ass.

I shook my head, throat closing as my heart pitter-pattered like a love-sick girl—because I was. I was head over heels for this man who had me forgiving him the moment I woke up from my near-death experience.

"Okay." He kissed my forehead, then stepped out, leaving me gasping for words. "I'll be outside your room if you need me."

I nodded and shut the door again. Reaching behind my head, I pulled on the string at my neck, letting the gown fall to the floor, and looked in the mirror.

Black bags tainted the skin under my eyes—my cheeks hollowed pits. I didn't look emaciated, but my bottom rib poked out like it didn't belong.

How did I get like this?

I'd eaten and drank water but also vomited... a lot. Some days, I hadn't been able to hold anything down. But I thought women gained weight when they were pregnant?

I stretched my poor muscles and pulled my shirt over my head, foregoing the bra. There was no way I'd be able to reach back there and clasp onto those little hooks. Let's not forget the concentration it took to line those things up behind your back.

My shorts came next, then my socks, when the door to my room opened. "I'm almost done."

Did I imagine the noise, or did he just not hear me?

"Jake?" I said, sticking my head out of the bathroom door.

A man in hospital scrubs, too tight to be comfortable, stood beside my IV bag next to the bed.

"Oh, sorry. I thought you were someone else."

"No problem. I'm just adjusting your IV. Are you ready to get hooked back up?" His deep accented voice, with wavering vowels, struck me to the core. My stomach dropped, and the room blurred.

"I'm-I'm almost done. I'll have the nurse do it when she comes back in."

It was him, the man with the banded tattoo. It was darker in person, with a thick, solid band and a thinner one below. I shut the bathroom door and twisted the lock in place, a squeal escaping me.

But how? How did they find me?

"Everything okay, ma'am?"

I bit my knuckles, biting back the scream clawing at my throat. "I'm fine," I said, my voice breaking. "Just stubbed my toe."

"Let's get you hooked up and resting."

The silver door handle moved down, and I reached out, holding the handle in place. "I'm going to the restroom. I'll have the nurse do it when she comes back."

"Okay, I'll wait."

"That's fine. *Really*. I'll be a while."

"It's not a problem."

My breath caught in my chest as I kept my hand on the door. If he tried to come through it, he'd be able to. There wasn't much I could do in my weakened state.

I needed a weapon, but there wasn't anything of use in this sterilized bathroom except the foaming hand wash, and unless I put it in his eyes, there wasn't much else I could do with it. I was helpless against the giant man waiting to kill me.

Silence on the other side of the door killed me slowly as time passed by. Did he leave? I didn't hear the door close. I exhaled, took a step closer to the door, pressed my ear to the wood, and then held my breath.

Air conditioning whirring.

Distant beeping.

A stagnant roaring of vacant space.

Knock.

Knock.

I jumped in place, my heart bursting in my chest.

"Ma'am?"

Even if he were a legit nurse, there's no way I'd be able to answer him. My throat constricted as my heart worked overtime, pumping blood into my brain.

What if I'd mistaken his identity? How many people had similar tattoos? If he was here to kill me, wouldn't he sound angrier or at least try to wrangle me out of the bathroom with a little more desperation? Had my overheated brain caused more paranoia or hallucinations?

My heart rate skipped as it sped, my feet inched away from the door.

Knock.

Knock.

I vaulted backward, jerking my hand to my chest as if the sound bit me and stumbled, my spine slamming into the towel bar.

"Adelaide? Are you okay?" The door jiggled as he rattled the knob. "Why is the door locked?"

I rushed for the door and opened it, throwing myself into his arms.

"What's wrong?" he demanded.

"He was here," I mumbled into the crook of his neck as I tried climbing the length of his body.

"Who was here?" His voice lowered, sending chills down my legs as he gripped my shoulders.

"The guy with the banded tattoo on his arm. The mercenary."

He pulled me from his chest despite my desperate grasp to keep him close to me. "What guy? There wasn't anyone in here."

"He'd dressed like a nurse. He tried to get me to come out of the bathroom."

"Adelaide, I was at the nurses' station across the hall the entire time. No one came in or out."

"He was here," I cried, refusing to believe my mind deceived me. "I know he was. He messed with my IV bag."

I wiped the tears from my cheeks.

"Okay. Okay. Don't cry."

"Can we go home? I don't want to be here anymore."

"We're working on it. Come, lay down for a minute. You're going to work yourself into exhaustion again."

"Can you grab me a tissue, please?"

He nodded, walking me back to the bed where the ominous IV bag that once provided a helping hand now stood before me with death written all over it.

Jake disappeared into the bathroom as I removed the tape on my port, pulling the fine hairs from my skin as I jerked it free.

He walked back with a tissue just as I yanked the catheter from my vein.

"Jesus Christ, Adelaide," he said, grabbing my arm as blood splattered onto my palm and dripped onto the floor. "What are you doing?"

"He can't poison me if I don't have an IV in."

"Goddammit." Jake pressed the tissue hard into the back of my hand. "Hold this while I find some tape."

I placed my hand over the tissue, the sight of blood turning my stomach while he dipped into cupboards, but came up dry.

"I'll be right back—"

"No. Don't leave me," I said, standing from the bed too fast. "He'll come back."

"*Sweets*. I'll stand in the doorway and have your nurse come back in. Relax."

How could I relax when I was fairly certain I was a door's width away from becoming another statistic? Why didn't he believe me?

"I'm not lying."

"I believe you."

He did?

Jake opened the hospital room door and kept to his word, standing in the doorway, and asked the nurse across the hall for some gauze and tape.

The woman from earlier walked in behind him and shut the door, applying sanitizer to her hands as she stepped further inside. "I would've taken it out when we finished this IV bag."

I shook my head. "I just want to go home."

She gloved her hands, then picked up my arm, peeking under the tissue. "You should wait for a nurse to do this next time. You could damage the vein by ripping it out like that."

There wouldn't be a next time if we didn't get out of here.

My head swam as she bandaged up the hole in my hand. "There you go."

"Is the paperwork ready?"

She glanced at Jake, who stood over us, his arms crossed like he was ready to lay into someone—most likely me. "We have two more papers that need signing by the doctor, and then you can go."

"We need to go," I said with a lowered voice as she left the room.

"I'm working on it. Just lay back and rest."

"I can't." I raised my arms above my head and yawned as he tipped my feet onto the bed. "He'll come for me."

"I'll be by your side." He covered me up as I stared up at him. "Don't worry, sweets. I won't let anything happen to you." Jake pressed his fingers to my knuckles. "You're safe."

Jake

24

Why would they come here? What was their purpose?

We had a deal. A deal Adelaide still didn't know about. I wanted to keep her safe. She didn't understand how much I wanted that. Maybe because I told her I wasn't protecting her, which was the furthest thing from the truth.

She'd scared me like I'd never been scared before, and I knew the moment they wheeled her body beyond the double doors and left me out in the empty waiting room that I couldn't be without her. Never again.

I didn't understand those feelings. Not yet. For now, I had to keep her safe and find Holeo... but most importantly, I would keep her *safe*.

Adelaide laid curled into a ball on the bed, her eyes darting back and forth beneath her closed lids as she did what I'd instructed—rest. She wasn't asleep by any means, but at least she'd complied with my request—that was something.

Flashbacks hit me from her stint in a medically induced coma as they regulated her temperature. For the first twelve hours, my heart stopped beating, unsure if hers would continue.

It was the first time since my parents died that I'd feared death.

Even though death was a friend to me, I'd had that inescapable terror he'd come calling for her, which had me holding her tighter, watching her longer, and caressing her hair while she slept.

But now, she rambled about Yervant slipping into her room. It couldn't have been them. They wouldn't back out of our deal when I was so close to finding Holeo.

I glanced at my phone as a knock sounded at the door, and nurse Maddy walked in with a handful of papers. I placed my finger to my lips as Adelaide jerked and Maddy slowed, taking lighter steps through the room.

"Glad to see she's getting some rest." She handed me her release form as I stood from my chair.

"I'm not sleeping," Adelaide said, keeping her eyes closed and her hand latched around the bed rail.

Maddy smiled and pointed toward the papers. "This is all the information you'll need for at-home care," she whispered. "The doctor recommends coming back if her condition changes or you note any confusion, trouble speaking, or lack of consciousness again. Do you have any questions?"

"No." I shook my head and dropped the paperwork on my lap.

"Okay, well, you are free to go anytime."

She turned and walked out of the room, tossing the curtain to the side as she passed through.

One less thing to worry about. Now we could get her home where she can rest, and her parents can see her.

I'd kept in contact with them, giving them updates each time Linda called or if there was anything I felt was worth mentioning. Convincing them to stay home and not grab the first flight out was challenging, but I'd told them she was in excellent hands—my hands—and I'd let them know if anything changed.

Adelaide sat up as I stood from my chair, her arms stretching over her head. "Can we go now?"

I bent over and rubbed my thumb against her freckled cheeks where her long lashes touched her face. She exhaled through her nose, her warm breath steady against my wrist. My thumb moved to her supple bottom lip, missing how it felt against mine.

Clearing my throat, I wiped the nostalgia cloud from my vision and brushed her hair with my fingertips as her gaze fluttered up to mine. "Yeah. We can go."

I helped her out of bed and slipped her shoes onto her feet.

"Home. To my parents?"

"You'll stay at my place, but your parents want to see you. They can meet us there."

Adelaide stood, taking the papers I handed her, then wrapped my arm around her waist and stepped out of the room.

"Wait. *Um*," Maddy said as she rounded the nurse's station. "Hospital policy says we have to wheel you out. Just in case something were to happen."

I waved her off and pressed the button with the blue handicapped drawing. "Hospital policy is not my policy."

"I insist."

"So do I. Thanks for your care, Maddy."

We walked through the automatic door and to the elevator, where we waited for a couple to exit, then stepped inside.

"I can walk, you know," she said, leaning into me, her voice fragile yet strong.

"I do, but I want to make sure you don't fall and hurt yourself or worse."

We rode down the elevator, my arm never leaving her body until I had her sitting in the front seat of the overly cleaned rental.

"I'm sorry," she said as I slid into the driver's side. "I keep messing up while trying to do the right thing, but everything goes to shit, and once again, I'm a fuckup."

Adelaide caressed her tattoo, and I covered her hand with mine, interlacing my pinkie finger, so my King of Hearts touched hers. "I've been trying to tell you this. Maybe not in the best way, but I'm here to protect you. I won't let anything happen to you if you just give me the chance."

She shook her head, her eyes glistening with unshed tears. "I just didn't see how that was possible with how much you hate me."

I pinched the bridge of my nose and sighed, squeezing my eyes before opening them. "I don't hate you, Adelaide. There's just so much shit that's happened between us. I need time to process all of it."

"I know. I'm sorry." She hung her head, casting her gaze to the floor as she moved her tongue to her lip. "Where's my lip ring?"

She'd been awake and alert for the last three days, and she hadn't noticed the damn thing missing? "They had to remove it when they intubated you. I have it in your bag."

"Mom will jump for joy when she sees it's gone." She pinched her lip in its stead, substituting that action for her typical self-soothing.

"Speaking of parents..." I glanced at her as we pulled up to a red light, debating whether I should bring it up. But I'd wanted to shake her awake from her coma for an explanation, and now that we were alone and on our way home with her strength returning, my mouth decided it was the perfect opportunity. "Can you explain why you asked about my parent's death when you already knew from reading their police file?"

She frowned, her brows knitting together in a transaction of confusion and wonder. "What are you talking about?"

The light turned green, and I pressed on the gas with too much enthusiasm, jolting us forward. "The little job you did for Nico. You did a little more than that, didn't you?"

"Nico?" She braced her hands against the dash. "How do you... how do you know I did a job for him?"

"You think I wouldn't find out that Nico Moreno hired you to erase the evidence against Charity from the police database?"

"But... how?"

"I've known them for years."

She reared back. "You're friends with the mob?"

"Associates."

I wouldn't go into detail about how Luca had been our number one seller of drugs and guns for the last several years, or how Charity dated my friend, or how I grew up in this town hearing about the notorious Moreno Mafia. That wasn't important. What was, was me getting an answer I'd waited five excruciating days to hear.

Adelaide pressed her hand to her forehead and rubbed her temples with her fingertips. "Any other criminals you 'associate' yourself with?"

"Including you?"

She gave me a lopsided smile and glanced away, tucking her unruly hair behind her ear, which brought a smile to my face.

How was it I still craved to be inside her, despite all the evidence pointing towards her betrayal? Eventually, I'd overlook it all just so I could stay with her and witness her beauty every morning, but for now, I'd stay... cautious and reserved.

"I do some things... in my time off that others would find... less than savory." I shrugged.

She turned to me with brows furrowed, her fingers pinching her lip. "What does that mean?"

I sighed. Was she ready to hear this? "Another time, sweets."

"Don't you think I should know which monster to fear?"

I laughed as I switched hands on the steering wheel and scratched the five-day-old scruff on my face. "Let's just say... you should be happy I'm the monster who got to you first."

Her throat bobbed as she swallowed. "My head hurts," she said, wincing and rubbing her temples again.

I reached into the back seat and pulled out a Gatorade, placing it in her lap. "Drink this. You need to stay hydrated."

"Thank you." She grunted as she struggled to snap the safety off the lid, then took a sip.

I groaned, watching her lips touch the bottle, her head tipped back, and her throat bobbing up and down, and she drank. My mind shouldn't be so sexual towards something so innocent as drinking, but it was. I cleared my throat, bringing my tight fist to my mouth as I did. "So tell me, what were you looking for in my parents' file?"

"Jake, when I hacked into the police station, I had Holeo's help. Believe me when I tell you, the first time I'd heard about your parents was the time *you* told me about them."

I clenched my jaw, pulsing my muscle as I contemplated the possibility.

"What's that?" she said as I drove through the private airport's opened security gate with my fist squeezing the steering wheel.

A plume of fiery black smoke, like ink in blue waters, rose to the sky, casting shadows across the land.

"Shit."

Two big red fire trucks sat parked next to my hangar, spraying their foamy fire retardant onto my plane, and another sprayed the building beside it, preventing the fire from spreading.

I'd bought that plane when I'd made my first legit million, and now it'd gone up in flames.

I pulled the car to a stop and put it in park. "Stay here."

Her eyes went wide, her fingers gripping the drink between her legs. "Where are you going?"

"I'm going to find out what happened. Just stay in the car."

She nodded, and I wondered if she'd listen this time or if we'd end up in another race against the clock type situation.

I stepped out of the car, locking it behind me for good measure, and found a firefighter.

"What's going on?"

"Are you the owner?" he asked, opening a metal drawer on the side of his truck.

"Yes."

"Some type of explosion. We won't know yet until we get the fire put out." *Fuck.* "If you want to talk to the officers in charge over there," he pointed to a group of officers in black short-sleeved uniforms standing around gawking. "They can help you."

"Thanks."

An explosion... it had to be them.

I glanced back at the car, unable to see inside from the tinted windows. It made my heart skip a beat and my stomach sink with unease, which had me marching back to the vehicle and ripping open the door, only to find her exactly where I'd left her.

"What's happening? Is that your plane?"

My stomach settled when my gaze clashed with her alert and focused eyes.

"Yes." I slid into the car, slammed the door shut, and drove toward Charity's home. "We need some place to lie low for a moment until I figure things out."

"It was them, wasn't it?" She shoved her drink onto the floor. "I told you they were at the hospital. How did they find us?"

It'd make sense they'd follow around their leverage. How else did they ensure I'd keep to the deal? My question is, why, though? It's not like anything had changed. Why would they not only come after her in the hospital but also blow up my plane?

What changed for them?

And how did I tell Adelaide I made a deal with not only the devil but his entire entourage?

"I don't know." Gripping the steering wheel tighter, I made my way onto the freeway, checking the vehicles moving behind me. "Shit."

"What? What's wrong?" Adelaide turned in her seat and watched the white car moving across lanes in sync with me.

"We're being followed."

I pressed on the gas, darting in and out of traffic until I exited off the freeway and turned right towards Luca's home.

"What does that mean?"

It meant they were coming for us, and I didn't know why. We were out in the open without a place to hide yet, and if they caught up with us, we were screwed.

"Just hold tight."

I turned left and blew through a stoplight, then right and through another, the car still trailing behind me, until I pressed on the gas and slid around the corner. The white car blew past us, missing his turn as I rushed towards the driveway.

"Why are we at Luca's?"

Vito stood next to the door as I stopped the car, and hopped out, getting Adelaide out by the arm. I don't know what happened in the six days since we talked, but clearly, they weren't the patient kind.

"What's going on?" Vito said, holding his hand out to stop me.

I looked over my shoulder at the empty street. "Things have changed. I need to speak to Luca."

The front door opened, and Charity walked out, with Max in tow, her boisterous laugh claiming the scene around us.

"Jake? What are you doing here? I thought you were leaving today?" Charity said, tossing her keys into the air and catching them.

"Change of plans. I need a safe place to put her until I get some things cleared up."

"Not a problem." Charity smirked. "I have a safe room in the basement."

"That's not a safe room, Charity..." Max said, narrowing his eyes.

"It's *my* safe room."

She turned on her heel and walked back inside, motioning for us to follow.

"That's not the same thing. No one else is safe in that room but *you*."

Charity chuckled, and I finally understood.

"Jake, let's just take a commercial flight home."

"We have an actual safe room. Do you want her in there?" Max asked, placing his hand on his hips as Luca and Nico stepped out of the office.

"Can she get into trouble in there?"

"If she's anything like Charity, yeah."

I shook my head. Adelaide wasn't anything like Charity, not even close. Adelaide was innocent, to a degree, but the sins of life tainted Charity.

Car doors slammed outside, and Adelaide flinched. An abrupt commotion, followed by a litany of gunfire, erupted outside.

Charity and Max stepped towards the door, guns drawn, when Vito slipped through the front door and slammed it behind him, engaging the lock.

"Get to safety," he said, his hand holding his arm as blood oozed from between the creases of his fingers.

"What's happened?" Luca marched towards him.

"Five cars, all armed men in tactical gear."

The thick wooden door shuddered at his back as something hard and heavy collided with it.

"This way," Nico said, rushing down the steps in the foyer, followed by Charity and Max.

"Jake. I'm scared." Her whimpered plea twisted me up inside, stroking my darkness that beckoned me to let it out. To show everyone what I was capable of when I'd become cornered, when someone I loved was in danger.

"We'll be okay, sweets."

We moved faster, Luca and Vito taking the steps at the front as the front door burst open, followed by a barrage of bullets hitting the ground at our feet and the walls above our heads.

Adelaide screamed, and I grunted, nearly tumbling down the stairs and taking everyone out before me like a rogue bowling ball.

The back of my thigh burned with a fiery high-strung pain that quickly morphed into agony.

I'd been hit.

Adelaide

25

I screamed, my throat raw and dry, as gunfire erupted behind us, pinging their bullets in every direction imaginable. Jake stumbled, falling to his knees beside me, dragging me down along with him, which fed into the terror thrumming along my skin like rogue electricity.

Charity and Max turned and stood above us, returning fire as I struggled to pull Jake to his feet, his hand moving to his thigh as he limped into a room on the right.

"Let's go."

"What was that for? I could've gotten at least five of them when they came down."

"Now's not the time for you to play target practice on the enemy, Charity," Max said, engaging the safe room door and stepping inside.

Jake hobbled to the wall and sunk onto the floor, leaving a trail of blood in his wake. "*Fuck. Fuck. Fuck.*" He slammed the side of his fist against the wall with each scathing word.

"What the hell is this about?" Luca said. The Don for the Moreno Mafia sat on a cot, his personal bodyguard beside him, bleeding from a gunshot wound to the arm.

"I thought I lost them."

"You're bleeding." My heart ached deep in my chest—the ringing in my ears was akin to a symphony of broken flutes. "You're bleeding," I repeated with a whisper as I stared at the puddle under Jake's thigh.

"Lost who?" Luca said from behind me.

"The people Adelaide pissed off."

The floor swallowed me up, my stomach sinking as I watched blood soak his pants and drip out onto the floor. "Where..." I reached for him, grabbing at his pants, his hand quickly catching mine to stay my search.

"My leg."

I yanked my hand from his and snagged his belt buckle when he stilled my hands again.

"It's not that bad. I'll be fine. Max, grab me a towel, would you?"

Max walked around Charity, who watched the security monitors, and grabbed a hand towel from a tall gray metal cabinet.

"Just let me see. You're bleeding everywhere."

Jake tipped his head back against the wall and shimmied his pants down his hips with a growl and pulsing jaw muscles as Max tossed the towel to his chest.

"It was stupid for them to come here," Luca said.

"Do you have another medical kit in here?" I asked over my shoulder, seeing Nico working on Vito's arm.

Charity grabbed another kit off a shelf and brought it next to me, placing it on the floor.

"Jeez, Jake. Ever heard of a tanning booth? Your legs are as white as milk."

"Fuck off, Charity."

I ran my hand over the back of his leg until I hit the jackpot. Bright red viscous blood covered my fingers, sending my vision on a tilt-a-whirl.

My chest constricted, and my lungs collapsed as I stared at my crimson hand. *Where did all the oxygen go?*

Jake grabbed my shoulders and forced me to look at him as though he could sense my impending panic attack. "Adelaide. I'm fine. Why don't you sit down and take a few deep breaths?"

Guilt stabbed at me like a vengeful lover. I should be the one to comfort him. Instead, I sat like a useless bimbo, trying to see straight and shake my swirling vision back to normal.

"They're trying to say something in the camera," Charity said, breaking into my dread and morphing it into something else entirely.

"Turn it up," Vito said, standing from the bed.

"I'll only say this once." The deep accented voice slithered through the speakers like a poisonous gas. "Come out, or there will be more bloodshed. Do you want the death of your new friends to be on your hands as well?"

How were we supposed to respond to that? I stood from Jake's arms and froze as my gaze landed on the man who'd been in my hospital room just a couple of hours previously.

"How about a little motivation?"

The man placed his phone screen up to the camera just outside those safe room doors and turned the volume up.

A man and a woman sat in chairs, their eyes and mouths covered at a kitchen table—the same kitchen table I'd dined at my entire life.

Muffled protests numbed my body from the inside out as I watched my mother struggle against her binds.

"Mom!" I stepped back and covered my mouth, my heart thudding in my chest.

"*Fuuuuck*," someone muttered.

"Send her out now, and we won't kill them."

A man on the tiny phone screen stepped into view, his pistol pointing at my mother's skull.

I rushed forward, my hands pounding against the door. "I'm in here. Don't kill them. Please."

Tattooed arms wrapped around me as I reached for the spinning handle to give them exactly what they wanted. A sacrifice, someone they could pin their woes on.

I'd willingly offer myself and my unborn child to save them. My parents. The only people in this world who had always supported and loved me unconditionally. Who held me when I cried and encouraged me when I felt like giving up. Who taught me to do the right thing and be a good person.

"Open this fucking door," I said, tugging on the handle again.

My mother's cries burrowed into my soul as Max's tattooed arms pulled me from the door, my legs kicking in protest.

"Let me go! They're going to kill them."

Charity stood in front of me and pointed to the security panel on the side. "You can only open it with a code."

"Adelaide, you can't go out there," Jake said from the floor, his breaths labored.

"You have thirty seconds, or I'll kill them."

"Let me out of this room now, or I swear to God I'll murder you all in your sleep."

Jake shook his head. "No, Adelaide. I promised to protect you." He slid his back up the wall until he stood, pulling his pants up along with him, the blood leaving his face in a white rushing wave.

"You're not protecting me." I jabbed my fingers into my chest and pulled at my shirt. "You're killing me. You're killing me. I'll never survive this."

"Twenty seconds."

"Jake." My gaze flicked wildly back and forth from the screen to Jake, my voice distorted with desperation.

He shook his head again. Could he really watch my parents die and not do anything to save them?

"Luca," I said, giving up on Jake and going to the person who had all the power in this house. "Please." I ripped my body from Max's grip and kneeled down before Luca. "Open the door. I'll do anything." Luca turned his gaze from mine as though I'd never spoken.

"Charity... Nico. Help me." Wet, hot tears streamed down my face, burning my eyes with their salty bitterness. "What if it were *your* parents?"

"Ten seconds."

A torturous scream tore from my throat as I rushed to the door again, pounding my fists into the steel. "Please don't kill them. I'm trying." I sobbed.

"They can't hear you," Luca said.

"*Five.*"

"*Ahh.*" I kicked the door, my hands and feet working together to get a message across to them that this wasn't my doing. They forced me in here, and I was at their devilish mercy.

"*Four.*"

"Jake!"

"*Three.*"

I rushed back to him and fisted his shirt. "I'll do whatever you want. Just let me out."

"I can't do that, sweets. I'm sorry."

"*Two.*"

Glancing back at the screen, the man lowered the phone and shook his head. "I didn't want to have to do this," he said.

Jake seized hold of me and buried my face in his chest as though he prepared for them to blow up the door and use his body as a shield.

"*One.*"

Two gunshot blasts, one right after the other, drew a startling anguished sob from my chest. My knees gave out, and I collapsed. Jake's hold on me slipped as I folded in on myself, my sobbing dying in my throat, leaving my mouth gaping as the tears fell. The world stopped spinning, and a piece of my heart crumbled to ash. I sucked in air, croaking from the harsh intake.

My parents.

My flesh and blood.

Dead.

Because of me. Taken away before my eyes, without remorse from a monster who bore no consequences.

"I told you that if you reneged on our deal, I'd come down on you. Let this be your final warning. Find the hacker or your sister and Adelaide are next."

What deal?

My ears rang with a high-pitched cadence as the silence in the room hovered over us like a weighted blanket. Only it didn't offer comfort, just death and the stench of betrayal.

Something brushed against my shoulder. "Don't touch me. *Don't.*" My hands covered my ears as I rocked, tucking my knees up to my chest. "Don't touch me," I whispered with a desperate plea.

"They're leaving."

I pulled on my hair and slapped my face, sobbing, needing to feel the pain of something else other than the despair tearing at my chest.

My psyche.

My very being.

Nothing mattered.

"Adelaide, stop. You're gonna hurt yourself."

What did it matter?

Jake's hands wrapped around my wrists as he prevented my physical assault. Little bits of hair popped from my scalp as he pulled my hands from my hold.

"This is your fault," I screeched, slugging his chest with my fist as he pulled me to my feet. "You did this. You let them die." Jake didn't stop my onslaught but held still, his face contorted with pain. "I hate you!" I raked my nails down his cheek, seeking retribution.

"That's enough." His bruising grip wrapped around my upper arms and shook me like a rag doll. "You'd be dead if it weren't for me."

"*Jesus,*" someone whispered.

Pebbled beads of blood formed on his cheek from the angry red slashes running down.

I tugged on his punishing grip. "I'd rather be dead. Why couldn't you just let me save them?" I dropped to my knees with a sob, his hold pulling my arms above my head as he prevented my collapse. "I begged you. But you didn't listen to me." I jerked against the cold cement floor as a blast of gunfire came across the security speakers, causing a violent tremble to chatter my teeth.

"Adelaide, listen to me."

I shook my head, scrubbing at the tattoo on my finger, needing to get its dirty reminder off of me.

Jake dropped to my level with a strained grunt and pulled me into his arms, and I let him, burying my face in his chest and wailed a muffled anguished cry of a breaking heart.

"Listen to me."

I leaned my forehead against his chest—his intoxicating scent nearly smothering me and rocked my head side-to-side.

"I'm so sorry, sweets."

Don't say that.

I was willing to sacrifice it all, but he wouldn't allow me to do the right thing for once. My body sagged as he squeezed tighter, my shoulders dropping, the fight in me dissolving along with my will to live.

This was too much.

I'd wait for the earth to swallow me up whole, take me away, and eviscerate my existence from this world. My headache grew worse, my eyes swollen and itchy, the pounding in my temples beating against my skull.

My parents were gone, and they all sat by and let it happen.

Adelaide

26

I flinched as his hand came down on the back of my neck and smoothed my hair. "I'm sorry, sweets."

The safe room door opened, surrounding me in a whirlwind of chaos, like a corrosive tornado whirling with shuffling feet, metal clanging against hard surfaces, and men shouting.

Damage control.

A creeping numbness settled over me, blocking out thoughts, smells, and sounds. It staunched the flow of tears, dampening my face, the last tear falling from my chin, and I sniffed.

What if they weren't dead? He didn't show us the screen when we heard the gunshots. What if he just wanted us to believe they were? A flutter tickled my breastbone as Jake's arms fell away with a grunt, tearing me from my thoughts as he held his head, his face pale, like white sheets flapping in the wind.

He leaned back, his hand slipping through the crimson mirror beneath him, sending him onto his ass.

My stomach swirled as he closed his eyes and rested his head on the cement. "Jake?" I pulled myself from my stupor, swallowing the hurt, anger, and pain, and leaned over him, placing my hands on his chest. "Jake, what's wrong?"

"He's lost a fair amount of blood," a man in his late fifties said as he walked in carrying a black bag. "I'm Doctor Dan."

The doctor kneeled beside him and rolled Jake onto his side. Jake worked his soaked pants back down his hips, smearing the blood along his skin.

"Looks like it's a graze. It's pretty deep, but it's nothing we can't fix here. You got lucky."

Charity stood in the doorway, a gun in hand. "He's taken care of me when I should've died," she said as if it would make me feel better.

I swallowed hard and released the sob I'd held back, silently crying into my hands. This couldn't be my new reality. I needed air. This stuffy room bled with Jake's blood and the memories... I stood as the doctor worked on his leg and stumbled out of the room, my palm leaving bloody streaks as I caught myself along the door frame.

There wasn't enough air that wasn't tinged with the metallic stench of iron, and the hallway wasn't better.

Drops of blood beside spent shell casings. Bullet holes littered the walls like an empty honeycomb.

"Where are you going?" Jake said, his voice labored and pained.

My heart raced in my chest as I moved along the damaged hall, and with each boisterous punch against my breastbone, it spiked dread to blistering degrees.

"Charity," he called out as I hit the stairs.

"On it."

"You shouldn't leave," she said behind me.

"I need some air," I hissed.

I took two more steps, my feet slapping against the concrete with purpose when she pounded behind me and pulled me to a stop.

"Your boyfriend is down there bleeding. What are you doing?"

"Get out of my way." I pushed her to the side and continued my ascent, my stomach swirling with nausea. The electrolyte drink I'd consumed threatening to come back up.

"I didn't want to have to do this," she said as I hit the top of the steps.

Her body wrapped around me, and I fell to the ground with her legs wrapped around my hips.

I braced myself for impact, my hands hitting the floor for only a second before she'd twisted us around. Her legs pinned mine down as I lay on her, my back to her chest. Charity's arm swiped across my neck, her elbow bent at my throat and squeezed.

The blood in my skull throbbed, adding sharp pulses to my temples. I clawed at her, running my nails down her arms, pulling against her forearm, but she'd locked herself in like a boa.

My body twitched as the pressure moved from my temples to my eyes, then my cheeks.

"Charity? What are you doing?"

"Putting her to sleep."

"What? Why?" Nico said.

"Jake wanted me to stop her."

"Let her go. I'm sure that's not what he had in mind."

Black spots, like tiny gnats, swarmed the corners of my vision, foretelling my brain shutting down. I jerked again, a full-bodied shudder.

Charity's hold loosened, and she shoved me off of her.

I gasped, rolling onto my belly and pushing myself up to my feet.

"You fucking psycho! What's wrong with you?" I said, my voice cracking.

Jake hobbled up the stairs, the doctor trailing behind him. "I'm not done yet."

"What happened?"

"You told me to take care of her—"

"She tried to choke me."

"I didn't try. I was working on it."

"Jesus, Charity. I asked you to stop her, not assault her."

"Technically, you just said my name. All else was implied."

"Not implied."

Jake hobbled towards me as I rubbed my throat, where her ghostly touch constricted against my skin.

"When you try to help a friend out..." she mumbled.

"I think we need to give you lessons on social cues or something, Bella," Max said.

Luca stepped up behind her and put his hands on her hips. "Charity. *Giuro su Dio.*"

"She's crazy," I whispered as Jake wrapped his arms around me, the inky black rage boiling inside of me subsiding, making way for his warmth and comfort.

"I'll take care of this. I promise," he whispered in my ear.

"Jake, why don't you and Adelaide go up to the second floor and hit the guest room? It's been a long couple of days, and we have some cleanup to do." Nico said.

"I still need to finish his stitches." Doctor Dan held two metallic medical instruments in his hand, wearing a tight frown.

"Do it upstairs."

I followed them up the steps, to the left, and along the corridor. The bedroom door opened to reveal a spacious room with a king-size bed to the left, a headboard made of industrial pipe, and two lamp-post-like end pieces.

Jake laid across the width of the dark blue comforter on his belly and groaned as the doctor set back to working on his stitches. I lay beside him, his breath on my cheeks, and grabbed his hand.

This was where I should have been. Beside him, not seeking an escape but breathing the same air as him. I should've swallowed my grief, held his hand as I was now, and comforted the only person I had left in the world.

Well, maybe not the only person anymore.

Max walked in with the doctor's bag and set it down beside him, then walked away with a sympathetic smile and shut the door.

Were those the looks I'd get now? Would people see me differently, pour their sympathy over me, walk on eggshells around me, or guard their words?

"Okay, make sure you keep it clean and call me if you need anything."

"Thank you," Jake said as he released my hand and stood beside the bed.

He nodded. "I've left two pills on the nightstand for you, Adelaide. Get some rest. And Jake, this bottle is yours." He tucked it into his medical pack and pulled out an orange prescription bottle. "For the pain."

I couldn't take those, could I? I'd heard there were only certain things you could take while pregnant, and although it didn't bother me last week about what I put into my body, it mattered now.

The doctor left with a pinched smile and gentle nod, leaving Jake and me alone. This would either be the beginning or the end for us.

There was no turning back now.

Adelaide

27

"Come here, Adelaide," Jake said when I shut the door behind the doctor.

My feet stuck to the floor with sticky hesitation as renewed grief washed over me.

He was okay.

I was okay.

Our *baby* was okay.

But my parents weren't, and our safety was far from guaranteed.

I should tell him.

No. I can't.

He should know.

My mind warred with me, back and forth, right and wrong, until I walked into his arms, his palms cupping my face. "I'm going to fix this. I promise."

He believed those words as easily as I could stare into his blue eyes, but it was a promise he could never fulfill. My parents were dead... because of me, and they'd never get to hear what should be jovial news.

I tilted my head to the ground and blew out a heavy, shaking breath, puffing out my cheeks. "Jake, I wish there was a reset button, and you could be the hero and press it, but that's not possible. This is..." my voice choked in my throat, and my chin quivered, "my fault." I took his hand and brought it down to my stomach, placing his palm flat against my belly. "There's only one promise I'd ask you to make."

He furrowed his brows, his head tilting to the side. "What are you saying?"

I sniffled as he sat on the edge of the bed, his hand shifting against my stomach. "Adelaide?" His low, rumbling voice sent shivers down my legs, with gooseflesh following like marching ants.

Shaking my head, I bit my lip, unable to bring forth the words and give him the answer he demanded.

My parents' faces flashed before me. They weren't the type to kick me out, and they'd welcome this baby and me with open arms. My parents loved me unconditionally, through thick or thin.

"How do you know?"

I swallowed, bracing myself for his unleashed anger at my supposed decep-tion. "The nurse at the hospital told me." When he didn't move or make a sound, I continued. "I wanted you to—"

"How far along are you?"

"Um..." I mumbled. "Eight weeks, give or take a few days."

"Eight..." he said, exhaling his words. Jake shook his head, the disbelief on his face as clear as the Pacific waters.

I froze, my heart aching as he tipped his head and pressed his cheek to my belly, wrapping his arms tight around my waist. I reached for the ends of his darkened hair with my fingertips, hesitant to touch him and ruin this foolish paradise, but I remained steadfast. He either let me touch him when I really needed it or not at all.

Heat rose from his scalp as I threaded his strands through my fingers and held him against me. Hot tears rolled down my cheeks as I bit my lip, forcing back the sobs that beat against my breastbone.

What was he thinking? What wicked thoughts ran through Jake Murray's head right now?

He pulled back but wound his hands around my hips, his thumbs brushing the exposed skin from my bunched-up shirt. "Why are you telling me this now?"

I squeezed my eyes closed as my chin trembled. "Because," I wiped the tears from my cheeks, "we could have died down there, and you would've never known." My face tightened, and my breaths rattled my chest with an uneven canter. "I already hate myself for my..." I broke down and covered my face with my hands, hiding from him—from the world that despised me so much.

Jake took me in his arms, standing from the bed, and held me tight as I wept into his chest. "I'm here, sweets." His hold tightened.

"Jake," I shook my head, "stay with me. Just for tonight? I don't want to be alone."

If I let him walk out that door, it could very well be our last conversation—the last time I saw him without him divulging his thoughts on my revelation.

"You don't want me to stay, Adelaide." He smoothed my hair over my head and gripped the back of my neck.

"Yes, I do." I bit my lip as my breaths quickened. My heart palpitated in my chest.

I ran my hands up his chest, and he didn't move.

"Sweets," he growled. His saddened gaze faltered for a transitory moment, then fell away completely as he looked down at me. "What do you want from me?"

I shook my head. How do I answer that when I don't know? The guilt ate through me as I contemplated the answer. "You..." *for a single night, even if that's all I'll ever have again,* "to hold me."

He sighed and wiped his hand down his face, then walked me back toward the bed, stripped off my clothes, and tucked me in like the first night he'd taken me home.

Nostalgia assuaged me as I lived in the past for a fleeting second, only for his bounce on the bed to throw me back like unwanted trash.

He slipped in behind me and wrapped his arm around my waist, his hand resting near my face.

"What would you ask me to promise you?"

I frowned and tucked the side of my face into the plush pillow. "I want you to be there for your child, even if you hate me."

His warmth heated my back as he squeezed me tight. "That I can promise you." He kissed the back of my head, prompting a smile I shouldn't have.

A sob escaped from the painful lump in my throat. My shoulders shook, and agony ripped me open from the inside out.

"*Shh*, sweets."

I turned in his arms and rested my forehead against his bare chest, my arms tucked between us. Jake's warm thighs heated mine as I slipped them between his.

Life wasn't fair, but I wasn't even close to being at the bottom of the pits yet. I still had a long way to tumble. The question was, would I be able to climb back out, or would darkness swallow me up?

I tipped my chin towards him and stared at his glacial blue eyes through my blurry tears. Our gazes locked in silent conversation until the urge to touch my lips to his became overbearing.

His soft lips brushed against mine in a gentle caress, reciprocating what I'd hoped wasn't one-sided emotions. Our lips moved in tandem like a slow dance between old lovers as his hand wound up my spine.

"Make me forget," I whispered as our lips teased one another.

Jake tucked my hair behind my ear. "You need to remember."

"Not tonight." I shook my head. "Please."

"You'll regret it in the morning," he said while studying my no doubt red splotchy face.

Sadness glossed over him, dragging a spiky rake of anguish down my insides. Don't reject me. Not when I need this.

I needed him and his comfort like I needed air to survive.

Wrapping my hand around his neck, I pulled his lips to mine and forced his doubt, or chivalrous deeds, away while rubbing my core against the top of his thigh.

A moan rose from my chest, fueling my need for him. "I've never regretted a day with you." My center skimmed over his leg, igniting a fire in my belly and zings of euphoria from between my thighs, right down to my toes.

If I continued, I'd come before he even touched me.

He dipped down and sucked my nipple into his mouth, his tongue swirling around the hardened nub.

My mouth fell open as I tipped my head back, my hips moving harder and faster against him, relishing the pressure building low in my abdomen.

"Come for me, Adelaide. I need you ready."

He seized my hips and dragged me against his leg. Our open mouths absorbed each other's breaths as I hung on tight with the ecstasy that flowed through my body. His hand slid down to my lower back as I arched, my toes curling, my eyes pinched tight, and rode my climax. "Jake."

"God, you're so beautiful." His hands dipped lower, sliding my underwear down my hips, his teeth nipping my breast as he bent and pulled them off my feet.

My slick core dampened my thighs as I whimpered against his knuckles, brushing the seam of my sex. My body shuddered, and ripples of gooseflesh spread across my skin.

Jake dipped his finger in his mouth and sucked off my juices. *"Mmm.* Just like I remembered."

"My God."

Wrapping his hand around my thigh and dragging it over his hip, he positioned the head of his cock at my center.

My body ached for him with a carnality that rivaled even the hungriest predator.

"Hold on to me, sweets. Don't let go."

My heel pressed into his plump butt as his lips slammed against mine. Jake sucked the life from me as he plunged deep inside, my body stretching and burning around him, his thick length filling me to the brink.

"Oh my god. *Fuck*," I gasped against him, his slow, hard thrusts drowning me in bliss while taking away my pain.

What I wouldn't give to have this feeling forever. It was better than drugs or any dopamine rush.

Jake grabbed the back of my knee and swung it off his hip. "Turn." His low and raspy voice sent shivers down my spine.

I shifted, doing as he ordered, and pressed my ass against his hardness. My body needed him as much as his hard length proved he needed me. He pressed back inside, hitting deeper than before.

"*Oh*, Jake," I purred, grabbing his ass as he thrust with a torturous tempo that had me begging for more. "I need more."

Jake nibbled on my neck, his heady breaths burning my skin. "You want more, sweets?"

"Yes. God, *yes*." My body clenched around him as his hand dipped between my legs and circled my clit with his fingertips. I exhaled with a moan, releasing his ass, and gripped the hairs at his nape.

My heart palpitated with chaos while he set a devious order to my world. A temporary order guaranteed to dissipate the moment he stopped.

"I'm close," I whimpered.

Jake snaked his arm beneath my neck and pinched my nipple, dropping my soul into an earth-shattering orgasm. I curled into a ball, my body constricting around him.

He groaned and pinched harder. "God, you're so tight." He pumped into me, my climax waning as he jerked.

Warmth shot through my core as he came inside me—a unique sensation that set me on fire. My tense muscles relaxed against the soft mattress and his chest.

I closed my eyes. My body drained of energy, my emotions crippled with instability and grief.

"Sleep, sweets," he said as he nibbled my lobe.

"But..." He was still inside me. His cum seeped down the crease of my thigh. *How would I sleep this way?*

"Close your eyes, and don't argue."

Jake's hand slipped from between my legs and settled on my belly.

Tears flooded my eyes with pinpricks of pain and sadness.

He was right. I would regret it. Not because it was with him, but because I'd chosen to forget.

I wept with his arms tucked around me and his cock still inside me until my heavy lids won the battle my stubborn mind was too weak to wager.

28

I'd woken in the middle of the night, my limp dick still pressed between her cum covered legs.

This wasn't supposed to happen—her parents dying, me holding her while she cried herself to sleep after fucking her. What was I thinking, letting my desires get the better of me? Emotions were high, adrenaline crashed, and one thing led to another. At least that's what I'd tell her when she woke up.

But for now, I let her sleep a little longer, in peace where the reality of her new and ruined life was tucked far away amid shadowed dreams.

The sun had barely come up when I'd opened my eyes for the second time, with my arms still wrapped around her slender frame and my dick tucked away in my briefs.

I rolled away, the loss of her heat against me like a knife to the chest. I dressed in my bloody pants, still not having my luggage from the car, and limped down the steps, expecting a bustle of activity.

Where was everyone?

Stepping outside into the bright morning sun, I opened the trunk with my key fob as I passed Vito, his arm in a sling tucked against his body.

"Morning," I said. "How's the arm?"

Vito chuckled, then raised a brow. "How's the leg?"

I tugged my suitcase from the back, along with her pack, and dragged them to the door.

"You know where everyone's at?"

Vito cleared his throat. "Family meeting."

Right.

I nodded and walked back inside with our luggage when a blood-curdling scream resounded across the pictured walls.

Adelaide?

I bolted up the stairs, ignoring the searing fire on the back of my thigh, and threw open her bedroom door.

Adelaide thrashed the tangled sheets around her, her eyes wide with fear. Tears rolled down her freckled cheeks.

"What's wrong?"

"The blood. Get it off me." She held out her hands, palms up. Her brows pulled together, her breaths ragged. "It's everywhere."

"There's nothing there, sweets." I tugged her towards me, placing her head on my chest, and ran my hand down her hair like I do with Becca when she has her night terrors. "There's nothing there."

Her mournful cries tore my heart from my chest, her tears wetting my skin.

"Look at me, Adelaide."

I held her hands in front of her face, hoping she was awake enough to see her mind drowning her with fictitious visions. But that was the problem with night terrors—they'd loosened their hold when her mind was ready and not a second sooner.

"What's going on?" Max said from the bedroom doorway, his chest heaving.

"Bad dream. She's fine."

Max slid his hand down the door frame and rubbed his eyes. "I'm not used to that kinda shit so early in the morning." Walking away, he grumbled something indistinguishable, his voice dissipating with distance.

"Adelaide," I said, holding her rocking body in my arms. "You're okay."

She blinked.

Once.

Twice.

Her lids fluttered as she awakened, her trembling intensified. A tear dropped to her raised knees before she wrapped her arms around them and buried her face.

My throat tightened as her shoulders shook.

We were one and the same now. I understood her pain more than anyone, aside from Becca. The pain of losing a parent was something I didn't wish on my enemy—a loving parent, that was.

"I'm sorry," she said, sniffling in the hollow space between her knees and chest.

"Why are you apologizing? This is normal."

She shoved me away with her arm and moved off the bed. "Nothing about this is 'normal.'"

"You're right. That was the wrong thing to say."

Shouldn't I be well versed in this? I've comforted Becca hundreds of times in the last fourteen years since our parents' death but failed at the first chance I got with Adelaide.

I slid off the bed towards her and pulled her crossed arms from her chest. "I'm sorry."

"Stop apologizing to me." Her anger hid the broken, sorrowful woman under the surface.

Anger was normal.

"What do you want me to say?" I got down on my knees before her and wrapped my arms around her naked waist, placing my head on her belly where *my* child grew.

My scent from between her legs filled my senses, making me swell in my pants.

"Nothing."

Her hand swept through my hair, the weight of her arm growing against my back.

"Everything will work out in the end. I promise."

She groaned. "*Please* don't say that."

I'd made promises before. I'd broken them too. But this was a promise I was willing to keep and do anything in my power to make it happen.

We created our futures.

Sure, obstacles would be thrown our way, but that didn't mean we couldn't get to where we were going in the end. It'd just take some time to get there.

I stood and ran my hand down my beard. She needed time in this phase to work out her anger and come to terms. I understood that. I'd been there before. "I need to make a few phone calls, and then I'm sending you home."

"What?" she cried. "You're... you're leaving me?"

"I'm not leaving you. I'm sending you to our home, where you're safer."

Our home?

"And what will you do?"

I gripped her hand in mine. "I'm going to make them pay."

"You can't," she said, shaking her head. "They'll kill you."

"I have more people on my side. They won't get away." I brushed her hair away. "When I'm done, I'll come back for you."

Her chin quivered as she hung her head, shaking my hand off her face. She spun on her heel and marched into the bathroom, slamming the door behind her.

"That didn't go over as planned," Luca said from the door.

"If it was planned, I'd say it was a failure."

"What do you propose then?"

How about ripping your head off for listening to our conversation and staring at her naked body when she was mine?

They may have been okay with sharing, but I certainly wasn't.

"I'm going to find them and kill them."

"Sounds like something you'd want to think long and hard about."

"I have."

Did all night count?

"Quando il diavolo ti accarezza, vuole l'anima."

"Does it look like I speak *Italian*?"

I tossed my suitcase I didn't remember carrying up the stairs onto the bed and threw open the lid.

Luca scoffed as he tucked his hands into his pockets and leaned against the door, making himself a fixture. "It means the price for giving in to the temptation may cost more than you're willing to pay."

"The only temptation I've given into is crying in the bathroom because those fuckers killed her parents after we made a deal." I tossed on a clean shirt and shucked off my ruined jeans.

Blood soaked my bandage. I must've opened it up when I ran. I'd worry about it later.

Throwing on a clean pair, I sat on the bed and slipped my socks over my feet.

"What do you hope to gain from this?"

I sighed. "To wipe them from the face of the earth so no one will ever know they existed." And if I was going to do it, I'd need his help.

"No one really knows they exist, anyway."

"Not helpful."

"It's the truth."

I slipped on my shoes, picked up my phone from the nightstand, and called Tonk. He answered on the third ring with a gruff, "What?"

"I need you to pick up Becca from her apartment and take her to the safe house."

"Give me a scale."

"One to ten? Eleven."

Luca disappeared from my doorway while Adelaide stayed in the bathroom.

"Okay."

"Should I let Alek know?"

"Yeah. We'll be making our way home on the ground."

"What's wrong with the plane?"

Adelaide walked out of the bathroom, her eyes red-rimmed and puffy.

"I'll explain later."

Hanging up, I pushed my phone into my pocket and limped towards the bedroom door, slamming it shut so no one could see her plush breasts and supple ass.

"I'm going where you go," she said, crossing her arms over her exposed chest.

"I figured," I said, sighing. "Get dressed. We're going home, and we have a long drive ahead of us."

She took three long strides to the bed where her pack lay and dug inside, pulling out an outfit. "Why are we driving?"

"It's safer. Airplanes have one destination."

"They also have more security in place."

"There's no security outside of an airport, and if they know you've been on a plane, they know where you're going to land."

"You think they'll come after us?"

I nodded. "Better to assume so."

"What about my parents?" she said, her voice lowering to a murmur.

I exhaled and stopped zipping my bag halfway around. "I'll have Alek call it in. We'll take care of them."

She nodded, keeping her gaze on her bag as she sniffled. "Will I be able to have a funeral for them?"

"Adelaide," I said as I reached out for her. Gripping her shoulders, I tipped her chin up with my finger. Her red, irritated eyes enhanced the darker green ring around her irises. "I'll take care of everything. I promise."

If only I could turn back time and take away her pain—to press a button and be her hero like she said. But that wasn't possible.

"How long will it take for us to get home?"

"Not long."

"What then?"

"Then we get you someplace safe while I handle them."

"I don't think you exactly qualify as a vigilante, Jake. Why don't we just go to the police?"

I smirked. "Why didn't you go to the police instead of running away?"

It may be hypocritical, but she wasn't the only one who kept secrets, and I wasn't about to let her in on mine just yet.

She shrugged. "Because I would've incriminated myself just to tell them about a suspicion I had." She glanced around as if her mind ran wild, as did mine. "Why did they threaten Becca? How did they know about you?"

I sat her down on the bed. "I made a deal with them. Your safety for Holeo."

"Why did you do that?" she demanded.

"It was the only way to keep you out of harm's way. They think I've gone back on that deal. But it's too late. They burned what bridge we had between us when they killed your parents."

Her eyes lowered, and she covered her face with her hand, then swiped it down as if it'd stop the flow of tears pooling in her eyes.

Shit. I shouldn't have said that.

"Get dressed. I don't want to lose more daylight."

I zipped her bag and mine and hauled them out of the room after she slipped on a pair of shorts and a t-shirt—my t-shirt. *God, she looked good in that.*

When we reached the bottom of the steps, I took in the scene before me with a growing irritation beneath my skin.

"No." I shook my head.

Charity stood with two packed bags, Max next to her with one of his own.

"Morning, sunshine. Ready for a road trip?"

"No. You're not coming with us."

"Actually, she is," Luca said as he walked out of the kitchen. "You dragged us into this, and they struck my home, killing two of my men."

"He's given me permission to have fun, Jake. Do you know how often he's allowed that outside of the bedroom?" She leaned in and made a circle with her fingers. "This many times. Don't be a party popper."

"Isn't it pooper?" Adelaide asked behind me.

Charity laughed. "Sorry, inside joke."

"She's not coming." I continued walking outside to the Bentley and tossed our gear in the back.

Charity and I didn't get along. They all knew that. So sticking us in a car together was bad news. It's not that I didn't appreciate her help finding Adelaide, but we had a long history together, and there were things we couldn't fix—like her loud mouth.

"This isn't an option," Luca said.

"And if I refuse?"

A smile that reeked of warning bells tipped his lips. "Is that something you want to try?"

Things kept getting more complicated the more time went by. "Fine."

"Great. It's settled then," he said as if we just decided on a vacation spot.

Charity and Max brought their gear out and struggled, tossing it in the back, along with ours.

"What's in that?" I asked as Max stepped in and lifted it for her.

"Guns, grenades, knives. The whole shebang." She wiped her hands as though her suitcase contained a year's worth of dust.

I groaned. If we got pulled over with all of that shit...

"Come back in one piece," Luca said, grabbing Charity's ass and pulling her into him.

I rounded the car before they sucked face. "Get in. We're wasting time."

Charity and Max slipped into the back seat while I opened Adelaide's door and set her inside.

My thigh ached with a burning sting as I shut the door, glaring at Luca for putting me in such a position, and walked around to the driver's side.

This would be a disaster of epic proportions, and we were at the center of the storm.

Adelaide

29

My world peeled away, rotting layer by layer until all that was left was a raw, bloody coating of singed nerves. The color in the sky hemorrhaged into the background as I stared at the scenery zipping by.

We'd been on the road for three hours, and Charity hadn't stopped bobbing her head to the music pounding away in her headphones.

A burning hit my chest. She felt happiness, heard music, and moved so carefree. It wasn't fair.

After all, I'd only tried to keep everyone safe, and it backfired. Now more people were involved in solving a problem they shouldn't be part of.

My lids bobbed the moment we put tires to the road, but I refused to let them close. Instead, I played with my lip and stared out into the colorless abyss.

Jake wrapped his fingers around my hand, resting in my lap. "What are you thinking about?"

I snorted. "Nothing."

If I thought about anything, I'd only cry. Most of my thoughts returned to my parents, and I thanked God I spoke to my mother before the hospital.

"Why don't you get some sleep?"

I shook my head, keeping my gaze out the window. "I don't *want* to sleep."

"Sleep deprivation will only make things worse, you know."

My swollen lids partially blurred my vision. I pulled my hand from his. "I. Don't. Want. To. Sleep."

Didn't he understand the nightmares that came to me? The blood, the screams, the horrific visions of my parents' blood burning into the kitchen table? How was I supposed to walk back into my home and not see the stains, the terror on my father's face, the tears on my mother's?

I couldn't do anything to stop it. He wouldn't allow me. *They* wouldn't allow me, and now I was stuck in a perpetual game of horrors.

Jake jerked the car down the exit, crossing the suicide lane and nearly clipping the sand barrels.

Charity squealed.

Max's hand came down on the back of my seat as he pulled himself forward. "What the fuck, Jake?"

Jake brought the Bentley to a skidding halt on the side of the road in the middle of nowhere and got out of the car. He rounded the front with a limp and a look of pure ire clenching his jaw.

What have I done now? Jake ripped open my door and disconnected my seat belt before pulling me out of the car by my elbow.

"Stop. What are you doing?"

Jake moved me towards an abandoned gas station with a Route 66 vibe, my feet scuffing up dust from the sand-covered earth as we rounded the corner.

The blue and red paint peeled from the cylinder walls with weeds waist high and rustling that gave me pause, whether it was a snake or reeds rubbing together.

He pushed me against the wall, glanced around the corner from where we'd come, and then back to me.

"I understand you are going through some tough shit—"

"Tough shit? I wouldn't call my parents being mur..." my voice shattered.

"Adelaide. I've been there. Trust me, I get it. But you have someone else that's relying on you now. Neglecting your health because of your grief doesn't just affect you, but also our baby." His hand cupped the side of my face, his fingers dipping into my hair. "I won't allow you to disintegrate before my eyes. Do I make myself clear?"

My eyes burned as I chewed on my lip and rocked my foot from side to side, bending it at an angle as he stared at me with an intensity that rivaled the southern sun.

"Don't act like this pregnancy makes you happy. Don't act like you care. You wanted to destroy me for what I did to you. Congratulations. You got what you wanted."

"I'd never wish this on you, Adelaide. Never." He stepped in closer, his heat overtaking the chill that settled into my soul. "I'd take this pain from you if I could." His thumb brushed away the slipping tears. "I love you, sweets, and there's nothing you can do that would change that."

He didn't just confess his love for me now. Not in the height of my grief, when I can't tell reality from dreams, or night and day. This was just part of my nightmarish Hell. I'd wake up from this for it to all be a lie—a figment of my warped imagination.

"That's not true," I whispered through panicked breaths.

"It is. And you can choose not to believe it, but I'll be there every time battling your doubts for you."

"Why? Why are you doing this? You hate me. I lied to you and tried to steal from your company. I stalked you and your friend." I swallowed the softball-sized lump in my throat.

"Those are lies, my sweet angel. I couldn't hate you. I tried. I really did. But I can't."

My mind swirled like a tornado, destroying everything around me.

"You said it. You said I meant nothing to you. I didn't exist."

He shook his head, his hand cupping the other side of my face. "I'm so sorry. I was angry and confused. But I didn't mean it. You're the most important person who's ever entered my life, even though it was like a fucking cataclysmic storm that wiped out any sense of *normalcy* at every turn." His lips brushed against mine, but I turned from him, ripping away his touch.

"Don't. Don't do that."

"Do what? Fight for you? It seems like that's all I've been doing since I met you. You'll never get rid of me no matter how much you try, Adelaide. I'm here forever, so you better get used to it." He slid his hand down to my stomach and rubbed his knuckles along my belly button. "And the next time you say I'm not happy about this baby, I'll bend you over my knee, little girl. I made you a promise, did I not?"

How? How can he flip so easily, being furious and wanting to ruin my life, to wanting to be with this baby and me? He sent my mind on a tailspin, my rudders smoking and on fire, hurtling towards the ground at full speed. I thought I'd hit the ground before that night when he found out, but no. This was it. I was near impact, *ready* to make contact.

"Say something."

I shook my head and leaned to the side, away from him. He slammed his hands next to my face, his palm connecting with the cylinder with a meaty slap next to my ears.

"You're not going anywhere until we get this situated."

I placed my hands on his chest and sighed. His warmth dipped me into the past by my toes when things were easier between us before he broke me, and then I shoved him.

"You want to work on our 'relationship' while my parents lay dead in my home?" I cranked my jaw to the side as my nose stung with renewed tears.

"That's not what I meant."

"There are people after me that want me dead, and the top tier of the mob is sitting in the backseat of your car." I pushed him a little harder.

"Adelaide."

"You have some fucked up priorities, Jake."

"Would you just listen to me?"

I shook my head. "I did listen to you until you pinned me to the wall and strangled me. I almost bought the fairytale, but that's all it was. The honeymoon is over, and now we have to deal with the consequences of a good time."

My chest tore in half as I shoved him again, his jaw clenching. I loved this man wholeheartedly, but anger slipped through my lips, and my teeth gnashed with hatred.

Grief locked me in place.

Fear stole my reasoning.

I didn't want to die. I didn't want *him* to die. But for the last week, I'd knocked at death's door too many times, and that's all that consumed me. If I could free my mind of any thoughts, I'd take that drug. I'd grab the closest rocker and become an insane woman who rocked in the corner staring at the wall.

"I shouldn't have put my hands on you; you're right." He crowded my space as he towered over the top of me, my neck bent backward. "And it'll never happen again, not out of anger or malice. I'm sorry."

The air whooshed from my lungs like a broken window on an airplane. An apology I'd heard before, but this one hit a little different like I could believe the promise he wrapped up with silken honey.

His hand hovered near my face. I turned my gaze to his healing palm where I'd cut him at the bus station, ironically to keep him safe. The moment I realized I'd done everything to protect him and my family because I loved him.

I grabbed his wrist and brought it closer to my tear-streaked cheek. If I let him in, that was it. No turning back. Like what he said that night in his garage. I was his, and he was mine. No more of this back and forth, still trying to figure out what *this* was.

Sighing, I turned my face into his palm, kissing the injury I'd inflicted.

"You fight me so hard, but in the end, you know this is right. You know we belong together, even if getting there has been a bumpy road."

'Nothing worth fighting for comes easy.' Dad said that all the time.

I leaned closer to him, his heartbeat calling to me as I placed my head on his hard chest. My arms wrapped around his waist instinctively, as if deep down my soul knew he was my only salvation. Fresh tears escaped my closed lids as he hugged me back, his lips kissing the top of my head.

"We'll get through this together, sweets. Let me handle everything else. You take care of yourself and our baby." He rubbed his hand down my back, sending soothing waves up my spine. "Okay?"

I nodded against him, needing to stay in the silent confines of my fucked up mind for a moment longer.

"Let's get back on the road. We have a long way to go."

I sniffled and nodded.

"And let's get you a tissue."

A laugh escaped my pursed lips, and it felt good, almost normal.

"There she is," he whispered, wiping a tear from my chin.

I followed him back to the car, my pinkie locked with his, our heart tattoos smashed together in a symbolic merging of two becoming one.

The king to my queen.

He opened my door and settled me back inside before shutting the door and whipping around the front to get back in the car.

"Now that you two got that out of your system, can we find a real gas station, please? My bladder is about to explode," Charity said, popping a gummy worm into her mouth.

Jake pulled onto the road, and I exhaled like I'd left all my terror of the unknown on the side of the road. He slid his hand across the center console and took mine in his, his thumb caressing my sensitive skin.

"Sleep, please."

I closed my eyes and leaned my head against the headrest. Hoping everything he'd said to me wasn't a manipulation tactic or a lie but a genuine revelation of his feelings. Because I wasn't sure my heart could handle another destructive moment.

Jake

30

Six hours turned to seven, and seven turned to eight. She'd listened and took my advice, sleeping to gain her strength and, in turn, making the trip run smoother and faster.

"There are two bedrooms upstairs," I muttered to Charity and Max as I pulled into my driveway. "Sleep wherever you want."

"Finally. My back is killing me. These vehicles aren't meant for traveling," Charity said, stretching.

The sun dipped below the horizon before I'd pulled onto my street, and now the darkness crawled towards us like spirits from the underworld, escaping their hellish dwellings for the evening.

"How's the security here?" Max asked.

"Hopefully better than what you have in your castle, princess." I turned to Charity. "Don't take your grenades into my house."

"Aww." She feigned a pout, then succeeded when I narrowed my gaze. "Fine."

Adelaide stirred, jerking forward with a sharp inhale through her nose, followed by a muted whimper.

"We're home, sweets."

Max and Charity left us alone in the SUV as they grabbed their suitcases and made it inside. Hopefully to find a room and scamper off for the night.

Adelaide rubbed a deep indentation on her forehead from the car's sidewall. "How long did I sleep?"

"Sevenish hours."

We stepped out, and I grabbed our bags. "I have a phone call I need to make," I said as I dropped our luggage next to the door. "I'll be in a second. Get settled."

She nodded and looked around the living room as if it were her first time stepping inside my home... our home.

There was that word again.

I stepped back outside, shutting the front door, and called Alek.

"Hello."

"Hey, we're back."

"Any trouble?"

"Nothing that I couldn't handle," I said. "Did you go to her parent's home?"

"Yes, it's been settled."

"Dead?"

A major part of me prayed to God it was a bluff, but then I remembered who we were dealing with, and it shot the thought down faster than I could conjure happy thoughts.

"Yeah." He cleared his throat. "Shot to the head."

"*Fuck.*"

I sat on my steps and braced my elbow on my knee as I drove my hand through my hair. I clenched my jaw as emotions and memories I'd worked to suppress for fourteen years tickled my spine.

"The coroner picked them up. What do you need now?"

"If you could do the funeral arrangements, that'd be helpful."

"I'll get together with the funeral home and set things up. Does she want to pick things out?"

I shook my head even though he couldn't see me. "I think that would be too much for her. Just make it good for her."

"All right. Anything else?"

What would I have wanted my parents to have? I exhaled and rubbed the nape of my neck. "I'll let you know."

"Okay."

I hung up and dropped my head into my hands, running them down my face and scratching at the itchy beard that grew out all week. I didn't even recognize myself when I'd looked in the mirror.

Hoisting my exhausted body up from the steps, I walked back inside and found Adelaide sitting on the couch with a cheese stick in one hand and the bowl of applesauce she'd dipped her cheese in.

"That's... an interesting combination."

A small smile crossed her lips. "It's really good. I used to eat it all the time when I was a kid."

"Come on. I want to show you something." I held my hand out for her—something I'd noticed I'd been doing a lot lately. She shoved the rest of the cheese in her mouth with an extra dip of applesauce and stood.

"Where are we going?" She covered her mouth as she spoke around her food and took my hand with her other, following me down into the basement.

"You'll see."

This room was my sanctuary, one I'd not shared with anyone, including Becca.

"What's in there?"

"You'll see."

Slipping my hand from my pocket, I typed in my eight-digit code, ready to share this for the first time.

The door swung open on its well-oiled hinges, and I walked her inside the darkened room before flipping the switch on.

Green neon lights glowed from beneath the long three-man desk where two separate computer systems ran their searches, hunting for a man who was the key to all of this.

Two black chairs sat side by side, one for the more intense days of cat and mouse and the other for more relaxing days of strategic planning.

Five flat screen monitors covered the length of the table, along with two mounted overhead, all of which were interconnected, allowing me to work on multiple tasks at once.

Adelaide's eyes widened as she took it all in. "Holy shit."

"I want you to help me."

"With what?"

I squeezed her hand and brought her closer to the comfy black leather chair with lumbar support and armrests. Sitting her down, I turned her towards the computer screen.

"I want you to help me find them."

Taking the seat next to her, I moved the mouse, waking up the screens on the right.

I offered her a way of distraction.

I offered her a way of revenge—in a safer way without her putting her life in jeopardy.

I offered her a modicum of control in a world that offered her none.

"Why? I mean, I don't understand."

"They made the wrong move, Adelaide. Now we'll make a better one."

She shook her head, her chair turning side-to-side as she gripped the desk.

"Jake. No offense, but you're just a tech CEO. What are you going to do with a group of mercenaries that are trained to kill?"

Was there ever a right time to tell someone you were a broker for the criminal underworld?

Probably not.

"Let me worry about that. I want you to focus on finding out everything you can about them. I want their bank accounts, habits, and leader's name." As I listed my demands, I pointed to each finger. "I want to know who they're fucking, their sleep schedules, and their next targets."

And when we were done with recon, we'd sacrifice the pawn to kill the king.

"And what stops them from coming here, where they know we are, and shooting us?"

I leaned forward in my chair, my hands wrapping around her legs. My thumbs brushed her inner knees, and she shivered, raising goosebumps against her pale skin as I thought her question through.

She had a point, although I'd see them coming before anyone could break through here. You couldn't approach my home from any direction without an announcement hitting my phone. The lights in this room flickered to red if a door opened, and alarms sounded, and the lights flickered to blue if a window broke. The police had a five-minute response time if the alarm went off.

I stood and walked to the far wall, slid the wireless wall monitor to the side, and used a thirteen alpha-numerical passcode, opening up my vault behind it.

"Whoa," Adelaide said as she came up beside me.

"It'll take nine-hundred-thousand years to break this code to the safe room. We'd die of starvation before they could get inside."

The vault was fireproof, weatherproof, and impenetrable. It had its own ventilation system that ran on its own power source and a water filtration system. Should they decide to cut the electricity to the house, this room would still operate as if nothing ever happened.

It paid to be paranoid.

We stepped inside the safe room with a kitchenette, bed to the side, and a full bathroom in front of us.

I'd had three companies install this room, each one with a different layout, each one with different specs, capabilities, and sizes. Once one area was finished, I hired a new company until only one room remained. That room lay beyond the bathroom and now held three years' worth of rations for two individuals.

At the time I'd thought of this, it was for Becca and me, but now that she was staying with Alek, it was for Adelaide.

"This place is insane."

"I only showed you this because I want you to feel safe here. I'd never put you in harm's way. Ever." I swallowed the rising lump in my throat as I glanced at her belly. I'd never put either of them in danger. "Do you understand?"

She nodded as she ran her hands over one of the twin-sized beds. Her gaze wandered over the flat-screen TV, which was tied into the security system, then over to the kitchenette. "I understand."

"Good. Let's get started in the morning."

I put my arm out as I walked toward her, wrapped it around her shoulder as I came near, and took her out of the room, closing the vault behind us.

"What about Holeo?"

"We'll find him and let karma decide his fate."

Assuming that what she'd explained to me was true, he deserved whatever the hell came his way. You don't put your crew at risk.

"Why do you want me to help?"

"Because it'll be good for you." I led her out of the computer room and up the hall to mine. "We'll start early in the morning. The faster we get this done, the safer we'll all be."

"Okay."

"Until then, get some rest. It's going to be long days without caffeine."

She stopped and turned. "What do you mean 'no caffeine?'"

"Caffeine isn't good for the baby."

Adelaide scoffed and swiped her hands out in front of her like a referee calling shots. "I may be pregnant, but I'll be damned if you take a cup of coffee away from me. I'll stop the energy drinks, but I will not go without a cup of coffee."

"Even if it was for the health of our baby."

She sat on the edge of the bed and kicked her shoes off. The button on her pants came next. "Listen, if I don't wake up with some sort of caffeine, you won't be around to experience this bundle of joy. *Comprehendo Cap-ee-tan.*"

I chuckled as I shuffled forward, then grabbed her pants at her hips and jerked them down along with her panties. "Half and half," I said.

"You're not one of those daddies who goes overboard, puts padding on all the edges, controls what mommy eats, and buys only organic, are you?"

I picked her up and tossed her further up the bed, coming to land between her thighs. "The only thing organic I eat is between your legs." I ran my tongue between her lower lips and nipped her clit with my teeth. "All the other things are a 'wait and see' kind of moment."

She moaned as I licked her again, lapping her sensitive flesh with the flat of my tongue. If we didn't have a terrorist to destroy, I'd keep her in my bed from sun up to sun down, devouring every delectable inch of her body until she and I couldn't walk. Then I'd do it all over again the next morning.

"Jake. God."

My chest swelled as she issued my name like a seductive queen. Threading her hands in my hair, I pushed my tongue inside of her and fucked her. She raked her nails against my scalp and tensed her thighs against my ears as she came.

"*Fuck.*" Her breathless cries caused my balls to ache. I'd unload like a misfiring cannon into my jeans if I didn't get inside her.

"Hard and fast, okay?"

I rose above her and she nodded, giving me the okay to loosen the collar around my neck and dive into her with abandon.

Grabbing her hips, I flipped her over onto her stomach, pulled her ass into the air, and smacked her hard. She cried out, her fists clenched in the duvet. I'd kiss the red palm print marring her ass when I'd had my fill and not a second sooner.

I stripped my jeans as I bit her other ass cheek, spreading them as I dove in for another taste. Her juices coated my chin and lips, her arousal like silk on my tongue.

Pushing her knees together, I pressed the tip of my cock at her entrance, grabbed the headboard for stability, and slammed my way deep inside of her.

Adelaide curled in on herself, her face contorting as her mouth fell open. Helpless mewling filled my ears like a ravishing goddess.

"God, you feel so good."

She clamped around me, tightening as her rapid breaths halted mid-moan.

"Not yet, sweets."

If she came now, she'd finish me, and I wasn't ready to end this—to end the feel of her wrapped around me, her walls pulsing on my painfully hard cock. It was too good.

She released her breath in a huff as I gripped the headboard tighter and used her hips to bounce against me. My balls drew tight, sweat prickled my spine and the nape of my neck.

I reached for her, wrapping my hand around her throat, and pulled her back against my tattooed chest. "I'm ready for you now, sweets. Come on my cock like a good girl," I growled as I thrust into her. "Let me feel your pussy squeeze me." I pinched my thumb and forefinger against her jugular, cutting off the blood supply.

Wrapping my arm around her waist, I kept my other hand tight against her throat and powered into her with a need the likes of which I'd never experienced.

She whimpered through suppressed breaths as she brought her hand to the nape of my collar, her nails biting into my vertebra.

I staggered, sweat running down my spine, my injured thigh burning as though someone shoved a white-hot iron through it.. Her fingers wrapped around my wrist, pulling my hand free from her throat.

On a gasp, she screamed as she clenched tight around me.

I bent her over, my hand pressed between her shoulder blades, the other gripping her hip as I thrust into her. On the third deep plunge, I released all I had within her.

"You're like a sweet candy." I nibbled at her ear. "You know it's bad for you, but you can't help but indulge."

Adelaide laughed breathlessly. "Then you're like getting a tattoo. The allure is intoxicating, but once you're under the skin, it's impossible to get rid of it."

"I'm taking that as a compliment," I said, biting her shoulder. She collapsed to her belly, and I followed, keeping my cock fixed inside her.

"We keep falling asleep like this, and I'm gonna get a UTI or something."

I pulled her closer to me, tucking her ass against me. "Okay, just tonight then."

I'd make no promises because falling asleep with my dick inside her was the most intoxicating drug.

Our sweaty bodies stuck together, and I welcomed the feel of her. I closed my eyes. The drive home and into her had worn me out. Sleep consumed me before my heart rate settled back to normal.

Adelaide

31

I raised my arms above my head and turned my mouth into my arm as I yawned. "We've been going at it for hours. I need a break."

"Let's try one more time, okay?" Jake said, wiping the loose hair from his brow.

I groaned and leaned forward, placing my head inside my palms, my elbows against my knees. "Fine. But we're not getting in today."

"Try, try again."

"William Hickson? Really?"

"Well, aren't you well read?"

I snorted and grabbed the third Gatorade for the day while his incessant reminders to stay hydrated played in my mind. "No. The dude died like a hundred years ago, yet my English Lit teacher insisted we study him. That's the only thing I remember about him and his poem."

Guzzling my drink, I twisted the lid and set it back on its coaster. Because God forbid my bottle left a water stain on his immaculate desk. The man was more anal about things in his secret computer room. And the longer we spent in here, the more his OCD and paranoia smothered me.

"Maybe you should've paid more attention in school."

I snorted again. "So I could... what? Sit around and not use the education." I shook my head. "Besides, it's not like I didn't graduate with full honors and a scholarship."

"Because you hacked it."

"You know," I pointed at him and laughed. "I regret telling you that."

In the last five days since we'd been home, I'd divulged things to him I hadn't told anyone. The truth bug was out, and I enjoyed the freedom it equated.

"Only because I hold you accountable."

"Yeah," I sighed.

My gaze turned down, and my heart staggered in my chest. The smile on my face re-opened the festering wound of grief as a constant reminder that I shouldn't be joking around, smiling, or acting like life was okay. Because it wasn't. Today we'd put my parents to rest, and I hadn't even gotten dressed yet. I'd chosen to ignore it altogether and pretend as though it'd never happened.

Out of sight, out of mind.

But life didn't work that way. It had its subtle ways of throwing baroque reminders at me, and so did Jake. He wouldn't let me stuff it down until it consumed me.

"It's okay to smile, Adelaide," he said, as though he could sense my inner turmoil.

"No... it's not." I swallowed the stinging swarm in my throat. "We haven't even put them in the ground yet." I stared off beyond him toward the TV monitor that hosted several camera angles inside and outside of the house.

"Once you allow yourself to be happy, the healing process will begin. I promise."

Jake's promise of healing made it sound seamless, as though it were easy enough to hit the start button and begin. But how would someone know they'd started or not? Where was the measurement stick?

I turned to my computer screens with the Armenian-Swiss bank website taunting me.

We'd worked tirelessly for the past twenty-four hours to get into the account they'd used to pay Blackstone Tech. I'd hoped to have accomplished the task before the funeral, but that wasn't looking so hot.

"What time is it?"

"We still have another hour and a half until we need to be at the service. So how about this, go get ready, and if there's enough time left, you can try accessing the account before we leave. Sound good?"

I shook my head for the umpteenth time. "Sounds like a terrible plan." If I stood from this chair and searched for a black dress or anything forlorn,

I'd break down and never recover. Much like when Charity had to pick the bathroom lock and pull me out when Jake had left for 'errands' with Max.

"Adelaide, you will face this today. You'll regret it later if you don't."

I rolled my lips, wishing I'd put my lip ring back in after the heat stroke incident. "And what if I can't?" I whispered, my voice a pathetic broken mouse of a sound.

"I'll be by your side the entire time."

"How about we focus on getting ready first? *Hmm?*"

Jake stood from his chair and dragged me out of mine, voiding my choice in the matter.

Maybe that's what I needed—someone to force me to confront my fear, and right now, that was seeing them in a coffin and accepting this was real.

I forced a shaky breath as he pulled me from my chair and out of the room with berating thoughts pounding me down.

I'd done this to them, and there were no do-overs. No *respawning* and returning to home base. Life was a permanent mess; your choices were final, and the outcomes were devastating. I made the wrong move on the game board, and now I'd suffer for eternity because of it—and so would my parents.

All I wanted was to sit in the neon room with my computer screens in front of me, escaping the dimensions of my new reality, and find the men who destroyed my picture-perfect life.

But between the bouts of morning sickness, lack of sleep, and caffeine, I wasn't getting to do much of it. Jake had to pick up the slack.

"I really *can't* do this."

Sweat slicked my skin, leaving my palms a dewy mess and my brow beading with waves of hot and cold.

"You can."

"And what if they are there?"

I'd thought this question through long and hard ever since he told me his friend had taken care of all the arrangements. What's stopping them from wiping their hands clean of us and bombing the church like they did the school kids in Mexico?

"You'll never know. You focus on your family while I take care of everything else."

I stopped just outside his bedroom door. "And how am I supposed to ignore the elephant in the room?"

He glanced up the stairs, grabbed my arm, and pulled me through the door.

Jake's conversational skills outside closed doors dipped into the non-existent stage since Charity and Max came home with us.

"They need us, and taking you out in front of a hundred witnesses isn't exactly advantageous."

My sinuses burned as the tears formed in the corners of my eyes. "Really? You think they cared about that when they killed kids?" I yelled, pressing the side of my fists into his chest with grinding teeth.

He took hold of my wrists with his thumb and forefinger and squeezed the divot below my thumb and wrist bone, making me flinch.

"Why didn't you just kill them right there when you had the chance?"

He pulled me to him, and I buried my face against his hard chest, letting the tears soak into his graphic t-shirt.

"Because if I killed them, it wouldn't have changed the outcome. They're smart, but we're smarter. We'll find the leader, the real one, not the face of it all, and destroy him. Only then will we be safe."

"And what if we can't?"

He ran his hand down my hair, soothing me. "Failure isn't an option."

"But it's always a possibility."

"*Hmm*," he grunted, a low rumble beating my eardrums. "I bought you something for today."

He released me before disappearing inside the closet and came out holding a long black garment bag. He tossed it onto the bed and unzipped it.

Jake held up the modest, short-sleeved maxi dress with a rounded neck, and I nearly choked on the surreality of it all. The material hung down to the floor with inclined silver buttons running up the slit in the front to the hip with a nude-colored fabric beneath, hiding any skin the slit might've shown.

"This is for me?"

He nodded and gave me a warm smile that had my toes tingling and my aggravation melting off of me like ice on a hot summer's day. "I thought you'd want something to wear instead of one of my t-shirts."

"Jake, you didn't have to do that. It's beautiful." I fingered the wool dress with detailed stitch work. "But you know I'll never look at it or touch it again after today, right?"

"I figured as much." He laid it out on the bed and walked back into the closet, returning with a pair of short nude heels to match the peeking fabric beneath. "Do you want me to have Becca do your hair?"

Jake plopped the shoes down by the bed as I shook my head. "I think I'll put it in a bun. That's simple enough."

"Okay, just let me know if you need anything."

He turned towards the door. "Jake?" I wrapped my arms around him, trapping his arms beneath my hug. "Thank you. You have no idea how much you mean to me."

Jake turned in my arms, and with a delicate touch, he palmed my face and brushed his lips against mine, his tongue licking the seam of my lips. "And you have no idea what lengths I'd go to to keep you by my side."

I smiled and stood on my tiptoes, pressing my lips back to his for one more kiss before dressing for the most depressing day of my life.

His hand slid down my back and palmed my ass, pulling me against his hard length. My arms wrapped around his neck, needing that sexual therapy where he fucked me out of my mind and left me dazed and confused. It was better than any prescription on the market.

Jake pulled away from me, wiping his lip with his thumb. "Nice try." He adjusted himself and stalked out of the bedroom door, leaving me sexually frustrated and fucked in the head.

I exhaled through my nose and snatched the dress off the bed, taking it into the bathroom with me. Hanging the modest gown on a hook, I stripped down and stepped into the shower, turning the water on cold.

Deep down inside of me, there was a need for the numbness to consume me. If it weren't for this little bean growing in my belly, I'd pound back drink after drink until it did the job.

My parents would understand.

I braced my hand against the side of the tile as I bent over. Tears spilled from my eyes as if someone had turned the dial on full blast, my chest battling to contain the explosion inside of me.

Would this pain ever end? They say grief gets better over time, but how was that possible? I'd never speak to them again, hear their voice, or feel their loving arms wrap around me when I came upstairs.

How could I face their coffins, knowing I was why they were there? My knees buckled, and I collapsed to the chilly tiled floor as shivers wracked my body.

I couldn't do this.

The air in my chest stuck in my throat, suffocating me until spots burned my vision. The space between my shoulder blades pinched like a knife twisting back and forth without reason—just because it could.

I drew my knees to my chest and hid my face as I wrapped my arms around my legs, holding them close as I wept. Soon the lack of oxygen would have me sinking into the darkness, and I could avoid all of this.

Footsteps drew near. The canter of his step, the scuff of his heel at the end of his second step was a dead giveaway, but still, I wept, hiding my face from view, my ankles crossed at my butt, my knees held tight.

Please don't force me to do this.

"Adelaide. Sweets." His soft, sympathetic tone had my shoulders shaking harder. "Come on."

Jake turned off the icy water that had numbed my skin and chilled me to the core, depriving me of the much-needed emptiness that would get me through the day.

His fingertips wrapped around the backs of my upper arms as he hauled me to my feet and lifted me out of the walk-in shower. Grabbing a towel from the hook, he wrapped the plush material around me and rubbed me dry while I stared at the expensive flooring.

"I'll be with you every step of the way."

I nodded as the words caught in my throat as my breath did moments ago, only now my body betrayed me by not giving me the one thing I could use... unconsciousness.

It forced me to face my deepest fear, regret, anguish, and sadness. This was too much for a nineteen-year-old to handle.

Jake tossed the towel after having dried my pliant body, then pulled the dress over my head and down my hips without underwear or bra. Not that I needed either. The dress held my breasts in place, and it's not like anyone would know I didn't have panties on.

He pulled my hair out from the back of the dress, letting the wet stringy strands hang around my shoulders.

"You look beautiful."

A small twitch lifted my lips—hollow and without substance.

He drew me out of the bathroom, a comb in hand, and sat me on the bed.

Jake sat behind me, running the comb down my hair with slow and precise downward motions, careful not to tug on my scalp. I'd welcome that pain. It might even send a twinge between my legs, which I'd also welcome.

Once he finished combing through my long splotchy black locks, his fingers brushed against my scalp from the top of my skull, taking turns on each side of my head until he was down to the very end. He tied off my hair, preventing it from unraveling.

"Where did you learn to French braid?"

Jake ran his hand down the plait, then finished with his fingertips against my spine until they fell away at the mattress. Shivers raced across my flesh.

"I had to learn when Becca became my responsibility."

"How old were you when your parents died?" I cleared my throat, the squeeze tight like a noose.

"Fifteen."

I hung my head. "When did it not hurt anymore?"

Jake exhaled and pulled me into him. "I never had the opportunity to grieve for my parents. Becca and I didn't have anyone, and I wasn't about to get separated in foster care." He ran his knuckle down my cheek before grabbing a heel from the floor. He placed my foot inside the nude heel, then braced it on his black suit slacks.

I'd been so busy inside myself that I hadn't noticed his suit. Black shirt, tie, jacket, and slacks. The only thing out of place was the shine of his black dress shoes.

"So, what did you do?"

He worked the strap around my ankle. "I learned how to hustle. I was already good at hacking. At that age, I'd hacked the police department to rid the world of Ruby's existence, so I learned how to make money doing it. Then I started selling fake IDs, and I found out how much I liked the criminal world."

I shook my head, suppressing a laugh. Jake... a criminal. "I can't see a straight-laced man such as yourself as a criminal."

"There's still so much about me you don't know, and when the time is right, I'll share it with you."

My stomach flipped into a sickness. "What *exactly* does that mean?"

A knock sounded at the door, drawing his attention away from my finished second strap. "We'll discuss it later."

He stood from his crouched position, then held his hand out for me.

Jake took a shriveled-up mourning girl and turned me into a beauty before I comprehended what had happened.

"Are you ready?"

I hung my head. Couldn't I just cave in on myself right now and become a figment of everyone's imagination?

"No."

He tucked his hand in mine and patted it. "Just hold my hand. I'm here for you." He squeezed. "Okay, sweets?"

I nodded as he dragged me towards our bedroom door.

Becca stood on the other side in a modest black dress that hung down to mid-calf and sleeves to her wrists. In one hand, she carried a black quilted purse with a silver chain for the handle. Unlike my swooping one, her neckline hugged the base of her throat, where a dainty platinum chain hung, contrasting the blackness of the dress behind it.

How could one look so elegant going to a funeral?

She gave me an empathetic smile.

"The limo's here."

Jake

32

There were cars as far as the eye could see crowding the parking lot and side of the street, showing the world just how important the deaths of these two individuals were. But there was one in particular that had me clenching my fist, and there wasn't anything I could do about it. No sense in drawing attention to them and letting Adelaide know they'd arrived, just as she thought they would.

A woman a few inches shorter than Adelaide rushed towards us. Her black dress, which hung to her knees, and curled red hair wavered as she weaved through the crowd. My body tensed, and I wrapped a protective arm around her waist to pull her into me.

"Adelaide?" She placed her hand on Adelaide's arm as she studied her. "I thought that was you. I almost didn't recognize you with that black hair of yours."

"Hi, Auntie Mable."

My hold on her waist loosened as Mable pulled her in for a hug.

"Where have you been? I've been trying to get a hold of you all week since the police broke the news." She pulled back and gripped her shoulders. "This is horrible. Just horrible. I'm so sorry, dear."

"Thanks."

Adelaide wiped the forming tears from her eyes with the back of her hand as I grabbed the travel pack of tissues from my pocket and handed them to her.

"Thank you," she whispered.

"Who's this gentleman?"

"He's um..."

I reached forward, extending my hand, and Mable shook it. "Jake."

"It's nice to meet you. Although I wish it were under better circumstances."

"Likewise." I nodded.

"I'm going to find my—"

"Addy. Oh my God. Addy." Monica rushed forward, squeezing Mable out of the way, and wrapped her arms around Adelaide's neck as she rocked her side to side. "Where have you been? What did you do to your hair..."

"Who is that?" Becca whispered as Monica blasted her with question after question, drawing irritation right up to my tightened collar.

"Her best friend."

"Gotcha. This is a huge turnout."

I nodded. "They were honest people." I rubbed my freshly shaved jaw and pressed my hand into Adelaide's back. "Let's go find our seats. The pastor is taking the podium."

Adelaide nodded and wiped her eyes with her tissue, smiling as her friend's mouth ran a million miles a minute. I'd stop her if it weren't for the rare smile she'd put on Adelaide's face.

"I'm going to sit," Monica said, sympathy drawing her brows into a wrinkle between her eyes. "We'll catch up after. Okay?"

Adelaide's feet stopped moving at the doorway, the vacant aisle giving her a wide view of the double caskets at the front.

"I can't go in there."

And just like that, the joy she'd had from seeing her friend died on her lips. She stiffened her spine as I pressed her forward. "I can't see them like that." She shook her head, tears drizzling down her freckled cheeks. "I just can't."

She spun, attempting to escape, but I held her firm and brought her to the entrance. "You can, and you will." I pressed my lips to her cheek, her salty tears spreading across my tongue as I licked them from my bottom lip. "Look at me, sweets."

I took her wet, tear-stained face into my hands and forced her gaze to mine. "You are a strong, brave woman, and although this may seem impossible and like your life is ending, it's not. You can do this. Take one step at a time and put your parents to rest." I wiped the solitary tear that fell with my thumb as she nodded. "Today is the day to say goodbye, ask for forgiveness if you feel the need, and tell them how much you love them. Give yourself what I wish I could." I pressed my lips to her forehead, circled my arms around her shoulders, and drew her into me. "Whenever you're ready."

Adelaide sniffled as she nodded, bringing the tissue to her nose as she hugged me tight and then pulled away. "Okay."

"You can do this, Adelaide," Becca said, startling me.

I'd nearly forgotten her standing beside us, soaking in the scene. When Adelaide cried, it drowned out the world around us until only she and I stood together. No one else existed at that moment in time.

I could've told her pretty lies and let her believe this would be easy, but the result would be the same. I'd be on my knees picking up her broken pieces as she wandered around our home like a decaying porcelain doll.

She took two steps forward and breached the church's opened doors towards the two oak caskets waiting in the front, her shoulders shaking as her head hung.

I swallowed through a tightness forming in my throat as I imagined my parents ahead, not hers.

This may be harder than I thought.

Adelaide

33

A heavy dizziness formed in my temples as I took a step, then another, and another. My limbs tingled as my heart throbbed in my chest. My parents' closed caskets sat before me with an array of flowers that were all wrong.

Those weren't her favorites. They were dark, with tight roses twisted together to form a wreath of sorts. She would've wanted something yellow to make people happy.

My father hated flowers. He said they were weeds that took away from the beauty of his green lawn.

Daddy would've never approved of such a thing.

People lined the pews, their weeping sniffles echoed around the chamber, their swollen gazes fixed upon me as I walked down the aisle.

This was all wrong.

"This seat, sweets."

Jake's hand pressed into my back, pushing me towards the front pew from the center of the aisle just before I reached out to touch the shining glossy wood.

"What the hell did I do to deserve this?" I whispered, shaking my head. "What did they do to deserve this?"

This wasn't right.

It wasn't fair.

Jake sat me down, my body numb, my hands hanging limply at my side. Agony paralyzed me from the inside out, burning a hole through my gut and searing my flesh with anguished sobs. If it weren't for him, I wasn't sure I'd be able to find my way or make my feet move.

A man in a long white robe placed his hands on the podium, his fingers wrapping around the sides like they were his anchor. A purple cloth hung around his neck down to his waist and would sway side to side as he moved.

"Brothers and sisters, we are gathered here today..."

I covered my mouth and wept in silence as he spoke about the sanctity of life and how the blessed are only resting from their work in God.

Jake wrapped his hand in mine and rested it on his muscular thigh. His other hand covered the one he held. His thumb caressed my wrist with a welcomed distraction.

I pulled in on myself, tugging my conscious self into the deep recesses of my mind until I'd lost myself in thoughts that weren't of death and sadness.

Waist-high grass slipped through my fingertips as I walked through a field. The bright sun burned my eyes, making me squint at the illusion forming before me. A vast ocean in the middle of a meadow—out of place in the scene like me. I walked up to my hips in the crisp, cool waters, the gentle waves lapping at my belly as little fish gathered around me. The sky darkened, casting violent shadows into the water surrounding me.

Something nudged my elbow, pulling me away from my internal sanctuary with a gasp.

"Adelaide, did you want to say something?"

"*Huh?*"

"The pastor wants to know if you want to say a few words?"

I glanced up, first to Jake, then to the caskets up front, and shook my head.

Auntie Mable stood from her seat, her now husband beside her, and walked towards me with a paper in her hand.

"Adelaide, come stand with me."

My stomach bottomed out as I stared at her hand, the little gold ring I'd seen a million times, around her ring finger. I shook my head as I pictured myself standing in front of everyone, their eyes spearing me in the chest.

"Come say a few words about your parents."

My breaths staggered as I looked at Jake and back to her wrinkled, uncalloused hand. I couldn't go up there.

I stood, wrenching my hand from Jake's, and ran down the aisle—leaving my aunt standing dumbfounded.

My heart clenched, pressing down on my lungs as shocked gasps and murmurs followed me. I burst through the door, throwing them wide until they smashed into the wall behind them with a thunderous boom.

The strength I'd gathered to race out of there dwindled, and I nearly crumbled down the cemented steps had it not been for the metal railing in the center. I used the rail at the bottom of the steps to catapult myself around and sprinted up the inclined sidewalk in unforgiving heels.

"Adelaide, wait," Jake shouted behind me.

I ran until my lungs gave out, leaving me panting on the side of the dirty street, the church doors still in view. He rushed up behind me as I bent over, clutching my chest, searching for the air not given freely, for the peace I sought. My hands trembled as I collapsed on the sidewalk, stained with blackened spots made of chewing gum. "How did it come to this, Jake? How can this happen? They didn't deserve this."

He sank beside me, balancing on his haunches, and rubbed my shoulders. "Some things are not made for us to understand."

"Don't give me that blanket bullshit answer," I snapped.

"It's true, Adelaide. You'll have to learn how to handle the shit end of the stick sometimes."

A pinched nerve fired off between my shoulder blades as I drew in a deep, ragged breath. Was that what I needed to hear instead of some syrupy sweet answer telling me life would be okay with time? Jake knew not to gloss over their death and how it broke me down to nothing but a grain of sand washed out to sea—flailing around without control.

"What do you need from me, Adelaide?"

I shook my head. It was such an impossible answer to give. What did I need? How about my parents?

My home.

My best friend.

Jake...

"I need you to help me feel..." I sniffled and glanced up at him. "To feel normal."

He hung his head and sighed before looking back at me, his longer strands on top brushing over his forehead. "Where would you like to go?" He offered his hand, and I took it, letting him hoist me up to my feet as I wiped the tears with the back of my hand.

Away from here. Far away, where I could disappear into a crowd of faces. Some called it purgatory, but to me, it was home. It was the numbness experienced somewhere between absolute happiness and pure torture. That's where I wanted to be.

I shook my head. "Anywhere but here."

He turned his palm in mine and walked me down the street, the incline steeper than I remembered.

Auntie Mable stepped out of the church doors with Becca and Monica beside her. She glanced at us and pinched her brows with a snarl on her upper lip.

Jake jerked me off the sidewalk and gave Becca a slight tip of his head to the left. She followed his direction, and I tightened my grip on his hand as he led us to the other side of the street.

Auntie Mable stepped down the stairs with fury in her eyes.

"Don't say a word," he said as he shielded my body from her marching towards us.

"What was that all about, Adelaide?" Auntie Mable crossed her arms over her chest as she tapped her foot on the ground.

"Adelaide has taken the death of her parents very hard." His stern but calm voice had her gaping like a fish and rearing back.

"We all lost someone here. I lost my brother and parents, and I've never acted this way."

I opened my mouth to reply when Jake squeezed my hand.

"I'm glad you could handle your grief in such a constructive manner, Ms. Leaver. However, Adelaide is allowed to grieve in her own way. If you don't like that, it's best to step back until your emotions have simmered down."

Monica glared at Auntie Mable as she walked past her and hugged me. "Are you okay?"

I nodded, swallowing hard as I glanced around at the gathering crowd.

What have I done?

Jake's tempered tone left my pulse thrumming in my ears like a drum about to go to war. I hid behind him with Monica's arms wrapped around me like a cowering child, afraid of the consequences.

"This is the problem with society these days," Becca said as she looked down at my aunt. "You have a certain expectation of what people are supposed to look like as they process their grief. No one should have to sit pretty and grieve. Shame on you and your judgmental friends."

My mouth fell as Becca spoke to my aunt. I'd never heard her say anything to anyone that wasn't kind and respectful. She was the good-natured one, in contrast to Jake.

Auntie Mable's ears turned crimson, matching her rosy cheeks as she adjusted her stance. "I'd... I'd like to s-speak to Adelaide. I don't even know who you p-people are." She turned her shoulder slightly as though she'd garnered courage and lifted her chin, snubbing her nose at us.

"You know who I am," Monica said. "And what you're doing is gross. Especially on a day like today."

"And it doesn't matter who we are. You won't be speaking with her today." Jake twisted his gaze to mine. "You two get her in the car."

Monica nodded and rubbed her hand up and down my arm as we followed Becca to the blacked-out limo with a driver holding the door open.

"Thank you, Monica. For coming and standing up for me."

"She's a witch. Don't listen to her."

I glanced back. Jake stood a foot away from Auntie Mable, her face pale and stricken, as though he'd threatened to kill her cat.

"I'm going to get back in there and tell everyone what a cunt she is and how you need more time," she chuckled, which brought a smile to my face.

"Thank you."

"Anytime. But *uh...* you'll need to pick up your phone if you need backup." She smiled and gave me another hug.

"I'll send you my new phone number."

"See ya."

I gave her a saddened wave as I climbed inside the limo and sat next to the window, watching Jake's lips moving and my aunt's gaunt face tremble.

"What's he saying to her?" I asked Becca, who slid in beside me.

She leaned over and peered out the window. "I imagine he's explaining how wrong she is, and if she doesn't want to ruin a relationship with the only blood she has left, it's best to leave you alone for a while."

"You think so? She seems a little pale for that."

"It's something I'd wished he'd say, but knowing Jake, he's probably threatening her."

The blood washed from my face from the confirmation I'd been afraid of.

"I'm kidding," she said, patting my arm. "He's just talking to her, that's all."

I guess it didn't matter. Auntie Mable would form her opinion all the same, and I'd be lucky if we held a relationship after the funeral, anyway.

It's not like we were close.

Aside from the occasional get-together and me being the flower girl at her weddings, we didn't have anything in common, and we certainly didn't talk to each other outside of family events.

Jake spun on his heel, leaving her standing like a stone, and entered the limo. Becca slid over to the other leather bench seat, making room for Jake.

"What did you say?"

He slid in next to me and pulled me against him after shutting the door.

"I told her if she ever brought up this moment again, she'd never have a relationship with her niece or great niece or nephew. I'd see to it." He kissed the top of my head, and Becca's eyes widened.

"Why would you..." She plopped her hand into her lap, looked away from us, and then back. "Are you..." Her brows pinched together, then widened as her eyes grew larger. "Oh, my God. Wait..." Becca held her hands up in front of her as if she were stopping traffic. "Oh, my God. Are you pregnant?"

I sunk in my seat a little further and closed my eyes tight. We hadn't agreed to tell anyone. In fact, it was the elephant in the room we sort of ignored, except when my insecurities got the better of me.

"She is."

"Well, that explains some things."

My closed eyes stung with tears as I focused on a small meadow with spring flowers bursting through the ground with rebirth.

Nausea swirled in my belly, and my body tensed as I waited for her to say how awful he was for getting me pregnant at such a young age or how we'd never make it. Uncharacteristic for Becca, but I braced for it all the same.

"She's had some morning sickness, but that's it."

"This must be even harder for you."

I sniffled and wiped my tears again with the back of my hand, thanking God I didn't put on makeup.

It *was* hard.

I'd never get to pick up the phone and call my mother for advice on the nasty morning sickness plaguing me or the anxiety that had doubled since I'd found out. But Jake made it easier. In fact, I couldn't take my eyes off of him some days.

The way he walked or sat in a chair with his broad shoulders squared and intimidating. How he'd hang his pants low on his hips, teasing me with that V-shaped muscle that disappeared into his waistband, or even the way he moved the mouse on his computer. I'd become infatuated with him.

But mostly, it was the way he held me when I wept.

I sat up and used the tissue to wipe my nose. "Thank you."

Becca tilted her head.

"For sticking up for me. I wouldn't have been able to talk sense into her."

"There's no talking to someone who thinks grief should have a uniform reaction. You did nothing wrong," Jake said. "Except run away from me when I told you to stop."

A small smile spread across my lips. The limo lurched forward. "Where are we going?"

"We'll drop Becca back off at Alek's, and then I'll take you home."

"Are you staying?"

He nodded. "I'm not going anywhere, sweets." He gripped my hand, resting in my lap, and pulled it to his.

I crossed my legs at the ankles, the heels a hindrance but comfortable, and leaned against his hard shoulder. I couldn't wait to get this dress off, sit in normal clothes, eat normal food, and watch TV.

Do normal things on this abnormal day.

The minutes ticked on like hours until we arrived at a modern two-story home with some fake grass in the front and a bright red door with a wreath hanging in the center.

"This is their home?"

"Yeah, it's new. He had everything moved in while she was in the hospital with the baby," Becca said. "It's nice. You should come see."

I sat forward, ready to get out, but faltered.

"Just a peek."

Becca moved to the edge of her bench seat with a smile and waited for the driver to open the door before sliding.

"Why is she staying with them?" I leaned in and whispered.

"It's safer than her apartment right now. And Liz enjoys having Becca around."

I followed Becca to the front door and walked in with Jake behind me, his hand placed low on my back.

"We're back."

A distant wailing baby screamed in one of the back rooms as muffled spoken words drifted through the tall foyer, which opened up into a living room.

"We? Who's *we?*" Alek asked.

The intimidating, hulking man with a smoking skull tattooed into the back of his hand stepped out of a back room with a half-naked baby whose arms flailed in the air, followed by a woman fixing the top of her shirt strap.

"Hey," Jake said.

"I thought—"

"We came to see the baby," Jake said through clenched teeth.

Was he upset? Why?

"Perfect timing. She's just been fed and needs to be burped."

"And dressed," Becca said. "She can't be naked. No wonder she's crying."

Becca took the crying baby in her arms and cuddled it to her chest as she gently bounced while patting its back.

"She spit up, and we were changing her," the woman said.

So this was the couple I'd taken a picture of at the ice cream parlor. It's no wonder why Jake was so furious when he saw that.

"Liz, this is Adelaide," Jake said, interrupting her grumblings.

"Nice to meet you."

I gave her a tight-lipped smile and a small jerk of a wave as Becca walked toward me.

"And this is Hannah—who we're really here for," she said, lowering her voice as she came closer.

The baby quieted in her arms, and she took hold of the tiny hand and moved it up and down in time with her soft, bouncing knees.

I leaned over and took in the raven hair she must've got from her father.

Liz peered over Becca's shoulder with a small yellow blanket for her to wrap the baby in.

"Well, since you're here, I'm going to take a nap."

"Okay," Becca said as she took the blanket from Liz, then spread it out on the couch and swaddled the baby. "Do you want to hold her?"

I looked back at Jake. Was she talking to me? "Me?"

"Yes, you."

"Can I talk to you for a minute?" Alek said to Jake.

He nodded as Becca put the baby in my arms. "I'll be right back." He kissed the top of my head as he walked outside with Alek and shut the sliding glass door behind them.

"They're so secretive..."

I shrugged as I walked with careful steps to the fluffy loveseat and sat with the newborn in my arms.

Her large dark eyes looked around while her milk-stained tongue darted in and out of her opened mouth.

"She's sweet, isn't she?"

"Yeah," I sighed, afraid of any loud noise that might set her off into a screaming fit.

"I can't believe you're going to have one of your own."

My heart jumped in my chest as I studied her tiny wrinkled lips and dimpled chin.

Me either.

34

A lek's tired eyes watched the swirling amber liquid in his cup as he poured himself a full glass of scotch while I sat across from him in a wicker chair.

"Not getting much sleep?"

"No. She's got colic or something."

What the hell was colic?

"What did you want to talk about?"

"I want to call it quits. Go legit."

My stomach flipped. How would Luca take this information, or any of our other sellers, for that matter?

"Have you talked to Tonk?"

He shook his head. "Not yet. I've had my hands full."

"Is she the reason?" I tipped my head towards the floor-to-ceiling windows, where Adelaide sat with the baby in her arms. My chest seized. Tightening around me as I watched her nuzzle the baby.

That'd be us at the end of the year, which sent a cold sweat dripping down my back.

"Partly."

"And the other part?"

I took the glass he handed out and sipped it. The burning liquor swirled around my tongue like a fire tornado before swallowing it.

"There isn't a reason for us to continue. I have a family now, we have a more than successful business, and the risk is just too great to continue."

I rested my elbow on the armchair, took a full mouth of scotch, and held it, relishing the burn before gulping. Wincing, I adjusted my leg, easing the pressure off the wound I'd periodically forget was there.

It wouldn't be all that bad to stick to our business, not take the risks life afforded us before these women came and turned everything upside down.

"And when would we do this?"

He shook his head, taking a seat across from me. "As soon as we can. Why not now? We don't have another job lined up."

I glanced back at Adelaide, who stared at the baby in her arms. A gentle smile across her lips ripped my beating heart out of my chest.

Damn.

This girl had me by the balls, and I liked it.

But how would life be without the darkness surrounding us? To step out into the light and bury our past behind us—to walk among everyday citizens and be one of them.

It was plausible.

"I have a job to do before we do."

"The mercenaries?"

I nodded. "They were at the funeral today."

"That's pretty ballsy."

My shoulders rose as I scoffed. "It's something."

"So, what's the plan with them?"

It was already in the works, but it would take some time—Rome and all.

"Straight out of John Boyd's playbook."

Alek crossed his ankle over his knee and rolled his shoulders as he relaxed into his chair. "We want to take the long route?"

"I don't think it'll take long with us working together."

"You don't think they'll see it coming?"

I laughed. "They made a deal with me because they're desperate. They can't find Holeo because they're inferior, technologically speaking."

A fact that brought about the giddiest sensation inside. We had the upper hand and could digitally destroy everything they worked so hard for.

If we couldn't win at hand to hand, we'd start with disconnecting them from their allies, taking all their means of resources, then drive them into hiding.

A man will wither and decay when disconnected from allies and society.

"So then what?"

"We have to make sure they regret ever threatening me and mine."

"And you think we can pull this off?"

I guzzled back the rest of the liquor and stood from the wicker chair. "Without a doubt in my mind."

"When do we begin?"

I placed the cup in the outside sink. "It's already begun. Now we wait and see." I waved my fingers in the air like I used to do when I was a stupid teenager. "I'm Merlin, remember?"

Alek chuckled and swallowed the rest of his contents as he rose to his feet and followed me inside.

"Let's go." I ticked my head towards the door when Adelaide turned her gaze to me. A bright happiness shone on her face, her smile beaming. That wasn't an emotion I expected to see today. The baby lay sleeping in her arms as she cuddled Hannah to her chest, making my stomach swirl.

If we survived all of this, that would be us, and she'd hold my baby with a look of love that rivaled God.

"Do you want to hold her?" Adelaide kept her red-rimmed eyes on me as she swept her tongue over her bottom lip in a move so innocent yet it caused my dick to harden against my slacks.

I shook my head. "No."

I'd never held a baby before, and something about their tiny bones had me cringing. Not to mention, the first child I'd hold would be my own.

Her freckles popped out on her cheeks as they reddened with a look I couldn't decipher. She dropped her gaze to the babe, then handed her off to Becca.

"Thank you. This was a good idea."

"You're welcome." Becca positioned the baby in her arms. "I'm sorry about today, sweetie. If you ever need someone to talk to about it, come to me. Okay?"

Adelaide nodded. Her sadness renewed.

Goddammit.

I wrapped my arm around her shoulders and walked her out of the house and to the limo.

"Did it help?" I asked when we got situated inside, her thigh brushing against mine.

"Yes," she said in a hushed tone, her hand resting in her lap.

Would I be a selfish bastard if I took a piece of her today?

Definitely.

"Good." I grabbed her hand and brought it to my lips, kissing her knuckles one by one. "I'd do anything to help you, Adelaide."

"Anything?"

"Within reason." My tongue flicked out against her palm, and she gasped, her plump lips parting as she gazed at me through her thick lashes.

Her long leg slipped over my lap as she pulled her dress to her waist and let it bunch around her hips. "Is this within reason?"

My God.

I grabbed her around the back of her neck with a fierce hold and drew her into me, ravishing her lips with a fervent hunger.

Her tongue slipped across my lips, tickling them with light flicks, as she ground her hips against my hard length pressing against my pants. The vixen slid off my lap with a devious glint in her eyes and settled between my legs, her hands resting on my belt buckle as if she were asking for permission to take her sadness, guilt, and frustrations out on my dick.

"Don't tease me, Adelaide. If you want my cock, take it out."

Her fingers worked on my buckle and zipper as she worried her lip until I was certain she'd break the soft skin.

My cock pulsed with the thought of her lips wrapped around me. I brushed my knuckle down her cheek and rested my hand under her chin, guiding her gaze to look at me as she reached inside my opened pants and pulled out my hardened cock. "Open your mouth and put me on your tongue."

Her silky lips wrapped around my head, and I sucked in a gasp.

Adelaide's wet warmth spread down my shaft and encompassed my balls as she moved further down.

"God, look at you. You're perfect."

I twisted her braid in my fist and kept my other on her chin as she guided my length to the back of her throat while the corners of her lips stretched over my length. I'd go for a repeat performance like the first night I brought her home after our date when I told her she was mine and there was no escaping.

My cock buzzed as she hummed, the tip too close to the source. "You're a dream, sweets."

I tugged on her braid and forced her down deeper until she gagged. Only then did I pull her up for air with a groan. Once she had her fill, I pushed her back down and pumped her back and forth until I couldn't handle it.

I needed more.

Pausing mid-stroke, I twisted her body and straddled her chest. The back of her head rested on the bench while I kept my cock lodged in her throat.

"I'm gonna give you every last drop, sweets. Don't waste it. Understand?" I braced myself, then unwound her braid.

She nodded with her lips stretched around the base of my dick.

"That's my girl."

Wrapping my fingers around her hair, I used it to keep her head pinned to the bench and pumped my cock into her ready mouth as she closed her eyes and placed her hands on my thighs.

Sharp prickles of heat spilled down my spine like a cactus rolling across each vertebra. Sweat beaded against my forehead and tickled its way down my brow.

"Open your eyes and watch."

Her eyelids fluttered open, and she sucked my soul into her deep green gaze, holding it hostage by my command. She made me lose my mind. And with my sanity on the line, I pushed into her mouth and deep into her throat.

Adelaide ripped her head to the side, her high-pitched whimpers and heavy gasps all red flags I wasn't about to ignore, especially when her nails bit into my thighs. But this was what she demanded of me. And I was the selfish jerk who would do anything to make sure she got what she wanted, how I wanted it.

I caressed her cheek with my thumb, a string of saliva still connecting us. "All done?"

She shook her head, and I patted her cheek with enough force to elicit a response but not enough to hurt her. "I need you to tell me you're okay and want more, sweets."

Adelaide turned her head back to me and opened her mouth, her wet tongue making my cock pulse in my hand. I tapped my cock against it, the wet slap tightening my balls.

God, she was nothing short of perfect.

"Use me."

A wicked grin ripped across my face as I pushed a button on the roof of the limo. "Drive around." I released it and looked back down at her. "You have no idea what you're asking, but let's not spoil the surprise."

"Stop teasing me, Jake," she said, glancing up at me with those devilish eyes as she flicked the tip of her tongue across her lips.

"Oh, Adelaide," I sighed, taking her chin between my fingers. "Let's fuck that attitude from your mouth."

She jutted forward and licked her tongue along the smooth ridge of my cock, leaving a trail of slick warmth. She'd be the death of me, just as I thought before I had my first taste of her. And now that I had, I was addicted without needing rehab. Not that I wanted one. I'd happily die hooked on her. She was a drug that was worth the risk.

"Show me how wet you are, sweets. Show me how much you like my cock in your mouth."

Her hand snaked between us as she lifted her dress, making me jealous she could feel her silky-smooth folds while I'd have to wait.

"That's a good girl. Let me see." I glanced between us as she raised her glistening fingers to my lips and slipped them into my mouth. I groaned as my tongue stroked between her fingers, my teeth holding her in my mouth as I devoured her essence and drove my cock past her lips.

I bound my hand around her wrist and withdrew her fingers. "Touch yourself, sweets." Her slurping, wet gurgles drove me deeper until my swollen head knocked the back of her throat. I drew back slowly. "I want to hear you scream around my cock."

Saliva dribbled down the side of her mouth as her shoulder moved against the inside of my leg, her fingers working her clit. Her brows pulled together in a tight wrinkle between her eyes, her jerky movements matching mine as we drew near together.

Fuck. I couldn't hold out much longer.

Her muffled cries pulled me into a deep trance where it was only her and me in this limo of death, driving around town, no one the wiser. Her mouth popped open, and sloshing echoed around us as I plowed through the saliva pooling in her throat.

A high-pitched whimper bled through and cut my heart to shreds as her legs spasmed, causing her body to shake against my calves. I gave two more deep thrusts, her orgasm causing a violent shiver beneath me.

My balls drew tight against my body with a deep ache rivaling any need I've ever had. I braced my hand on the leather seat in front of me as my cum spurt into her mouth.

"You're worth everything and then some." My cock twitched, scraping against her teeth. As I drew out, my cum dribbled down her chin. "Be a good girl." I ran my thumb over it and popped my cum into her mouth. "And clean up your mess."

Her lips wrapped around my thumb and sucked, hollowing her cheeks, her tongue flicking against me.

Devious vixen.

I'd only just cum, and already I was hard again, ready to pound into her.

She glanced up at me as I dug my fingers into her cheeks and kissed her bruised lips with renewed hunger. My briny tang on her tongue, evidence of my unforgiving hunger.

Adelaide's tongue swirled as she sat up and pushed her dress over her hips.

"Where do you think you're going?" I said, breaking away with a breathless hiss.

"I thought—"

"You thought I'd get my fill of you so easily?"

She nodded, biting her bottom lip as I tucked myself back into my pants.

"I only had a sample, Adelaide." I slid down her body and pushed the end of her expensive dress over her face. "Lay still while I devour you."

I dove between her thighs and ran my tongue between her wet seam before nibbling her swollen clit.

Her gasp drove me into a frenzy, licking and sucking with determination as I dipped two fingers between her folds and dove deep inside her.

"Such a sweet pussy, Adelaide. You taste so good."

I spat on her clit and ran the flat of my tongue over it.

If only she could see how much her body had blood rushing to places that should be taking a break right now. She drove her hands into my hair and pulled as her body quivered around my fingers, rubbing against the small rough space inside of her with a come here motion.

"Jake. Oh, God." Her breaths escaped with sharp, exhaled hisses. "I think..."

Yes. I wanted her on my tongue—her essence, her flavor until I'd become drunk on her very being.

I moved faster, curling my fingers, licking her harder until her thighs slammed against my head and her muffled screams and the pumping in my ears were all the melody I fed off of.

My fingers lodged between her knees and pried her stiff knees apart, freeing myself from her succubus' grasp.

Pulling the end of her dress from her face, I latched onto her lips, making her taste her deliciousness.

A smile ripped across her face as I pulled away.

"There's that smile."

"I can't move."

"Don't tell me I broke you?"

She laughed like someone strummed the strings of an exotic instrument whose harmony hadn't been heard in centuries.

"No. But my muscles are like liquid, and I'm pretty sure you'll have to carry me inside."

"I think I can manage that." I pressed the button on the roof again. "Take us home."

This limo boxed us in, hindering my ability to exact the right amount of—

A whimper hit me like a sucker punch to the gut. Adelaide had curled her knees up to her chest on the floor, her hands covering her face, which only amplified her newfound sobs.

Fuck.

"Come here, sweets."

I sunk to my ass beside her and gathered her into my arms.

Her breaths hitched with rapid repetition as she hid her grief from me. "I'm such a terrible daughter."

My stomach twisted in knots at her admission. How many times have I thought the same thing about myself? I should've prevented it. I shouldn't have run like a coward. But life had a way of working itself out, and I finally saw the bigger picture. She'd see her need to grieve in her own way as imperative for her healing.

"Who told you that?"

"I just..." Her breath faltered like it stopped in her chest before escaping. "I feel guilty."

"Why?" I dipped down, cupping her cheek. "Because you didn't stay for the funeral?"

She nodded.

"Funerals aren't meant for the dead, Adelaide. They are for the living. And you don't need to be there to honor your parents."

"But I should have been."

I rubbed her back in soothing circles as she released another round of shuddering sobs. "Just because society tells you to attend doesn't mean you have to. It's okay. You handled it the best way you could."

"But they'll never forgive me."

"Adelaide, look at me." I pulled her up from my chest and wiped the tears from her freckled cheeks. She bit her lips, still swollen from my cock. "There is no right or wrong way to grieve. For anyone to tell you otherwise is a heartless asshole." How many times had I recited the same words of wisdom to Becca, yet she still felt guilty for her grief, having lasted fourteen years? "Do you understand me? I don't want you to feel guilty or unforgiven. There is no one here to ask for forgiveness."

She tucked her face against my chest and nodded. "I wish it was that easy. I feel like I'm going to go insane at the drop of a hat."

"Listen. You have every right to go insane, but you have to come back. And if I feel for a moment, just a single moment, you may not, I'll be there to make sure you do. Every time."

I held her tight, rubbing her back with comforting circles and smoothing out her hair, which had become crimped from her braid until the vehicle stopped in front of my home.

"Come on, sweets. Let's do something else to take your mind off everything."

She sniffled again, making me search for a tissue and handing it to her when I found them tucked inside the cubby.

"Can... we see their graves... when everyone's gone?"

"Whenever you want. You let me know, and we will."

She pecked a kiss on my cheek before the chauffeur opened our door, and we shuffled out with Adelaide wiping her tears and me straightening my wrinkled suit into place.

I wrapped my hand around her waist and walked her through the front door.

"God. Really you two? Get a room," I said as we stepped into the living room. Charity and Max quickly separated from each other, her hand wiping her mouth with her fingers as Max adjusted his pants.

"We didn't expect you to be back so soon."

"Good thing I was. I don't need you desecrating my furniture." I turned to Adelaide, who broke away from my hold and took the first step down the stairs. "I'll be there in a minute."

It took me a moment to pull my gaze from her sagging shoulders, and when I did, a sinking feeling settled into my bones with a startling realization—if she ever disappeared from this world, it'd be the start of a slow and torturous death for me.

"Listen up. I have a job for you," I said, turning back to Charity and Max, who had straightened themselves up.

Adelaide

35

I rubbed my shaking hand into my chest in a futile attempt to alleviate my stricken heart, which shattered faster than anyone could glue it back together.

How could I leave them there for everyone to gawk at their coffins like they were a roadside show? What kind of daughter was I? I should have stayed, but the thought of Auntie Mable pulling me in front of all those people drove panic to my bones and forced my legs to carry me out of there.

I reached behind me, my fingers digging for the zipper, but it disappeared as if it never existed. My arms burned as I ran my fingertips along the seam, searching for the elusive piece of metal. A strangled cry tore from my lips as I stomped my feet.

"Do you need help?"

I whirled around to find Jake standing in the doorway with a smirk.

God, I wanted to kiss him and slap him all at the same time. How could he smile on the worst day of my life? Why would he want to be my rock after everything that's happened between us?

I swallowed the pained lump in my throat and nodded. "Please."

He took two lazy strides and gripped my shoulders before turning me around. "Hold on," Jake whispered in my ear, his knuckles trailing from my shoulder to my wrist. Then, with a quick tug at the neckline, he tore the dress from my body, the ripping material trailing along the stagnant air around us. A soft metallic tink hit something in the room as he let the dress fall from my body to pool on the floor.

"That's better."

"You didn't have to ruin it."

He wrapped his arm around my waist and pulled me against his chest with his lips nibbling along my neck. His soft, warm lips kissed down my shoulder. "Now, you'll never have to see it again. And you won't feel guilty for getting rid of it."

How did he know me so well?

"Stop that," I said, elbowing him playfully.

"Stop what?"

"Getting in my head."

He wrapped his thick arms around my naked frame and hugged me tightly. "But you make it so easy."

I hung my head, accepting my defeat, then pushed his arms off me. "We should get to work."

"Adelaide."

"Yes, Jake?"

"Shouldn't you get some rest? Take the day off."

I shook my head. That was the worst advice. I needed out of my head and into the mind of someone else. If I sat around without taxing my brain, it would wander to my parents, and I couldn't stay in that abyss.

No.

I had a mountainous list of requirements that I needed executing and a bank account that needed draining or worse.

"I need to work. I can't sit around and twiddle my thumbs."

He sighed, his shoulders dropping. Did he just give in without a fight?

"Okay." He nodded.

I walked into the closet, pulled out one of his graphic t-shirts, and laughed as I found one that suited the occasion.

'My other computer is your computer,' typed out in red font on a black shirt, had me rushing to get it on.

"What's so funny?"

"I love this shirt."

"I'm going to start a collection for you."

My laughter died in my throat as I shook my head. "I'll just wear yours." I pulled the baggy shirt over my head, the long T ended mid-thigh, then slipped on a pair of black panties.

"Where are you going?" Jake said as I walked towards the door.

"To work."

"Not like that, you aren't."

"Jake…" I said, turning and leaning against the door with his chest in my face. "Max is out there, and he'll see you."

"A little hard for him to do that when his face is buried between her legs."

"If he looks at you, it'll start a war because I'll kill him. Are you prepared for that?"

I tipped my head back and laughed, my hand landing on his chest. "Don't be so dramatic."

Jake wrapped his hand around the back of my neck, his thumb pressed under my chin, forcing my gaze to meet his. "I'm dead serious."

His stolid black gaze wiped the gaiety from the atmosphere. I took in a deep breath and glanced toward the closet door. "He can't see anything."

"Is that a risk you're willing to take?"

"Fine. But you know this alpha-hole thing is not normal, right?" I sighed and rolled my eyes.

"Roll your eyes at me again, little girl."

"Or what? Are you going to spank me?"

His hand slid around the front of my neck, cupping my throat. "I'm not opposed to it."

My stomach swirled and dropped as though I had taken the biggest dip on a rollercoaster. Adrenaline burned through my veins as my heart rate hiked up from the prospect of his warm hand on my ass.

He glanced down at my parted lips and smiled. "I think you'd want that, sweets. You want me to spank you until your creamy ass is red?"

I clenched my thighs tight at the thought of it.

"Spankings are for children."

Jake pressed his thumb into the side of my neck as he reached down with his other and pulled me against him, his fingers gripping the thickness of my ass cheek. "Then stop acting like one."

I shouldn't egg him on, but I couldn't help imagining the pleasure I'd gain from it.

He dropped his lips to mine and kissed me like his life depended on it. As quick as he took my lips, he pulled away, leaving me breathless. "Get something on under that shirt, or I'll fuck you so hard I'll have to stab him in the ears just for hearing your cries."

Fucking hell.

Heat crawled up my neck and cheeks as I drew my lip into my mouth and sucked. I darted around him and to the closet before he said another word.

Finding my shelf, I slipped on a pair of shorts and lifted the shirt as I walked out to show him.

"Better?"

"For who?"

"Poor Max, who doesn't deserve your cruelty?"

"Anyone who looks at you without my permission deserves everything I give them."

My heart leaped into my throat, and I swallowed to keep it down. "How is someone supposed to function when you talk like that?"

"With caution."

Duly noted.

I smirked. "Well, now that I've done what you wanted, can I get to work?"

My shorts dug into my bloated belly, making me wish I could sit in my underwear.

"I don't know why you're so possessive about looking. Anyone can look. You can't go around killing everyone that sees me," I said as he ushered me out of the bedroom.

The two men in the parking lot faded into my mind as I thought about his excessively violent threats. His ability to manhandle two men with ease by himself was a situation that never crossed my mind in the thick of it all. What training did one have to have to take on two killers and come out on top?

"I've given in to the fact that someone had you before me. I won't allow anyone to touch you again."

"Are you jealous of Beckham?"

"Don't say his name."

"Beckham... Beckham... Beck—*ahhh.*" Jake grabbed me around the waist and threw me over his shoulder.

Without missing a step, he typed in his code and marched into the computer room. He slammed the door behind us, and before he took a seat in his chair, he grabbed my thighs and pulled me off his shoulder and onto his lap, with my ass high in the air.

"What the hell?"

A sharp *thwack* berated my ears, followed by sharp stinging ants crawling across my right ass cheek. "*Ahh.* Fuck."

Another hit my left, then another on the right, until I was certain the feelings I thought I'd have about such an act were no longer thoughts but warming prickles of pain that spread from one side of my ass to the other.

I squeezed my thighs together and moaned.

"Are you ready to listen?"

"Depends," I said breathlessly and grabbed hold of his ankle. "Are you going to do that again?"

"I can do this all day long until you stop being a brat." Another slap hit my left cheek before he picked me up and straddled me on his lap.

"No one's ever spanked me before."

Which should be obvious, since he was my first for many of our sexual activities.

He chuckled. "It shows."

He tugged on the bottom of my wavy hair, tipping my head back.

My chest heaved as I turned my playful glare in his direction, then stuck out my tongue.

"God, you are testing my patience."

I bit my bottom lip, enjoying my freakish behavior, but missing my lip ring. "I might be." I leaned into him and ran my tongue across his closed lips. *"Mmm."*

Jake grabbed my hips, shoved me off his lap, and spun me around. "Just remember," he said as he dipped his fingers into my shorts and tore them down my legs, "you wanted this."

"Yes," I gasped. "I do."

He shoved his hand into my back and pushed me down onto the other computer chair, leaving my knees locked and my stinging ass exposed for his carnal appetite. He grabbed my shorts and panties wrapped around my ankles and pulled them off, tossing them somewhere in the room with pink neon lights flashing all around us.

Weren't those green before? God, I don't remember.

His hands gripped my thighs, and his thumbs tucked into the creases where my pussy and legs met as he kicked my ankles wide and inhaled my scent.

"You smell like heaven, wrapped up in a dessert made just for me."

How does he make it sound like I'd even enjoy the taste of myself?

"God." I tipped my head back, my tendrils tickling the top of my sore butt.

"He's not here, but I'll be happy to take his place."

His warm tongue slipped between my folds, drawing a gasp from my tight throat.

"Fuck, Jake."

"That's better."

He swirled again, flicking my clit with firm motions, then sucked on it with his lips, his teeth grazing the sensitive nub. My knees buckled as a zing traveled to my toes, followed by a cry. I dropped my head, my hair tumbling towards the floor in a black wave.

"Don't fall." Two fingers plunged deep inside me, drawing a moan from my throat. "You wanted to play a game with me..." he said between flicks against my clit. "I'll make you regret it."

My mind went numb as his fingers worked inside my body, his tongue in tandem, building an unbearable pressure deep in my belly. He dipped in once, twice, and when I tensed for the third, it never came. Instead, he pulled out and ran his wet fingers against the circle of tight muscles. I jerked away, but his arm wrapped around my hips, and his teeth dug into my ass, causing a scream to rip out of me.

"Welcome to my game, Adelaide." His voice turned dark and sinister as his finger pressed against the tight ring of resisting flesh.

"I'm sorry," I said with a gasp. "I'm... *uhhh*." He pressed in a little harder.

The contrasting sensations scraped against the confines of my mind—a smoothing, rough texture pushed past my untouched barrier.

"You're so tight. I'm going to enjoy fucking your ass."

He couldn't be serious? I couldn't take him there. "No..." I gasped again. "I've never done that, Jake."

"I'll make you ready. Don't worry."

"What if..."

He pressed in a little further, stretching me to an uncomfortable fullness.

"What if I don't want to?"

"You will, sweets."

His lips brushed my clit, then licked, distracting me from his simultaneous assault on my ass.

The restless stretch soon dissipated, allowing a strange awareness to flood my system like a tsunami without warning.

"Jake?"

He hummed between my legs, never taking his lips off my clit. And as if someone opened the floodgates, my thighs tightened, my knees shook as I barreled over, my back arching into the air. My stomach muscles clenched as I drowned in bliss, my breaths a whimpered wheeze.

Jake ripped his touch from my body, my knees buckling beneath me. "Not yet, little girl." He picked me up from the floor, swiped a few things on the desk aside, and plopped my used ass on the surface.

Goosebumps branched out across my skin, intermingling with the sweat and heat that crawled across my open nerves.

His hand pressed into the center of my chest and eased me back onto the desk with a mixture of neatly organized cables, computer monitors, and keyboards.

Jake shucked his suit pants down his hips, not bothering to remove them from his ankles, and stroked his hard length.

"It's been too long."

It hadn't. He'd had me nearly every night since we'd been back, but he always wanted more.

He shuffled forward with two small steps and grabbed the back of my knees, allowing his erection to stand proudly on its own against his belly as he pressed my knees to my chest. "Hold still." He grabbed my hand and forced me to replace his hold. "Keep your hands there." His hand swung down, and my ass started with a new itchy fire. "Tell me you understand."

I nodded and gulped. "*Yes.*"

"That's perfect."

A soft pressure pushed against my wet opening, and I groaned from the loss as he pulled away, spit on my spread pussy, and rubbed it in with the head of his cock, sending wicked excitement through my belly.

"Remember, if he hears you..."

My eyes bulged before he slammed inside of me. My muffled cries swarmed the room like hundreds of bees finding a new home. He pumped in and out of me, his body slapping against my sore ass.

"*Yes. Yes. Yes.*" I whispered through gritted teeth, unable to maintain my silence.

A sharp slap hit my right ass cheek—once, twice, three times, sending a rush of moisture between my legs, his thrusts accompanying a wet slap.

"Your pussy tightens right up when I do that. Do you like that, baby? You like being spanked when I fuck you?"

I tucked my knees into my elbows and interlaced my fingers across my chest, helping my slick hands from slipping.

"Yes."

The computer monitor on the desk swayed back and forth in time with his thrusts. Its hypnotic motion entranced me.

Thwack.

Thwack.

Thwack.

My ass burned with sharp, itching tingles.

"*Fuck.*"

Jake grabbed my hips, pulling me closer to the edge. My heart leaped against my chest as my butt tipped toward the ground.

I was going to fall off the desk in a terrifyingly embarrassing sex moment.

Reaching out for him, he slapped my hand away. "I've got you."

His hands squeezed me, pressing me hard into the edge of the desk as he used me like his personal fuck doll.

"We're coming together, sweets."

Jake pressed his thumb hard onto my clit and circled with perfection.

My stomach dropped as the pressure to perform intensified the very motions he used to get me there. As if fear and anticipation swirled together to create this overpowering sensation of pleasure.

His thrusts, circular motions, and fullness had me teetering ever so close to the precipice.

Thwack.

I turned my head to the side and pinched my lips together. "*Mmm.*"

His hand skimmed up my shirt and pinched my nipple between his knuckle and thumb, sending a ripple of warmth between my thighs. All of it one step closer to destroying me.

"So close." I cried. "*Close.*"

"Yes, you are. I can feel it."

His motions slowed to a deep and punishing cervix bruising, fiery need as he interlaced his fingers behind my neck. It only added to his power position, but now he used my folded body to meet his demanding thrusts.

It only took a few more arduous thrusts before my inner walls spasmed around him.

A fraction of a scream broke through before I clamped down on my bottom lip, turning it into a tortured moan.

Jake grunted as he stilled. His warm spurts heated me from inside as he jerked his hips, his head tipped back, and moaned.

My jellied arms released my legs, letting them crash down beside him to dangle off the desk.

Jake pulled me up, his cock still twitching inside me, and claimed my lips, his thumb grazing my chin as he swirled his tongue against mine, tickling the roof of my mouth and sucking on my tongue.

He slid his cock from between my legs. The evidence of his possession trickled down my thigh.

"We can't have that," Jake said, pulling his pants up to his waist and into place.

"What?"

His fingers dove between my legs, scooping his cum and pressing it back inside.

"I'm already pregnant." I laughed. Would he have done this if I wasn't?

"It's not about that."

"Is this like a dog pissing on his territory?"

A smirk lifted the corners of his lips. "Something like that."

"Well, I assure you, no man will be putting his nose between my legs to smell your cum."

He wrapped his hand around the back of my neck and pressed his lips to my forehead. "You have such a way with words..."

"Do I..."

"Yeah. It makes me want to murder everyone that comes your way."

I gulped.

He withdrew his fingers from my pussy, then touched my bottom lip. "Open."

I kept them closed—the taboo thought driving me wild.

"Don't think; just do as I say. Now open."

I rolled my eyes like the brat he said I was, then opened my mouth.

He pushed his two fingers in. A burst of salt and tang spread across my tongue, coating my mouth. "Good girl. Taste what it's like when we're together."

I hollowed my cheeks and sucked his fingers into my mouth, my fingers wrapping around his wrist like he did in the limo.

His cock twitched against my damp thighs. "I think I could go for another round."

I pulled his fingers from my mouth and pushed against his chest before plopping to the floor. "You're gonna have to wait."

There was a bank account with their name on it that needed a quick reintroduction to inspections and taxes. Maybe an accidental transfer of funds to an unmarked account, and I couldn't wait to watch it all burn.

Adelaide

36

I wasn't upset. At least that's what I kept telling myself as I stared at Fruity swimming in his fish bowl. But somehow, the dirty feeling that I'd betrayed him crept along my brain with wicked tendrils spreading doubt deep down into my very substance.

Jake popped an M&M in his mouth as he stared at the code on his screen, passing by at a blistering rate. As much as I loved what I did, there wasn't any way I'd be able to watch the lines like that.

My stomach twisted, making stomach acid burn the back of my throat. I turned my gaze back to my screen and gulped. I needed to find the words to show him the three perfect lines on my computer. If—not if, when—I gave them to Jake, that was it. Game over. For everyone.

That was a good thing, right?

This was what we'd worked countless hours for. We'd spent *four weeks* with our eyes on our screens and hands on the keyboards, my mind and body numb to everything but the task at hand.

"I found him," I said, my voice barely a whisper.

As I turned my chair towards him, Jake leaned forward and turned his music down.

"What?"

"I said, I found him."

Jake pushed his chair in my direction and rolled to a stop in front of my screen.

"Holy shit." He laughed, a smile brimming across his face, and pulled me out of my seat into a spinning bear hug. "Do you know what you've done?"

I shook my head, but of course, I knew. I'd sentenced a man to death who was only trying to do the right thing.

"You just put everything in motion." He put me back on my feet, grabbed his phone, and pressed it to his ear as he seized my nape and kissed me full on the mouth, his tongue swirling with mine. He broke away only when the deep, garbled voice on the other end interrupted us.

"We've got him." His eyes bounced back and forth as he stared into mine, his hand still clenched around me. "Be ready to go in thirty..." He flicked his tongue across his lower lip. "Yeah. Get Dante."

Jake pocketed his phone and tipped my chin up with his pointer finger. "This is good. If we didn't find him, we couldn't destroy them. Do you understand that?"

I nodded, even though my stomach fought the very agreeableness he asked of me.

"Why don't you seem too happy then?"

"Because he was only trying to do the right thing. He doesn't deserve this, and I don't want anyone else to die."

Jake sighed and wrapped his arms around me as I tucked my head against his chest. His excited rhythm beat against my eardrum.

"Take out the reasons he did it and look at how he handled it. He kept you in the dark, abandoned ship and left his friends to die. *Correct?*"

But people made mistakes when faced with life-altering outcomes. I sighed, my shoulders sagging with defeat. "Yeah."

"So I hope you see that he's getting what he deserves."

I nodded once more and cleared my throat. Holeo didn't deserve to live while his friends feared for their lives because of him. While my life had been turned upside down and shaken, Skipper had lost his Torpedo... he may not survive.

"Good. Now..." He pulled me away from his hold and drew me out of the room after looking at the address on my screen again. "We've gotta get going."

"What are you going to do?"

"Turn even the slightest memory of them to dust."

"What if they expect that?"

"I'll be fine. I'll have a team with me."

"*Who are* you?"

He shook his head. His brows turned together as his head shook slightly from left to right. "I don't understand?"

"What tech mogul has a team of men at the ready to deal with moralistically corrupt mercenaries?"

Jake pulled back, his hand rubbing the back of his neck. "I'll have that conversation with you when I get back."

"You're leaving me here? I thought you said 'we?'"

He scoffed. "I'm not taking you anywhere near them. When I said we, I meant Max and me."

"And Charity?"

"She's staying here to protect you."

Jake and I slaved away on the computers while Max and Charity made themselves scarce, doing things I didn't want to know or ask about.

"You trust her to protect me?"

I'd watched their interactions. He didn't like her, and he certainly didn't have lengthy conversations with her. Besides, she gave me the creeps, like there was a light missing inside, which sent my warning bells ringing.

Jake propped his hand on his hip and ran his other down the length of his jaw, scratching at the scruff. He glanced behind me and then back at me.

He ushered me back inside the computer room. "You're going to stay in here until we get back."

"What? Jake. You can't be serious right now?" My chest constricted at the thought of staying there while he went out there into harm's way, dealing with men who did this for a living and thought he'd survive. "What if the house catches fire?"

"Then go outside to safety, Adelaide." He shook his head as if my fear was so comical and plopped me back in my seat.

"Don't laugh as though my fears aren't valid." Tears burned at my retinas. "What if you don't come back?"

"Adelaide." He bent down on his knees before me, his hands gripping my waist as he rolled my chair closer. "Stay here. Keep our baby safe. And know that when I come back—and I will—it'll all be over."

He bent down, his back curling as he pressed his lips to my stomach. I thread my fingers through his hair which had grown longer since all of this began.

"Okay," I whispered. "But I don't have to like it."

He stood, taking my face in his palms, and kissed me like it was the last time. My toes curled as his tongue caressed mine, our lips crushed together in a bruising touch.

"Stay here and be a good girl."

I smiled as a warmth flooded my body from his lowered tone. Biting my lip, I nodded, resolving myself to his command.

"I'll be back before you know it, but text me if you need anything. And don't be afraid. Charity's here, and the men guarding outside will still be here."

I swallowed as he walked out of the room, shutting the heavy door behind him with a snick.

The quiet beat of his subwoofer from the music he'd forgotten to shut off worked in time with the rhythm of my heart. It was like a war drum beating to his tune.

Jake would step foot in the same room as those murderers under the guise of handing Holeo over. The only question was, would they allow him to step out?

My skin dampened with sweat as I considered the possibility of never seeing him walk through that door again. A heaviness settled on my chest like the weight of a thousand elephants. Blood pulled away from my face, and my legs began to shake.

Breathe. Just breathe.

I gripped the edge of the desk and willed myself to control my fears. He'd come back. Everything would be fine. It'll be okay.

I grabbed my new phone off the desk and stared at Monica's name. After all this time, we'd had little phone conversations here and there, but other than that, she was busy in her new home in California, and soon she'd start up college.

Me: What are you up to?

My knee bobbed, and I stared at my computer screen, waiting for someone to bite on the emergency request forms I'd sent out as I waited for my best friend to respond.

Monica: Studying like mad before I enter this class. You?

Me: What do you think I'm doing?

Monica: Why sitting at your computer, of course. Say, when am I getting that picture?

Me: Picture?

I frowned. What the hell was she talking about?

Monica: Yeah, you know, the one with your pregnancy test.

Had I really forgotten to tell my best friend I was having Jake's baby? I grabbed a piece of paper and a marker, drew a rectangle—the shape matching the little tester we'd bought—and drew two pink lines with Jake's highlighter. I snapped a picture and forwarded it to her.

It was the best I could come up with.

Monica: Real funny. Show me the real deal.

I snorted and leaned back in my chair, crossing my ankle over my knee.

Me: I don't have the real deal. But I'm 13 weeks.

Monica: If I had a maid, she'd be breaking dishes right now.

A smile pulled at my lips as I recalled the memory before everything turned into a chaotic twister of misery and confusion.

Me: Probably a good thing.

Monica: We have lots to catch up on, but it's gonna have to wait. I need to study.

Me: Okay. Catch ya later.

Monica: Congrats, you lucky bitch.

I tossed my phone onto the desk before me and stared at the address listed on my computer.

Jake and his friends would capture and interrogate Holeo, and hopefully, he'd be able to give them useful information.

His logic rattled around in my brain like dice in a cup, and I no longer felt the guilt eating at me as I had before.

There was a peace inside of me I couldn't ignore. Did that make me sick in the head for feeling this way? For no longer accepting the responsibility of his demise?

I shrugged my shoulders to no one but myself, then set my fingers to the keyboard again, checking if anyone responded to the Emergency forms.

Not one.

I sighed, kicked my seat back, and interlaced my hands behind my head as I blew out a breath of air through my puffed cheeks.

This was impossible. How did he expect me to sit still and wait it out?

My stomach rumbled with hunger even though I'd eaten only an hour ago, and my tongue sat dry in my mouth like sandpaper despite the soda I'd consumed.

I wonder what...

Tears burned my eyes.

It'd happened again. The thought of my parents and wondering if they were sitting down to watch a TV show right about now. But reality hit me like a Mac truck.

They'd never finish their 'programs' again. The last time I'd seen my mother I was rushing out of my home with Crysis at my door.

He was older than I expected, but his behavior was that of a teenage boy—stunted by lack of interactions with his peers.

One could say I had stunted communication skills

"They are a lion on the hunt..."

Well, two can play at that game. I leaned into my computer and typed in the keywords 'bombing' and 'Mexico students.' An event I should've looked into long before now.

An unconscionable sum of articles popped up, making me wince. It'd take forever to sift through these to find the man Franklin said Holeo had recognized. Not that it mattered. According to Jake, it'll all be over when he returned, as though he had a card up his sleeve he hadn't cared to share with me.

I started on the first article dated back to twenty-sixteen. I was barely fourteen by then and hadn't recalled hearing about this on the news or any other website. At that age, I'd already submerged myself in the hacking community, and it would've been a big deal to us.

But the story was just as Franklin said—teens attended a hack-a-thon only for it to be bombed by what the article said was 'cartel retaliation.' But thanks to Franklin, I know that to be inaccurate.

Photo after photo of rubble-torn buildings, debris tossed into the road, vehicles burning on the streets, but nothing with a man Franklin had described. I skipped to the next article, then the next, until finally, after sifting for what felt like hours, I landed on pay-dirt.

The photo showed a car, blown to smithereens and on fire, much like all the rest, only vastly different. A Mexican officer in a black uniform cleared the street full of debris and what looked to be the dead body of someone lying in the street.

I gulped down the burst of sickness, then studied the crowd behind him. Children ran across the street from the burning building, followed by what I assumed to be police escorts. Beyond them were four figures walking across the street a fair distance from the children, seemingly unfazed by the surrounding chaos. What news organization was allowed to take pictures like this?

"The man with the banded tattoo."

I'd found him.

His blond hair hung down to his shoulders in waves, his black cargo pants and shirt now a creamy gray from the aftermath. This man was on the street the day I bought my father his tie. He was also in my hospital room, no doubt working on finishing the job he started.

A thick knot formed in my throat, causing an ache to form just below my chin. I rubbed at it, clearing my throat for relief, the tears from before burning with a vengeance.

All of this was so fucked.

Next to the tattooed man was another man, larger than the last. This one unnaturally darkened like those girls who sat in the tanning beds for far too long—their skin turning to burned leather.

I glanced at the man beside him wearing street clothes, only part of his face visible, but he didn't look all that happy, almost upset.

The fourth and final man walked at the back of the group, his hand touching the third man as if he were ushering him along.

My gaze drifted to his shoulders, then to his long wavy blond hair, just like the man with the tattoo, and further up to his mustache...

Chills bled through my scalp, pulling my skin tight.

"No..." I choked out a gasp.

He was at my home. The sick bastard spoke to my mother and looked her in the face.

My sinuses stung as the salty tears fixed to fall. What kind of sick game did he play with me?

I jerked away from the computer.

My mind was on fire, the connections snapping into place.

Is that why he asked me where Holeo was? Because he wanted to find him through me? He thought I'd be able to get to him when he couldn't?

But why would he try to take me three days before that? Why let me go? Why come after me and try to kill me when he knew I couldn't lead him to Holeo? Everything out of Franklin's mouth was a lie, except for one detail. My parents would get caught in the crossfire. It was a threat, not a warning, as I originally thought.

Franklin stood in front of me, knowing I didn't know where Holeo was and threatened my parents' lives.

I grabbed my phone off my desk and tapped Jake's name.

The phone rang as I paced the room, my stomach in knots, my chest tight. Voicemail.

I pinched my bottom lip, my feet eating up the carpet before me as I dialed again.

"Hello? Jake?" I said, answering the phone.

"What's wrong?"

"Jake, I don't think this is what it seems."

"What do—"

"Something's wrong. Do you have Holeo?"

"He's right here."

"Has he said anything?"

I sat down on the edge of my seat, my elbow resting on the desk as I stared at the picture on my computer.

"What's this about, Adelaide?" Jake grunted as though he struggled with something. A meaty *thwack* resounded in my ear. "Hold still," he said through gritted teeth.

"What does he look like?"

"Holeo? You mean Yergi? Black hair, mid-thirties, brown eyes—"

"Scar on his right cheek?"

"How did you know?"

I'd followed the description he'd rattled out to a T with the one in the article.

"He's one of them."

"If you don't stop speaking in riddles—"

"Put him on the phone. I need to speak to him."

"We're almost to the drop-off."

I slammed my fist down on the desk. "For fuck sake, Jake, listen to me, and put him on the phone."

He scoffed before an accented male voice came over the speaker. "Hello?"

"I need to know. Who is Franklin?"

"One of the most heartless, calculated mercenaries I know."

"Franklin came to me. He said he was Crysis, and he was looking for you. He said you were the key to fixing all of this."

"He isn't Crysis; he must've killed him."

"So, who is Franklin?"

"He's my second in command."

Second in command? That meant... My stomach bottomed out, then shot up, burning my throat with acid.

"You..." my chin quivered. "You killed my parents?"

My computer screen blurred as the tears pooled on my lower lid. My skin crawled as my fist clenched.

"I didn't do that. I'm working against them. We've been doing this together. Remember?"

"You..." I slammed my hand down again, sending a zing up to my elbow as my wrist bone caught the side of the desk. "You threw me to the wolves with no warning, and now my parents are dead."

"We all sacrificed something for the cause."

I shook my head, my heart battling against my chest. My vision blackened as I held onto the desk.

"I hope they fucking fry you alive, you piece of shit!"

"That's enough," Jake said in the background. "Adelaide." The sound of his voice settled deep in my bones. No one was safe if they were willing to kill one of their own. "Sit tight."

"I think it's a trap," I said, my teeth grinding together.

Jake

37

I hung up the phone and glanced at Yergi. "So you're the head of this snake, huh?"

"I used to be. I haven't been for quite some time now."

"You better tell me everything, or I'm going to gut you in front of everyone. Why are you here, in my city?"

"Be a little more inventive, Jake Murray." The man turned his glare on me. "They will be."

Tonk pushed the man against the backrest. "Torture isn't his specialty, but it is mine."

A frown dipped the corners of his lips. "Hmm." He nodded. "I see."

"Then you know when I tell you that nothing will stop me from taking pleasure in your screams, right down to the very last breath you draw."

"I believe you."

"Then tell him what he needs to know."

"I've been following them and observing their movements to see how much they've changed. This is the first time we've... they've all come together in a while." Yergi took a deep breath, his shoulders rising, then fell as he exhaled. "Sev Shun was my creation. From when I was a little boy, watching my country fight the control of Azerbaijan, I wanted to raise the strongest army to help my country. But as I grew older and watched how the government cared more about some damn piece of land than they did their own people, I dropped my desire to help my country."

"So you killed women and children? That's your solution?"

Yergi shook his head. "That's not how we planned our mission. The job in Mexico went wrong. Our targets were diplomats meeting to ally with Mexico. If they did that, it would give them power over the southern countries in North America. Our client, a powerful man in the middle east, didn't want that alliance."

"So you bomb a building full of kids and call it a good day?"

He sighed as the SUV came to a stop. "The meeting in the embassy was down the road from the convention center, but we couldn't get our car bomb in place before they left. I told them not to do it, but my crew revolted."

"Do what?"

"They followed them and blew their cars from the ground. They were okay with a few for the many. That's when I created Cryptonic. I worked with them, keeping my role as leader, but then they caught wind of my betrayal and drove me underground. That was about eight months ago."

"When you started working on hacking their systems?"

He nodded. "Listen, they locked me out of everything. I tried to make it right. I didn't agree with any of it, but I no longer had control." He held his cuffed hands up and begged with them clasped together. "Don't turn me over to them. They can't be allowed to continue."

Tonk chuckled. "Doctor Frankenstein turns against his creation."

"Wouldn't you?"

"I wouldn't have created the very problem I worked to resolve." Tonk removed his hand from Yergi's shoulder.

"What the fuck do we do now?" I faced Tonk and Alek.

"We stick to the plan. Nothing's changed," Tonk said firmly.

Yergi recoiled, his cuffed hands raised in futile surrender, his fear finally showing through his stolid face. "They'll kill us all."

"I'll kill you if they don't," I said, putting my hand on the pistol at my hip.

"After everything I just told you? Why? I'm not the enemy here."

"Because you recruited a teenage girl, knowing full well what kind of danger you were putting her in. And then after everything..." I clenched my fist, restraining from beating him to a bloody pulp. "You left her without the tools or knowledge to protect her."

"It wouldn't have mattered if I did or not. She's lucky to still be alive. We all are."

"I beg to differ." I squeezed my fist harder. "Now, if Franklin was your second in command, does that mean he's taken over?"

Yergi nodded as I pulled out my phone. "Which one is he?" I thumbed through a load of pictures we'd acquired on the men when we first met.

"If he's anything like me, he won't be there in person but watching from a safe distance."

Max chuckled from the driver's seat. "That figures. You let your team do all the dirty work while you take no risks." He shook his head. "No wonder they turned on you so easily."

"What does he look like, then?"

"*Um*, like his brother, Yervant."

"Yervant... the one with the tattoo, blond hair, big build?"

"The very one."

"Is this what we're doing?" Alek asked, his torso twisted in the seat toward me. "Your call."

I glanced around the SUV, Tonk as stoic as ever, Max gripping the steering wheel while he waited for the order, and Yergi staring straight ahead, awaiting his fate.

"We're doing this."

"Please—"

"Shut him up."

"I'm only trying—"

"To do the right thing. Yeah, we know. The problem is, I want them dead more than I want you alive."

"Get out." Tonk opened the door and grabbed Yergi by the arm, dragging him out beside him.

"Yergi," Sarkis said, clapping his hands. "It's been a long time." The man proceeded speaking in a language I didn't understand while I slid from my seat.

"We thought you'd never find him," Yervant said, his gaze following mine.

Was he sitting here watching like Yergi said? Or was he in some room in a far-off distance enjoying this very moment?

"Adelaide did."

The man tipped his head back with boisterous laughter, its pitch bouncing around the alleyway—the alleyway filled with Yergi's men who should be dropping like flies any moment.

If it weren't for Tonk and his brutal attention to detail, we wouldn't have had the element of surprise. As we spoke, our men stood behind us, above us, and all around us like an invisible cloak of protection, pinching in like a formidable vice, ready to squeeze the life from every single one of them.

I stepped forward, my grip on Yergi's elbow, and jerked him toward Sarkis. Yergi spoke quickly in his native tongue, then switched to English. "Where's Franklin? Was he good to you?"

"Franklin's..." Yervant rubbed his forefinger and thumb together by his side as he paused. "Tying up loose ends."

My stomach bottomed out when my high-pitched house alarm screamed from my pocket. Yergi turned his attention in my direction as my vision turned crimson red. I dropped his arm, wrapped my hand around my pistol, and pumped two bullets into Yervant's skull.

Adelaide

38

My mind played tricks on me with every wicked noise while I paced the neon computer room.

What was happening? What were they doing? Was Jake okay? Why didn't Franklin kill me that night? Why didn't he kill me when we'd spoken?

My stomach curdled as the lack of control tipped the scales. There wasn't anything I could do, and it twisted my mind and gut until fire licked my skin, forming a bead of sweat.

Jake left me alone with Charity, whose rogue footsteps bounced outside this room. And even though there were security measures to keep me safe, I didn't feel it.

My skin crawled with unease and hunger.

I slapped the back of my fingers against my other hand in time with my pacing feet. Control of the situation ripped free from my grasp, leaving me an unsettled mess. The image of Holeo and Franklin caught my peripheral vision with each pass I made, making the knot twist tighter in my stomach. I needed to get out of here, or I'd suffocate. I marched through the door, brushing past Charity, and made my way down the hall and to the kitchen with her on my heels.

"Where are you going? You were supposed to stay inside."

My stomach popped and groaned with hunger.

"I'll go back. I just need to eat," I said, gathering the ingredients to make a sandwich.

"This is why I don't babysit."

A muffled thump like a bird hitting the window gave me pause, followed by a harsh, shrilling alarm. I jumped, losing grip on the pickle jar in my hands, and it shattered against the tiled floor with pickles and green juice spreading out like a flash flood.

"Fuck," Charity said over the ear-piercing alarm with her shoulders hunched and her arms over her head. "Get down." Lights flashed, a siren blared down the hall, and a mechanical voice calmly uttered, "Intruder." I hunched over, following her direction as she rushed toward me and opened a double cabinet door. "Get in."

"What?"

"I said, get in!" Charity pulled the pistol from her waistband and motioned me inside. I pushed the products to the back and slid in, my knees crunched to my chest. "Don't move. I'm going to see what's happening."

"Don't leave me," I squeaked like an out-of-tune trumpet.

"I'll be back. Don't worry. I don't think I could handle Jake losing another girlfriend because of me."

"What?" What was that supposed to mean?

A smirk tipped her lips. "I'm kidding... sort of." Charity shut the cabinet doors, drenching me in darkness with nothing but my labored breaths and the stench of cleaning products burning my nose as she walked away.

I wrapped my arms around my legs and rested my forehead against my knees, pinching my eyes closed.

Thump. Thump. The same noise as before hit the enormous glass walls, and then the alarms died mid-crescendo.

A pang hit my breast bone from my heart, cranking into gear. My muscles froze, locking me into place as though fear encased me in cement until... a boot hit the marbled floor.

And then another.

And another.

I held my breath as I strained through the residual ringing in my ears, hoping to determine which direction the footsteps traveled until they stopped, leaving my heart rattling in my chest.

Where did they go?

I squeezed my legs harder, walking my feet back towards my butt, making myself as small as I could, then pressed my finger to the center slit in the cupboard and peered out through the sliver of light.

The cupboard door ripped open, and bright flashing lights temporarily blinded me. "There you are." The man clad in all black wrapped his hand around my hair, sending pins and needles spreading across my scalp. "I've been looking for you."

I screamed, my legs skittering across the floor as I kicked out at him, my heel connecting with his knee, giving me a satisfying cry from him. I pulled my hair from his loosening grip, my hair popping free from my burning scalp. "Charity!" I crawled across the pickle juice and broken glass on my hands and knees. The straight-edged shards slipped into my skin with deadly precision.

Where did she go? Did they get her?

"Where do you think you're going?" The man grabbed my ankle, twisted me around as he pulled me towards him, and then gripped me tight around my throat.

Franklin.

I wrapped my hand around his wrist. "The police will be here any minute."

"I almost wish that were true."

Jake's description of his automatic alarm system was his way of deterring me from leaving while he wasn't here to watch me. The question was, would it matter if the police responded? Franklin had gone through all of Jake's men he'd posted outside. What could a few cops do?

He yanked me up from the floor and pushed me towards the couch. "Have a seat." My eyes widened when he pointed his pistol at my temple. "Let's not make this harder than it needs to be." I collapsed onto the couch with bleeding wrists and forearms tainting Jake's red leather.

"What do you want, Franklin?"

"Have you figured it out yet?"

I nodded and swallowed hard.

"What tipped it off? Was it the gun or the outfit?"

"What do you want from me?" I cowered on the couch, wincing as my legs brushed against the glass infesting my flesh.

"Nothing. I've got everything I wanted."

"And what is that?"

"You here. Your boyfriend dead and Yergi out of the picture for good."

"Jake's..." I bit back a sob, and salty tears stung my eyes and sinuses. "He's..."

"*Shh.* You American women cry over everything."

My chest collapsed as I sucked in thin air, burning the bottom of my lungs. No, don't say that. Don't say that.

"Wh... why?" I wheezed.

"Let me tell you a story about a boy who only wanted to be enough. That boy grew up to become a leader. He ruled his men with an iron fist. But then something changed. He stopped leading and became nothing but a coward until his men snapped." He waved his gun back and forth as he spoke. "They turned against him, and he lost his control. But he wouldn't have that, so he worked against them until one day he slipped up, and they found out. Like the coward he was, he ran into hiding. He disappeared into the wind like the people of Ani. Only when his men convinced his new friends to tell us where he was, did we find out he—"

Shut up. "Shut up!" I cupped my hands over my ears, anger surging. "I don't want to hear about your stupid sob story when you made my life a living hell."

"You American women are so rude, too." Franklin's upper lip lifted in a snarl, wrinkling his nose. "If only your parents taught you better." A devious smile wrinkled the skin around his eyes as he studied the dagger from his words twisting my emotions into a raging inferno.

A scream erupted from my chest, and before I knew what I was doing, I lunged at him, my thumbs aiming for his eyeballs.

Franklin intercepted my attack, my hands so close I could feel his warm breath on my palms.

In a swift move, he released my hand and raised his. A solid *thud* bounced around inside my skull, and a heavy sharp ache tightened the skin around my left cheekbone. "I wouldn't try that again."

He shoved me backward toward the couch with his hands on my shoulders. I bounced, my body twisting off the couch and careening into the coffee table, my nose crunching against the edge.

Sharp agony stretched across my face and wrapped behind my ears, causing them to ring. A warm gush ran in torrents from my nose down my lips and chin. A groan ripped from my throat as I lay on the floor, my blood slicking the floor beneath me.

"That didn't have to happen."

My eyes burned as tears carved their sharp trail down my face, intermingling with the crimson debris. I groaned again, my need for escape moving my arms out in front of me as I army crawled to the end of the couch, my shirt mopping up the blood puddling on the floor. I pushed myself to my feet, my shirt soaked with blood.

"Are you faster than my bullet, Adelaide?"

My stomach sank into a bottomless pit full of venomous vipers attacking my nervous system.

"A little patience is all I ask. Until I get a phone call, then it'll all be over."

"What will?"

"Well," he said, using his pistol to direct me back to the couch. "That depends on what happens at the drop-off."

"But," I said, pressing the bottom of my shirt to my nose. "You said Jake was dead..."

"You misunderstood me. I said that's what I *wanted*."

"That's not what you said."

He shrugged. "Okay, maybe I fibbed."

"Don't hurt him."

An evil grin poisoned his smile. "Define hurt?"

"Don't kill him. Don't touch him. *Please*. I'll do whatever you want." I sat on the edge of the couch, my knee bouncing uncontrollably.

"That's all dependent upon him and whatever stupid choices he makes."

The faint sparkle of hope I'd had diminished as he spoke, spiraling me down into a darker abyss.

"Why did you kill my parents?"

Franklin sat in the chair, his elbows resting on his knees as he leaned over, his hands and pistol resting between them. "A misunderstanding."

"Between you and Jake?"

"We made a deal, and then he disappeared with no communication. I had to show him that wasn't how we did business."

"So you killed my parents?" I whispered, my throat aching as the words came out.

"It's not like they were our first choice." He leaned back in his chair, then leaned forward again as if he slipped up and remembered he shouldn't be comfortable. "We tried killing you... but you are a *tricky* little thing, aren't you?"

I shook my head. It was all luck. No thought or planning was involved.

"I've never underestimated an enemy so much in my entire life. But you?" He shook the pistol as he pointed it at me. "I couldn't tell if you'd ran away with Yergi or if you were telling the truth that you'd left the group." He sighed. "It just seemed odd that you left the group, and then he did. Almost like it was orchestrated."

Thoughts of escape bombarded me as he spoke, killing time as he waited for confirmation.

"I need a drink." I stood and took a small step back.

"Don't," he said, his gaze dodging to my feet. "I don't want to have to shoot you prematurely."

I took another step, solidifying my decision, then another, until I spun around and ran. A gunshot rang through the room, hitting the chair in front of me, puncturing the red leather with a narrow hole. I screamed as I raised my arms over my head, my ears ringing from the resounding blast, and continued running.

If I could get down to the safe room. I'd be okay there. Jake had added me into the system and showed me the safety protocols over and over. Use my thumb, go inside, and activate panic protocols.

I rounded the corner to the stairs and slammed into a solid frame. My eyes burned from the newfound agonizing shards licking across my nose. The massive man who'd thrown me over his shoulder the night my father saved me gripped my arms and stopped me from falling onto my ass.

"I told you—"

I screamed and kicked the Hulk before me, my bloodied hands pounding into his bullet-proof vest.

"What? You thought I took this fortress on my own? I'm flattered."

"Let me go!" Where the fuck was Charity?

"After I went through all this... *Nah.*" His pistol dangled in his hand at his thigh. "I worked too hard to keep my men free from your curiosity."

My head tossed from side to side, denying him. "I left the team. I didn't want anything to do with it anymore."

"Yeah, that's what they said. But you still know everything about us."

Franklin tipped his head to the man behind me. The hulking being wrapped his meaty arms around my chest, trapping my arms by my sides. My feet left the floor as he carried me back to the couch.

"You're a terrible shot for a mercenary," I said, struggling, my arms trickling with blood.

"Or my bullet went exactly where I wanted it to."

The Hulk tossed me onto the couch when two gunshots went off, and the flashing lights went out. I jerked my gaze towards the driveway where I was certain it'd come from, then back to Franklin, his hands gripping the pistol tight to his body in an act I'm sure he didn't have to think about.

"Well, it seems we're not alone anymore."

"Wha—"

Franklin jerked me off the couch by my upper arm and dragged me into the dark recesses of the room. His hand slipped through the blood coating my face as he covered my mouth. His lips brushed against my ear as he whispered, "Don't make a sound, or I'll paint the ceiling with you."

A cold hard metal dug into my ribcage, bringing about a muffled whimper against his gloved hand.

Rapid gunfire popped around us like suppressed popcorn, making me jump in Franklin's tight grasp. "*Shhh.* We have company."

My gaze darted across the room, searching for the culprit.

Was that Charity?

The bulky man ran towards the line of fire. His heavy black military-style boots pounded through my puddled blood where I'd laid beside the couch. He turned the corner, and two quick flashes of light illuminated the hallway, followed by the deafening blast of gunfire. My world slowed to a near standstill as the man tipped backward and crashed to the floor with a thud.

My deafening screams burst through Franklin's fingertips with chaos.

"Shut up."

Three men in full military gear stepped around the corner, their rifles drawn, as they searched the room until Franklin's laughter pointed them in our direction.

"I'll give you credit. For an arms dealer, you're quite resourceful," he said, ducking down behind me.

An arms... what?

I shook my head as a fourth man stepped between the others and pulled off the ski mask from his face, revealing Jake beneath the gear.

My body jerked forward despite the powerful arms wrapped around my body, and the gun pressed to my side. He was alive.

"*Ah-ah*," he said in my ear. "Not yet."

His hand slipped from my mouth as he gripped me tighter to his body and pressed us into a corner.

A door to the left opened up, and the barrel of a gun peeked through first, then Charity's bloody, beaten face walked through.

"Let her go, or you'll suffer a death you couldn't possibly imagine," Jake said, inching toward me.

"Jake. I'm sorry."

"*Shh*, sweets," He said, pressing his pointer finger to his lips while his other hand held out his pistol in surrender. "This'll be over soon."

"*Awe*, that's adorable."

I winced as he pressed the barrel harder into my ribcage, making me recoil from the pain.

"We had a deal, Franklin."

"We did. Until you started fucking with my accounts."

Jake shook his head, but before he could dispute Franklin's claim, he continued. "Yeah, don't think I didn't notice you meddling."

"If that was me, you wouldn't have known until it was too late." His gaze cut towards me. Because, unlike Franklin, Jake knew exactly who touched his bank accounts.

"Then who, Jake? It wasn't another random person who had a vendetta against me."

"How do you know it wasn't Yergi?"

"Yergi wasn't that smart."

"He was smart enough for you to feel threatened," Charity said, her feet inching closer to us, which made Franklin twitchy.

"You're surrounded. You might as well give up," Jake said as the other two men at his side flanked him. He pulled his gun back to his body and aimed it at us.

"If I die, so does she. Death with honor."

"Is it honorable in your country to kill pregnant women?"

"Even better. Eliminate the offspring of thy enemy. There is no higher honor. That's not from my country. Just a little something I picked up along the way." A sob broke my parched throat. "Come now. We knew this day would happen."

My knees threatened to give way. But the band of hope that diminished before sparked back to life like the brightest beacon.

In the three days I'd spent in the hotel hacking and watching self-defense videos, I'd learned a thing or two and I just prayed to God they had good aim.

Jake took two steps forward, and the gun dug deeper in response, my side bending away from the pressure.

My gaze locked with Jake's stolid expression as I grasped Franklin's arm and pulled as my legs dropped out from underneath me. My blood acted like lubrication as I turned my head to the side, allowing me to slip free from his grasp. A spray of gunfire erupted around me as my ass landed on the corner of his boot, sending a dull, aching knot of agony up to my throat.

I curled into a ball, covering my head and ears from the volley of gunfire as wet crimson droplets sprayed over my bare skin like a spring drizzle. My mouth hung open in a perpetual scream as my legs squirmed and jerked with each blast. I drew my knees up to my chest, making myself as small as possible until the gunfire ceased and the ringing in my ears reigned supreme.

The scent of gunpowder and fear stung my aching nose as I sucked in a wheezy breath.

Jake's voice roared from a dreary distance, as though I'd plunged into dark waters and the only sound breaking through was screams and him. The man who'd come to my rescue more times than I cared to admit because, for whatever reason, he loved me. And now, he'd nearly sacrificed his life for me—for us.

A strong vice wrapped around my wrists and pried my hands from my ears.

"Adelaide. Look at me. *God*. Look at me." Panic riddled his voice, forcing my clenched eyelids open. Droplets of blood splattered his forehead where his brows pulled together, causing a worry line between his eyes. "There you are."

Seeing him as tattered and broken as me broke the spell cloud around my head that made everything fuzzy and dream-like. I scrambled over and threw myself at him, wrapping my arms around his neck. I buried my bloody face in his neck, not caring about his bullet-proof vest scratching uncomfortably against my cheek.

Drawing him closer, I wrapped my legs around his waist and melted into him, sobbing. "I'm sorry. I'm sorry," I repeated as I squeezed.

My muscles shuddered, and my teeth chattered, and yet I repeated my apology while my cheeks cooled from the tears trailing down my face.

"It's okay, sweets. It's okay." He ran his hand down my hair, smoothing it over.

"I'm sorry. I should've listened. I love you. I'm so sorry."

"I love you too. Now shut up, Adelaide. You're okay. That's all that matters." His hand ran down the back of my skull again. "Are you hurt?"

"No." I shook my head against his shoulder.

There was damage all over my body. The bloody glass cuts on my arms and my most likely broken nose, but if I'd told him, he'd want to examine them, and that meant I'd have to let go of my life support, and I couldn't do that. Not now, probably never.

He wrapped his arms tight around me as the ringing in my ears drowned out the world until the only thing that remained was the scent of iron and gunpowder.

"Where's all the blood from?" he asked.

"I hit my n-nose on the c-coffee t-table."

"So he hurt you?"

I shook my head. "D-don't let go of me. P-p-please."

They'd killed a man—Jake, killed a man—who had stood behind me, my head no further than a foot away from his groin as they'd opened fire and annihilated the threat.

Was it over? It had to be if Jake held me in the middle of this blood-filled room. If he wasn't whisking me to safety, that must mean we were safe, and there was no way Franklin survived that massacre.

This nightmare—

"It's over, Adelaide. You're safe now."

Was I? Was it well and truly over?

"I'm just glad I don't have to clean this mess up," Charity said from somewhere in the room.

"You never have to clean up your messes," Max said.

I wrapped my legs tighter around Jake's waist and closed my eyes as he stood with me like I was weightless. His jarring footsteps, and the crunch of glass beneath a boot, assaulted my relaxing senses. One jolting step and a dip down made my stomach flip as the sensation repeated until his heavy boots hit the solid floor, my pained face still buried in his neck.

This was all my fault, and I couldn't escape the hollowed pain in my chest because of it. His home was destroyed, my parents were gone, and so many people died because of me—because of the team I thought did good things.

"I'm sorry," I whispered as light mutated into darkness. The unsettling in my bones diminished as if my body knew he'd brought me to a place of refuge, where prying eyes and death didn't exist.

"If you don't stop saying that, I'm gonna put you in a cold shower."

His hands came to my ribs and pushed my chest away from his as my ass sunk into something soft and bouncy.

Our room. My bed. Comfort.

Only then did I allow my eyes to open. Only then did I see his despondency.

Adelaide

39

Two months later

The bruising may be gone, but the heartache and agony stayed from the loss of everything I'd ever known. My parents lay beneath my dirtied knees as the tears flowed over my broken face, intermingling with the sod they'd placed over the settling earth.

I clutched my chest, wondering when the raw agony would disappear. *If it would ever get better, when did that happen?* How far away was I from relief? Would I ever feel normal again? I ran my fingers through the half green and brown grass where my mother's face should be, then wiped my tears with the back of my hand and stood.

Jake stood behind me, and I glanced at him when he cleared his throat. Tears formed in his eyes before he rubbed them with his thumb and fingers, holding them against his closed lids as if it'd take away whatever sadness affected him. He slid his hands over my round belly to where his growing son advanced his assault on my ribcage, battering me from the inside like a Mongolian seeking unfamiliar territory.

"Did you feel that?"

"I must've missed it," he said into my ear, his chin resting on my shoulder as I stared at my parents' headstone.

I squinted and raised my hand to my brow, shading my sensitive eyes to the high-noon blazing sun as I turned and glanced up at him.

"He'll do it again, don't worry." He always did. He spun around like an acrobat at practice all day long until I was sure he'd come through my belly.

"Are you ready to go?"

I swallowed and replaced the drooping flowers with fresh daisies and sunflowers—the ones my mother would've wanted at her funeral. They'd attracted the birds she loved, so when I visited every week, I'd catch a glimpse of them before they flew away and hid in the vast oak tree a good distance away.

"Yeah," I whispered.

"Everyone's waiting for us."

"Did we have to invite everyone?"

He chuckled and wrapped his arms around my shoulder, leading me away to his car. "It's a small gathering. That's all."

"But they intimidate me."

"What kind of friends would they be if they didn't stick up for me?"

I hung my head and sunk into the passenger seat. He shut the door and jogged around, hopping into the driver's side, his thigh fully recovered from the gunshot wound three months ago.

"Speaking of friends…" he said as he slid into the driver's seat and drove down the road. "Have you heard from Monica?"

I nodded and bit my lip. "She's having a hard time with her college classes, I guess. She said she couldn't make it."

"Ah, well, maybe she can come when Trevor is born."

"Trevor?"

"I like it. It's a strong name."

"It's an eighties name. We're not naming our baby Trevor. That sounds like a kid who picks his nose."

"Wow," he laughed, and I smiled.

I wanted to name our son something sentimental like my parents named me, but I wasn't sure what name yet. "Australia," I whispered with a smile.

"What?"

"My parents," I swallowed hard, "they named me after a place in Australia they always wanted to visit but couldn't afford. I want to name our son after something important like that."

"Maybe I'll take you in their honor."

I turned to him. "You'd do that?"

"I'd do anything for you. Haven't I made that clear yet?"

I sucked on my bottom lip to hide the girlish blush and looked out at the window, dreading the next moment.

"Do you think it will take long?"

"What? You can't wait to be back home hiding from society again?"

I laughed and interlaced my pinkie with his. "I don't have to hide when you're with me, but yeah, basically."

Jake pulled up to the courthouse, parking next to his friend's vehicles, then rushed over to my side, opened the door, and helped me out with an outstretched hand.

"Thank you." I adjusted my knee-length purple lace dress and grabbed my ID from my purse.

"Do I need to make sure it's the real one?"

Smirking, I thrust it towards him like when we'd first met. "It's real."

"*Hmm.*" He thumbed the ID card. "Adelaide Leaver," he said, reading off my name on the card. "Seems real enough to me."

"It's one of a kind."

"Yes, *you* are." He kissed the top of my head and took my hand, leading me through the courthouse doors, tucking my ID into his pocket.

Butterflies floated around in my belly like a sacred dance as we walked up to his friends waiting for us in the lobby. Becca stood with Hannah in her arms, giving her a little bounce as she slow-danced with the cooing baby. She'd been instrumental in helping me with my grief, stopping by every day, even if it was for a hug or to ask how I was feeling, if there was anything she could do. I'd never had a sibling, but I looked at her as a sister, just as Jake did.

"Look, Hannah, they finally showed up," Becca said.

"We took a slight detour." I glanced down and smiled as though we were out doing something we shouldn't have been.

My parents may not be able to be here, but at least I visited them beforehand.

"Has the clerk said anything?" Jake asked, looking at the tall white marble pillars that towered to the dome ceiling.

"She said give the judge about two minutes, and..." she glanced at her watch, "that was two minutes ago."

A woman with short curly gray hair stepped out and stood in a doorway, reading from a paper in her hand "Mister Murray and Miss Leaver?"

"Here." I raised my hand, then lowered it.

She glanced up at us and waved us forward with the paper. "Right this way, please."

We followed her down a brightly lit hallway with tiled floors and white walls with pictures of presiding judges, at least I thought they were, hanging in a triangle shape, then disappeared into a stuffy room.

Three rows of three chairs faced the quaint standing area where we'd be at the center of attention for approximately... *way too long*.

"We made the right choice," I said, leaning into Jake, who'd I'd latched onto when I stepped out of the vehicle.

He snorted and patted my hand.

The thought of having a large wedding where people sat back and scrutinized my choice of flowers, or my dress, or just having to interact with people I didn't know sent hives crawling up my arms.

"Judge Rascome will be here momentarily. Go ahead and stand here." She motioned to Jake and me, her eyes landing on my belly. "The rest of you can take your seats."

And then there was that.

My protruding stomach with our son kicking away at my innards. There was no way I could stand for a full ceremony while he stepped on my bladder.

We took our positions at the front while his friends sat down, excited to support him. There was no one here for me, aside from maybe Becca. She'd become the sister I never had, but that was it. Ivy kept to herself, not that I blame her, and Liz was busy being a new mom. That left Jake and me. Not that I'd complain.

He leaned into me, his breath on my lips. "You look beautiful." Jake traced the backs of his fingers down my belly, sending fire between my legs.

Lately, it was the simplest touch, and he'd have me panting like a dog in heat. I closed my eyes and chewed on my lower lip, imagining him pulling me into a hall closet and thrusting into me with my dress at my hips. He'd have to wrap his hand around my mouth because my moans of ecstasy were for his ears only. He didn't like to share, not even the pleasure I'd experienced from his touch.

"Your cheeks are red, sweets. What are you thinking about?"

His seductive voice drew me out of my daydream. "*Hmm?*"

"Finally," Alek said, breaking the trance between us.

I glanced away from Jake's penetrative stare and to the man in a black judge's robe billowing around him as he walked. His shiny black shoes peaked out with each step like obsidian reflecting the lights above.

Jake shook his hand as he took his place before us. "Thanks for doing this on short notice."

"It was hard to deny the check on my desk," Judge Rascome said, laughing. "Just don't ask me to do it again."

"Till death do us part, right?" Jake patted the man's arm, then let go of his hand. Apparently, they'd known each other for a long time. I guess criminal brokers needed friends in high places... well, *former* criminal broker.

"That's the spirit. Are we ready to begin?"

I nodded. "Yes, please." Leaning into the judge, I whispered, "Make it quick, please."

He chuckled as he gestured towards our locked hands.

"She doesn't do well in society," Jake said.

"Then let's make this quick." He winked with a lopsided smile. "Please place the rings on each other's fingers."

Tears burned my eyes as Jake pulled mine from his pocket and slipped a specially designed ring, combining both my mother's and his mother's sets into one unique band and setting.

I pulled Jake's out from between my swollen breasts and slid his father's warm metal band on his finger.

"Repeat after me. I, Adelaide Leaver…"

Jake caressed my hand with his thumb as tears burned my eyes with each profound word.

"And Jake…"

I glanced down at his polished shoes across from mine, his black suit pants hung perfectly tailored over the tops, leading up to his black belt and shining silver buckle.

"You may kiss the bride," he said, startling me as if it came out of the blue.

Jake slipped his hands around the nape of my neck, tipping my lips to his, and sealed our marriage with a sensual kiss that curled my toes and made my racing heart beat faster.

Cheers and rounds of applause erupted in the small room, bringing a heat up my neck and a smile to my face.

"Well, Mrs. Murray, should we have a party?"

"A party? Oh, no." I shook my head with conviction. Couldn't we just slip into our home and have a party of our own? Did we have to include others on this day?

"Too bad," Jake whispered in my ear as Judge Rascome placed our marriage certificate before him. Jake signed the document, then handed me the pen. "I have something for you."

I scratched my signature across the document and turned to him with a smile. "Oh, do you now?"

"A little wedding gift."

We were supposed to exchange gifts? Is that what Auntie Mable did at her weddings? She wasn't invited to my wedding, so I couldn't ask her, but I don't recall that ever being mentioned.

"Relax, sweets," he said as if he could sense the panic coursing through me. "It's just something I wanted to give to you on this day."

He took my hand in his and led me to the front of the courthouse, where I covered my mouth and gasped. I turned my attention to him, where he sat with a huge smile.

"You didn't."

"Go try it out."

I rushed down the steps as he yelled after me to be careful not to trip. I tuned him out as I made my way up to the black 1966 Chevrolet Chevelle SS 396, my dream car.

"You remembered?" I said as he walked up beside me, my hands hovering over the sleek paint job.

"I've been looking for it since you first told me."

The hood scoop in the center, the red-lined tires, the black leather bucket seats in front, and bench in the back were everything I'd pictured and more.

"But how?"

"It wasn't easy. I had to buy this off of a collector. He needed a little convincing, but money talks."

"Jake..." I gasped as I grabbed for the handle. I'd never seen one of these in person, and I couldn't believe it sat in front of me.

My heart warmed as I stared back at him, his hands tucked into his suit pockets. He remembered. It was the sweetest thing anyone had ever done for me.

"Now we can park it next to your dad's car, where we can look but don't touch."

I laughed. "Yeah, I don't think so. I'm going to drive this thing every day."

"Where would you go every day? You barely leave the house."

I chewed on my cheek as I tried conjuring locations but drew a blank. "Down the street and back is good enough for me."

Jake swiped my hand away from the door and opened it for me. "Take us home, Mrs. Murray."

I wrapped my arms around his neck and slipped my tongue into his mouth. He engulfed me in his arms, his scent overpowering with musky cedarwood and a hint of something else. My back hit the car. His hands dove into my primped hair and tugged. My bump between us was the only thing stopping him from crushing me with desire.

"Get a room, you two," Becca said from the courthouse steps.

Jake broke away, and we laughed, his face buried in my neck and mine in his chest as I gripped his lapels. "Maybe we should take this someplace private?"

"I agree, Mr. Murray."

Epilogue

One Year Later

"Okay, seriously. I said move to the left," I yelled, "My left, Jake, not yours."

"If you keep raising your voice at me, I'll stuff my cock down your throat and gag you."

I scoffed. "Please, you can't even kill the enemy. You think I'm afraid of you?" I grabbed my fruit roll-up off the desk and took a bite as I watched the enemy filter in and kill us. "Pitiful."

Jake stood, his shadow casting over me as I looked up at his towering stature. He turned my computer chair and knocked my controller from my hand.

"Excuse me, I was busy dying over here." I bent down to pick it up, and he grabbed my wrist.

"What kind of computer gamer plays with a controller, anyway?"

"The kind that likes to win." I took another bite of my fruity treat, then glanced at it and back to him. "Just how much are you wanting to gag me?"

"It becomes more likely each time you open your sassy mouth." He wiped his thumb over my sticky lip, and I pushed myself up, dedicating myself to the thought as I walked him back into his chair. He took a seat; our roles reversed as my nervous heart beat wildly in my chest. "What are you doing?"

"An experiment." I sank to my knees between his legs and bit my lip, eyeing his zipper.

"Should I be worried?"

His husky voice sent shivers down my legs, warming the part of me I'd beg him to take.

"Oh, very much." I pulled down his zipper and freed his thick, hard, weeping length. "Doesn't take much, does it?"

"With you on your knees and that look in your eyes." He bent over and cupped my chin. "Not at all." Raising my mouth to his, he pressed his soft lips to mine and devoured me with my hand, squeezing and pumping. "You taste like sugar and berries."

"Thanks, I got it from my candy." I smirked, wrapped my fruit roll-up around his cock, and took him in my mouth. He hissed, spurring me at a rapid pace, the treat dissolving into a sticky substance.

"Fuck, Adelaide." Jake dug his hands into my hair and tugged the strands at my scalp as my tongue swirled around, savoring the salty, sweet concoction in my mouth.

Our baby's whimper filtered through the speakers causing me to stiffen.

Jake squeezed tighter. "He's okay. His eyes are still closed," he said, pushing my head back on his cock. "Make me cum in that smart mouth of yours, and then I'll go get him."

I pinched my legs together as warmth flooded between my thighs.

Picking up the pace, I squeezed my fist tighter around the base of his cock. My tongue swirled the tip, and the candy melted, leaving behind a multicolored puddle in my hand. My lips stretched as I took him deep into my throat.

"Fuck, you're so beautiful on your knees," Jake groaned as he thrust his hips forward to meet my downward motion, hitting the back of my throat. His fist tightened as his muscles locked up beneath me.

Hot spurts of salty liquid hit the back of my throat in waves, and I swallowed him down with greedy need.

I pulled away with a pop, then licked the tip of his cock as he jerked. "That wasn't one of my better ideas." I held up my stained, sticky hand and grimaced.

"I beg to differ." His tongue dove into my mouth, swirling with contrasting tastes as he ate me up, leaving me begging for more. For him to take me on the floor, against the wall, or on the desk. However he did it, he'd leave me satisfied and wet. Except there was one little detail that needed to be taken care of first.

"Go get Ollie. I'll wash up." I broke away and smirked as I stood from the carpeted ground, hoping the liquid on my hand wouldn't drip onto the floor and stain it.

"What if I'm not finished?" He cupped my jaw and raised my chin with his thumb as he pushed me against the desk, his hips grinding into me. "I need more."

His tongue swept over my syrupy lips, and I moaned as he sucked on my lower lip, his teeth nibbling on my flesh.

Ollie's whimper pulled my gaze toward the video monitor. Jake's teeth scraped over my flesh until my lip popped free with a smarting sting. "I think your son has other ideas." I smiled.

"I think our son is cock blocking me." He groaned and laid his forehead on my shoulder.

"He's a little young to know what that means."

Jake gripped my hips, then tucked himself into his pants. "Fine, but I'll get what's mine when he's done."

"I expect nothing less."

Jake dashed out of the room, and I followed, breaking off to the bathroom as he continued to the nursery and washed my hands and face.

The cool water tightened my aching cheeks. There was a smile that no amount of finger massaging could wipe away, followed by waves of butterflies in my belly.

I stared at myself in the mirror, noting the maturity transforming my face. My skin was firmer and clear, my breasts had grown, mainly because of a ravenous child who never seemed to get enough, and the youthful glow I'd had before faded ever so slightly.

"What is this?"

I jumped and twisted, facing my husband, holding our seven-month-old baby in his two hands as though he didn't want to get a mess on himself.

"That's our son. Have you lost your mind in your old age?"

Jake peered around him in his outstretched arms and glared at me. "That's funny. I'll take that one out on your ass later." He took two steps forward while I gripped the edge of the sink. "I think you know exactly what I mean."

Ollie's smile warmed my soul as I reached out and took him into my arms. His black onesie with bold white lettering was obvious enough that Jake's question had to be rhetorical.

"Oh, you mean his shirt?"

Player number 4 just entered the game, scrawled across his shirt with a controller in the center and a loading time below.

"Sweets," he ran his hand down his face and sighed, his reaction setting my heart into a wild canter. "Are you pregnant?"

I bit my lip and swayed with Oliver on my hip, then nodded hesitantly.

Was he unhappy?

He stepped closer, his gaze fixated on Oliver, who reached out and slapped at his chin.

"Really?"

I nodded and contained the smile burning my cheeks. "Are you mad?"

He shook his head as he gripped me around the nape of my neck and pulled me in. "Of course not. It's not what I expected, but this is good news." He pressed his warm lips to my forehead as our son waved his arms between us, his squeals of excitement adding to the moment. "I hope you're ready to give up the tits, little man. It's time for you to share."

I snorted and walked out of the bathroom with my growing family in tow and my life slowly piecing itself back together as it emerged from the darkness.

"Daddy doesn't like to share, Ollie," I whispered, smelling his strawberry-blonde hair, soaking in his baby scent. "You better watch out."

"I heard that."

Thank you for reading the Blackstone Tech series. It's been two years in the making and I'm thrilled it's come to a satisfying conclusion. If you enjoyed their stories, please consider sharing with your friends and leaving a review. It doesn't need to be elaborate, a few words or sentences is all that's appreciated. It helps my books get seen.

Born on the Marine Corps Base Camp Lejeune in North Carolina, Ann-Marie grew up learning from strong, confident influences which translates in her writing today.

She acquired the love of writing when she was just 12 years old and at 19; she wrote her first novel, which remains under lock and missing key.

When she's not writing international bestselling books, she's traveling around the USA with her 3 children and a camper, tending to her garden and chickens, or fixing something on her mini-ranch. All with the wonderful support of her amazing husband.

★CONNECT WITH ANN-MARIE★
WEBSITE: www.authoramdavis.com
FACEBOOK: https://bit.ly/3tyZjzY
FB READER'S GROUP: https://bit.ly/2QmXasJ
AMAZON: https://amzn.to/3vLucmu
BOOKBUB: https://bit.ly/3tUgFrl
IG: https://bit.ly/3lIYEt6 | @authoramdavis
TIKTOK: https://bit.ly/3vMw7HK | @authoramdavis
NEWSLETTER: https://bit.ly/4190Kqb

Ann-Marie loves to hear from her fans. So email your questions or comments at AnnMarieDavis88@gmail.com.

www.ingramcontent.com/pod-product-compliance
Lightning Source LLC
LaVergne TN
LVHW041209050326
832903LV00021B/542